# Double the Numbers

# Double the Numbers

## Increasing Postsecondary Credentials for Underrepresented Youth

———————————

Edited by

RICHARD KAZIS, JOEL VARGAS,
and NANCY HOFFMAN, *Jobs for the Future*

HARVARD EDUCATION PRESS

Library of Congress Control Number 2004103338
Library Edition  1-891792-23-7
Paperback  1-891792-22-9

Published by Harvard Education Press,
an imprint of the Harvard Education Publishing Group

Harvard Education Press
8 Story Street
Cambridge, MA 02138

Cover Design: Anne Carter
Interior Design: Fish Tank Media

The typefaces used in this book are Horley Old Style and AG Old Face.

# Table of Contents

**SECTION TWO**
Lessons from the Field: Innovations in Systems, States, and Schools

## SECTION THREE
## Building Support and Public Will for Reform

# Foreword

## BY TOM VANDER ARK

Perhaps the most significant challenge facing our society today is the need to dramatically increase the number of Americans who graduate high school and go on to earn postsecondary credentials. This is an economic, social, and civic imperative — and it cannot be achieved without real changes in the educational opportunities and supports we provide low-income and minority youth. If we don't significantly improve high school preparation, college enrollment, and college completion rates among poor and minority students, our voting rates will continue to decline, family income will continue to stagnate, and we will continue to lead the world in incarceration rates.

Fortunately, the contributors to *Double the Numbers* are not content to specify the problem. Rather, in these short essays, some of the nation's best analysts, observers, and thinkers on educational policy and practice offer their prescriptions for what needs to be done if our nation is to improve attainment for underrepresented youth in both high school and postsecondary institutions. They also describe notable innovations already underway in states and districts around the country.

This book is an exciting collection of fresh ideas and reports on emerging schools, practices, and policies that can "double the number" of young people who obtain postsecondary credentials that have value in the labor market. I want to thank Jobs for the Future for commissioning and editing these essays and for organizing the national conference for which they were written.

The Bill & Melinda Gates Foundation is deeply committed to the agenda of improving high school outcomes and postsecondary success. The

Foundation launched the Gates Millennium Scholars program in 1999 because Bill and Melinda Gates believe that it is vital to our economy and society to develop diverse corporate, civic, and third-sector leadership. This cannot be done without more effective and equitable high schools and better transitions to and through college.

The focus of our philanthropy is to increase the number of American students — particularly poor and minority students — who graduate from high school ready for college, work, and citizenship. Doubling the number of disadvantaged students who graduate from college requires significantly better high school preparation for most students. We believe that every student should have access to a variety of high-quality options that offer a coherent, rigorous, and well-supported course of study. Toward that end, the Bill & Melinda Gates Foundation sponsors the creation of new schools and supports districtwide school improvement efforts.

We have learned that transforming large, struggling high schools is very difficult, almost impossible. At the same time, we are encouraged by the success of new small high schools that are proliferating in cities and communities nationwide. The most impressive of these schools start with the goal of preparing all students for postsecondary learning, work, and citizenship — and they organize themselves to accomplish that goal.

Momentum is building. Networks of like-minded school administrators are working together to strengthen their programs, so that innovation is not limited to isolated, unique institutions. Districts and states are beginning to see small high schools not as marginal "jewels" but as effective and efficient ways to improve secondary outcomes for more youth. New York, Chicago, and Milwaukee have adopted the expansion of new schools as the core of their secondary school reform strategies, and other cities have launched aggressive new school efforts, including Sacramento, San Diego, Oakland, and Indianapolis.

At the Foundation, we are particularly excited about the potential of early college high schools. These schools, which combine secondary and postsecondary learning in one place, embody the notion that with the right support systems every young person is capable of doing serious intellectual work. Early college high schools bring college learning and credits to young people who may not have had the expectation, preparation, or financial ability to continue their learning, and they do so in a highly supportive environment. We are investing in the expansion of this model — and we are watching its progress with great anticipation.

The authors who have contributed to *Double the Numbers* are looking for powerful change strategies in an era of shrinking resources and diminished expectations about reform. Theirs is not an easy assignment, but the ideas, proposals, and solutions advanced in these papers point the way to what a better educational system will have to look like.

The authors don't agree on everything. The reader will recognize in these essays some of the fault lines in current debates around standards, assessments, curriculum, choice, and educational finance. However, the authors start from a few shared assumptions: that incremental steps are inadequate; that fragmented reform of high school and postsecondary systems will fall short; that new practices, policies, and institutions are needed that bring K-12 and higher education into closer cooperation and strategic partnerships. Moreover, they share a passion for a common goal: a significant increase in the number of Americans who succeed in high school, get to college, and earn college credentials.

This is the right passion. It is the passion motivating the education investments of the Bill & Melinda Gates Foundation, investments that we hope will yield the kinds of improved educational outcomes, particularly for poor and minority youth, that are the ultimate goal of these essays and of the movement to "double the numbers."

Tom Vander Ark

*Bill & Melinda Gates Foundation*
Seattle, Washington

# Introduction

By Richard Kazis

This collection of essays is about strategies to strengthen our nation's public education pipeline, particularly our high schools and the postsecondary institutions whose credentials are the key to economic success. The focus is on policies and practices to reduce the unacceptably high costs of our nation's failure to prepare large numbers of young people for further education, productive careers, and active citizenship.

*Double the Numbers* is a call to action, a challenge to "double the number" of young people from low-income and minority families who succeed in getting to and through postsecondary credential programs. It is a call to narrow significantly the longstanding inequities in postsecondary success rates between higher-income and lower-income Americans, between white and minority students. The contributors to this volume recognize that there are no simple solutions to the attainment gap, and that a combination of approaches is needed. Consequently, the prescriptions and strategies advanced by these authors vary greatly. They are motivated by different underlying theories of change. They differ in their relative emphasis on innovations in practice or in policy. And they vary significantly in how fully they embrace incremental versus more radical strategies for plugging the leaks in the education pipeline.

Despite their differences, the authors of these provocative essays share a very important perspective: they are all interested in solutions, and they want to see improvement now, not in some imagined future. Their essays highlight federal, state, and local policies that can make it easier for more Americans to succeed not only in high school but also in postsecondary learning and careers. They write about developments in schools, districts, and states that are beginning to change the odds of success — particularly for low-achieving students, youth from minority or low-income families, and those who are the first in their families to go to college or for whom English is not their native tongue.

*Double the Numbers* sets the course for the next critical phase of education reform. The past two decades have witnessed a remarkable extended campaign, primarily at the state level, to improve the quality of K-12 instruction and learning. This has paralleled almost 40 years of federal higher education aid policies that have opened access to two- and four-year colleges for millions of low-income young people. Now, even as those efforts continue, our nation must raise its sights again, beyond high school to postsecondary credentials, beyond access to success, and beyond the top 25 or 30 percent to all young people. Toward this end, the essays that follow suggest both practical and bold ways to bring together the disconnected, isolated worlds of the K-12, higher education, and second-chance systems — for the sake of efficiency, fairness, and the long-term vitality of our economy and society, and for the sake of the next generation of young people who will need more than a high school diploma if they are to live a middle-class life.

## The Challenges We Face

Income and education are more closely linked now than at any time in our history. College graduates earn on average 70 percent more than high school graduates — a gap that has more than doubled in the past two decades even as the number of college-educated workers has risen. High school dropouts are four times more likely than college graduates to be unemployed. For states, this relationship has important economic implications. States whose populations have higher levels of educational attainment also have higher per capita income.

Yet despite the powerful connection between education and economic well-being, our state public education systems — K-12 *and* higher education — are not performing well enough to generate the full benefits associated with high educational attainment levels.

The statistics are by now familiar. Among Americans in their mid to late 20s, only 29 percent have completed a B.A. degree and 7 percent an associate's degree. Only 18 percent of African Americans and 9 percent of Hispanics between 25 and 29 years of age have earned a B.A. Low-income Americans have far higher rates of dropping out of high school and far lower rates of enrolling in college and obtaining a postsecondary credential than their middle- or higher-income peers.

A recent study from the National Center for Higher Education Management Systems has analyzed the difficulty young people have moving through the "education pipeline" quickly and efficiently. According to the study, for every 100 young people who enter ninth grade, only 67 graduate from high school within four years; of those, only 38 enter college, 26 are still enrolled in college after their sophomore year, and 18 graduate with either an associate's or a bachelor's degree within 150 percent of the required degree time (i.e., within three years for an A.A., six years for a B.A.). Again, the patterns are even more problematic for African American and Hispanic youth.

The leakage is unacceptable all along the educational pipeline.

*An astounding number of students fail to complete high school.* As many as 30 percent of entering freshmen leave school without a regular high school diploma. In some urban districts, 50 to 60 percent of ninth graders drop out

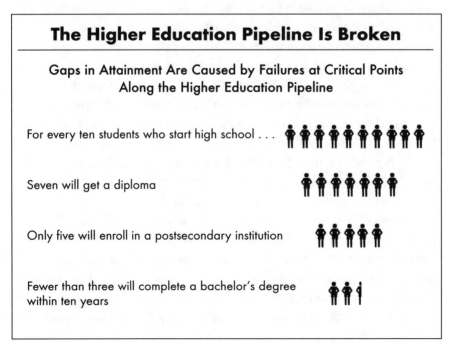

## The Higher Education Pipeline Is Broken

**Gaps in Attainment Are Caused by Failures at Critical Points Along the Higher Education Pipeline**

For every ten students who start high school . . .

Seven will get a diploma

Only five will enroll in a postsecondary institution

Fewer than three will complete a bachelor's degree within ten years

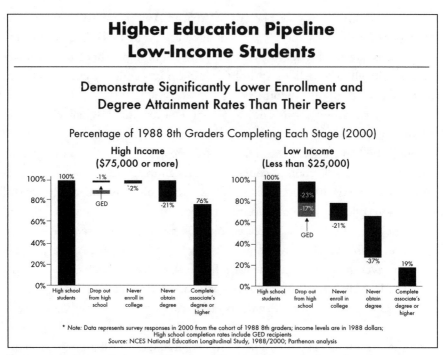

# Higher Education Pipeline
# Low-Income Students

### Demonstrate Significantly Lower Enrollment and Degree Attainment Rates Than Their Peers

Percentage of 1988 8th Graders Completing Each Stage (2000)

**High Income ($75,000 or more)**

**Low Income (Less than $25,000)**

* Note: Data represents survey responses in 2000 from the cohort of 1988 8th graders; income levels are in 1988 dollars; High school completion rates include GED recipients
Source: NCES National Education Longitudinal Study, 1988/2000; Parthenon analysis

before earning a diploma. The overall expansion of educational attainment has actually hit a plateau: the high school graduation rate peaked in 1970 and has not improved throughout most of the past two decades.

*Large numbers of high school graduates are unprepared for college work.* About one in three college freshmen takes at least one remedial course in reading, writing, or math. In urban community colleges, that percentage can be about three in every four new students. Minorities are less well prepared in high school than their white peers: only 47 percent of African American and 53 percent of Latino high school graduates were academically qualified for college, compared to 68 percent of white students, according to a U.S. Department of Education study of 1992 graduates.

*Attrition from postsecondary programs is unacceptably high.* While the proportion of high school graduates who begin college has increased dramatically in the past two decades, the percentage who complete any level of postsecondary education has yet to rise significantly. More than one-fourth of students who enter four-year colleges and nearly half of all who enter two-year institutions do not return for their second year. The percentage of 25-

to 34-year-olds who have successfully earned a college credential has not changed significantly in three decades. Nor has the 30-percentage-point gap in college entry between high-income and low-income students.

## The Costs of Inaction

These patterns bode ill, particularly in light of powerful demographic trends already in play. The skills employers need are increasing at the same time that the fastest growing segments of most states' populations — in school and in the work force — are those groups that have the greatest academic disadvantages: minorities, new immigrants, youth from low-income families. From 1972 to 1999, the percentage of young people of color in the public school population rose from 22 percent to 38 percent. Yet the high school graduation rates of the fastest growing population groups lag significantly. While more than three out of four white and Asian American youth graduate from high school after four years, the graduation rate for African Americans is only 55 percent and for Hispanics, 53 percent. The pattern holds for college graduation rates as well.

As the percentages of these groups in our schools and work force rise, extra effort will be needed just to maintain current aggregate levels of attainment and achievement, never mind to raise them significantly. In the past 20 years, the native-born work force grew 44 percent, primarily because of the entry of women, but, as Texas state demographer Steve Murdoch estimates, almost all the net change in the U.S. labor force between now and 2050 will be among Hispanics, blacks, and other nonwhite groups. Because of the lower average educational attainment of these rapidly growing groups, the share of workers with some post–high school education is projected to increase only 4 percent over the next 20 years, compared to a 19 percent rise since 1980. Some researchers project a net increase through 2020 in the number of people with less than a high school education.

Treading water is not good enough. Economist Anthony Carnevale estimates that by 2020 U.S. employers will need as many as 14 million more workers with some college education than our educational institutions are likely to produce, given current enrollment patterns. A shortage of workers with appropriate skills has serious costs. Employers weigh the quality of the available work force against the costs of operating in different locales when they decide where to locate or expand facilities, within the United States and globally. If work-force skills do not rise to meet the demand, employers will move to other states or countries.

Over time, the divide between those with and those without college credentials is likely to translate into deepening earning and income disparities. Educational and economic advantages snowball. Employers are much more likely to provide additional training to workers who already have postsecondary education. Individuals from lower-income families are much less likely to enter or complete postsecondary programs that can raise their family incomes. Better educated individuals are more civically engaged as well: they vote in higher proportions than do dropouts or those with only a high school education, electing candidates and supporting policies that further their advantage.

The fiscal health of our states and nation will be affected by how well we address the postsecondary attainment and achievement gaps. As baby boomers retire, they will depend on the productivity of a proportionally smaller U.S. work force to generate the revenue needed to finance their Social Security benefits. To the extent that the future work force poorly matches employer needs, thus constraining potential growth, retiring baby boomers will feel the pinch. On the other hand, narrowing the gap in college-going rates of the highest- and lowest-income Americans could help loosen our nation's fiscal straitjacket. According to one estimate, equalizing access to college among blacks, Hispanics, and non-Hispanic whites could add as much as $230 billion to the gross domestic product and generate $80 billion in new tax revenues, giving states the ability to choose between improving valued services or reducing marginal tax rates.

## Charting a New Course: Toward Postsecondary Success for All

Efficiency and fairness demand that states act decisively to improve the performance of their educational pipeline — from kindergarten through college. No Child Left Behind (NCLB) is important legislation in this regard, with its emphasis on academic achievement for all youth, particularly those from groups traditionally underrepresented in postsecondary education. However, NCLB is not enough. More and particular attention must be paid to the complexities of high schools and the needs of older adolescents than NCLB provides. Nor is a K-12 improvement agenda sufficient. State policies must promote dramatic gains in high school completion and in postsecondary success for all population groups, including those who traditionally lag in academic achievement.

The contributors to *Double the Numbers* see the need for progress toward two related goals: to expand postsecondary success significantly and to simultaneously reduce achievement gaps by categories that include income, race, and ethnicity. The call to double the numbers of low-income youth who attain a postsecondary degree is a way to quantify a practical, attainable goal for such efforts. About 19 percent of any year's eighth graders from low-income families (with family income around 200 percent of the federal poverty line) eventually earn a postsecondary degree. In 2003, according to estimates by the Parthenon Group, a Boston-based strategic consulting firm, about 410,000 low-income individuals earned a postsecondary degree. Working with publicly available data, Parthenon has determined that increasing the percentage of low-income individuals who earn college credentials by 2020 from 19 percent to 40 percent, which is the rate at which individuals from middle-income families earn degrees, would mean 460,000 more low-income college graduates in each cohort. This is not an insignificant increase, but it is one that could be absorbed by existing institutions, and it is not so rapid a change as to be beyond the realm of the possible. Doubling the numbers, as Ronald Wolk argues (see page 271), is both critically important and a fairly realistic mid-range goal.

Yet even this target cannot be reached without significant changes in both policy and practice that improve:

- the performance of K-12 education systems, including the second-chance systems that grant high school credentials to out-of-school youth and adults;
- the performance and outcomes of two- and four-year postsecondary institutions; and
- the linkages between K-12 and higher education, so that fewer young people are lost in the transition to and through college.

Each of these priorities poses significant obstacles. High schools are the

## What "Doubling the Numbers" Would Mean

| | 2003 Actual College Attainment | 2020 Projected Incremental College Attainment |
|---|---|---|
| **Low Family Income** College Attainment to increase from 19% to 40% by 2020 | 410,000 | +460,000 |
| **Middle Family Income** College Attainment to increase from 43% to 53% by 2020 | 880,000 | +260,000 |
| **High Family Income** College Attainment to increase from 76% to 85% by 2020 | 240,000 | +40,000 |
| **Overall Student Population** College Attainment to increase from 76% to 85% by 2020 | 1,530,000 | +760,000 |

Source: NCES National Education Longitudinal Study, 1988/2000; NCES Projection of Education Statistics; US Census Bureau; Parthenon analysis

segment of the K-12 system most resistant to innovation and improvement. Postsecondary education has traditionally been driven by enrollments and prestige, not by completion or learning outcomes. And the two components of public education — K-12 and higher education — have long been characterized by independence, a lack of connection or alignment, and few incentives to collaborate toward common goals.

The status quo is untenable. In the current fiscal environment, our nation cannot afford high schools that lose large numbers of students before graduation, extensive college remediation for students failed by the K-12 system, and publicly subsidized college loans and grants for students who never complete their educational programs. The costs are simply too high.

## Consensus and Contention

*Double the Numbers* responds to the pressing need to strengthen the educational pipeline that fails so many young people. These essays reflect the opinions and work of some of the nation's most seasoned experts on high schools, postsecondary education, and the weak links between them. Each author takes as a starting point the need for new policies and practices that can minimize the costly "leakage" of young people from our educational institutions — and that can reduce the disparities in educational attainment between different groups in society.

The authors share a set of common assumptions about how our K-12 and higher education systems must change if we are to "double the numbers" and reduce attainment gaps across different population groups. Their contributions to this volume also highlight significant areas of disagreement, differences in emphasis and priority, and varying assessments of the progress that is possible in the current economic and political environment.

## Areas of Agreement

All the authors would agree with the following statements as a starting point for the next phase of education reform:

• *It's not just about high school; it's also about postsecondary success.*
We can no longer accept high school as a terminal credential or learning experience for anyone. Policy must reflect this shift.

• *It's not just about access to college; it's also about completion.*
Too many policies focus on expanding access to college; too few focus on completion and success. Neither students nor society can afford this anymore.

• *It's not just about the efficiency of the pipeline; it's also about equity.*
Getting more young people to and through postsecondary education is critical, but to do so in a way that promotes social cohesion and addresses the demographic trends in our country requires strategies that improve attainment and achievement for those who are most at risk of failing in high school and postsecondary programs.

• *It's not just about attainment; it's also about learning.*
The standards movement of the past decade has driven home the point that "seat time" and making it through school is no guarantee of learning. This is no less true in postsecondary institutions, but policies that address the quality of college learning are in their infancy.

• *We are all standards-based reformers now.*
There is no turning back from the dominant framework of high standards, common assessments of learning, and accountability systems linked to those

assessments. Any reform efforts must start from existing policies and work to make them more flexible and effective. Much remains to be done to improve on what has been built to date.

• *Older adolescents need more high-quality schools and learning options.*
We need more and different models for reaching, motivating, and engaging older adolescents in learning. Policy should stimulate alternatives, fund them adequately, and ensure that they do not degrade into a new tracking system.

• *Policy matters: finance, accountability, and governance all need to change to bring K-12 and higher education systems into a more coherent whole.*
Stating this is the easy part. What is difficult is to specify the mix of policies that states can fit together to drive better postsecondary outcomes. These authors help describe the range of options and their pros and cons. But a lot of risk-taking and bold innovation by policymakers and practitioners are still needed to clearly identify the most effective and powerful levers for improved outcomes.

## Major Areas of Contention and Debate
Despite broad agreement on the above, the contributors to *Double the Numbers* shine a spotlight on important fault lines in education reform debates, with sharp differences in perspective, strategy, and priority. These include:

• *One path versus many pathways*
There is an implicit debate on the best strategies for ensuring that all high school–age youth have a learning program that enables them to succeed in college. Patte Barth and Kati Haycock of The Education Trust argue for a core curriculum that, in the short run, should be defined by a full set and sequence of college-prep courses. This perspective tends to focus on a single track — from high school to and through college. Robert Schwartz, former director of Achieve, Inc., and now at the Harvard Graduate School of Education, advocates a more streamlined and limited set of common expectations in math and literacy so schools could create distinctive identities that would appeal to students who might otherwise drop out before completing the required core curriculum.

To some extent, this debate is about short-term tactics: Barth and Haycock believe that school capacity to improve is so limited in many places that a core curriculum is the best way to raise standards and instruction levels in the weakest institutions, even as they recognize the risk of driving out diversity. Yet this debate also reflects competing views of how best to motivate and keep potential dropouts in learning programs (or bring dropouts back into credential programs that lead to postsecondary learning). Both the proliferation of options and the insistence on a core curriculum of Carnegie-unit courses have their drawbacks and tradeoffs: this is a legitimate and important policy debate.

Another aspect of the single-versus-multiple-pathways debate revolves around *when* multiple pathways should open up for young people. Should it be during high school or only after? Several authors would argue for a common curriculum through the equivalent of tenth grade, but then offer a broader range of choices once students make it over that bar. Yet advocates of charter schools, dual enrollment, and other variants that promote both curricular diversity at the high school level and the blurring of the boundaries between secondary and postsecondary education work from a different vision. They see program diversity as critical for helping many young people gain the skills they need to meet high school standards that prepare them adequately for postsecondary success.

• *"Hard" versus "soft" methods of signaling and alignment*
Marc Tucker, president of the National Center on Education and the Economy, presents one pole in this debate. He argues for a radical restructuring of U.S. education into three distinct segments, with clear rules and expectations for how one progresses to and through gateways to the next set of institutions. Stanford University's Michael Kirst and Andrea Venezia, taking a more pragmatic position, start from existing state policy and practice and look for strategies that states can use to improve the signals sent from college down to high schools and the incentives that might encourage higher education institutions to improve such signaling. This debate is about incremental versus radical change, about whether the very nature of our four-year high school and two- and four-year college structure must be remade. It is also a debate about whether improved information flows and

policy incentives can make our educational system adapt sufficiently, or whether a more aggressive reform strategy is needed.

• *Design of policies to promote options and choice*
Proposals on how to stimulate the supply of more and more varied learning options surface ongoing debates about choice, charter schools, and vouchers, and how new options should be encouraged and financed. Robert Schwartz argues for an individual education account that would provide more choice for individuals to pursue different pathways. Joe Nathan of the University of Minnesota believes that dual enrollment should be a pure "money follows the students" financing mechanism in order to drive school districts to compete for revenue by creating additional postsecondary options for their high school students. By and large, these papers do not confront head-on some of the more contentious aspects of choice and vouchers, including those most relevant to low-income students and their options and outcomes: Should a different value be assigned to different students based on the cost of serving them adequately? Should money-follows-the-student plans only be available to low-income students, or should they be more universal? Should private schools be included? Policy proposals designed to finance a significant expansion of secondary school options — or options that combine secondary and postsecondary courses and credits — will need to address these issues, which are so prominent in current state-level policy debates.

• *Individual versus institutional incentives for college success*
The authors here tend to favor one of two kinds of incentives to promote college success. One set of policy prescriptions for helping improve college outcomes focuses on the individual: for example, scholarships tied to doing well in high school (as in Indiana, Michigan, Georgia, and other states). The other emphasizes incentives to postsecondary institutions for improving outcomes: tying funding to performance, as suggested by David Longanecker and Peter Ewell, or providing rewards to institutions that graduate high numbers of Pell Grant recipients and other at-risk students, as suggested by Arthur Hauptman. These approaches are certainly not mutually exclusive. In fact, it is easy to envision ways in which states and the federal government could consider early interventions like scholarship

promises, financial aid, institutional support, and tuition policies as elements of a coherent set of incentive policies, all driving toward better completion rates and learning outcomes for lower-income students.

• *Universal versus targeted approaches*
This fault line — targeted versus universal approaches — is a longstanding one in policy. Should policies target those most in need, or are universal policies, though more diffuse, a better way to ensure political support and avoid marginalization? The dynamics of this debate can be seen in positions taken by a number of authors. John Bishop of Cornell University argues for a universal scholarship for all high school students who do well in meeting state learning goals, as in Michigan. But Scott Evenbeck and his Indiana colleagues would combine need and merit in awarding state scholarships, as in their home state. If money is to follow students to different learning options, should more money be "assigned" to those who are likely to require greater services and be more costly to serve? Some authors argue for this approach, fearful that to do otherwise would provide a disincentive to serve those with multiple risk factors and hamstring schools that want to serve at-risk populations. This debate also plays out in discussions about how best to provide support services to college students who need to strengthen their academic skills. In the current environment, universal policies can quickly become too costly (as with the HOPE Scholarship in Georgia), but targeted policies might be too easy to cut back or eliminate, since they will have less political backing.

• *Higher education accountability systems*
This final topic is the emerging hot button for state policymakers who see higher education as the next frontier for state policies designed to drive improvement and efficiencies. Right now, most state deliberations focus on costs more than outcomes, but there is a growing sense that if K-12 systems should be held accountable for how they invest public money, higher education systems will need a similar discipline and clear set of goals. The authors in *Double the Numbers* do not so much disagree with one another as express concerns about the development of accountability systems for higher education that either do not change incentives sufficiently or that fail to make increased attainment and completion the ultimate goal, particularly for stu-

dents from underrepresented groups.

## Acknowledgments

All but a few of the essays in this volume were prepared as background papers for a conference also called "Double the Numbers," which was organized by Jobs for the Future in October 2003. Held in Washington, DC, the conference brought together over 450 policymakers, practitioners, researchers, and others committed to improving low-income students' success in high school and postsecondary learning programs. It tapped a growing interest — across K-12 and higher education reform, among those working in local institutions, at the state level, and nationally — in addressing the leaks in the education pipeline more aggressively and more coherently.

The editors want to thank the many staff members at Jobs for the Future who made that event possible — and so successful. While the teamwork was exceptional, a few people deserve particular kudos: Lisa Dickinson, Sandra Jadotte, Sarah Kwon, Karen Ludwig, and Mindy Martin. We also wish to thank the presenters and panelists at the conference, a good number of whom are also contributors to this book. Working with the authors both before the conference and in turning conference papers into a book has been a pleasure: we could not have asked for a more cooperative and responsive group. Special thanks are due Marc S. Miller of Jobs for the Future, whose organization and focus enabled us to produce this book on a very quick time line, and to Hilary Pennington and Marlene Seltzer for their sage advice on structure and content.

Several national foundations have been supportive of Jobs for the Future's work on high school reform, the transition to postsecondary success, and strategies to strengthen the education pipeline. We appreciate the encouragement and generous support of the Bill & Melinda Gates Foundation, as well as the Carnegie Corporation of New York, the Ford Foundation, and the W. K. Kellogg Foundation, without whose help neither the Double the Numbers conference nor this book would have been possible.

Interest in the issues and approaches highlighted in this volume is growing. A vibrant network of organizations and individuals is emerging — representing education researchers, policy advocates, program and school leaders, state and national officials, foundations, journalists, and others — that sees the leaks in the education pipeline as one of the most important challenges facing our nation today. From the frequently insular worlds of high school reform, college access and success, work-force development, and alternative education, people are reaching across traditional boundaries, acknowledging the need to stanch the flow of young people out of our educational institutions and systems. As the contributors to *Double the Numbers* attest, looking at the problem holistically leads to a rich and powerful analysis of both the problems that need to be addressed and strategies that might have sufficient power and impact.

A final appreciation is in order here to all those who, through their daily work on the front lines of our educational systems, the halls of state agencies and legislatures, the offices of research and policy organizations, or the groves of academia, are working to increase the number of young people from low-income families who get to and through the postsecondary programs that are the gateway to educational and economic success. This book is written for them.

# SECTION ONE

Strategies for Improving Postsecondary Success:
High Schools, Postsecondary Institutions,
and Their Alignment

---

## *Introduction*

Any serious effort to improve secondary and postsecondary success for low-income young people will require changes both in practice — how schools are organized, teachers trained, and learning delivered — and in policies at the local, state, and national levels that affect the organization and delivery of quality learning. In the following chapters, the authors propose specific policy approaches and innovations that they believe can help break through the inertia that characterizes education systems and promote and encourage more and better opportunities for low-income youth. These authors focus on three aspects of the pipeline: the high school experience; the links between high school and postsecondary institutions and the transition to college credential programs; and the way colleges are organized and rewarded.

These chapters focus on policy levers that might be powerful enough to change the incentives that drive high schools and colleges and, as a result, might alter the priorities and practices of the governing boards, administrators, faculty, and staff. The authors also champion policies that change the incentives facing students and their families in ways that reward working hard, planning for college, and persisting in school to earn both a diploma and a postsecondary credential. And they promote policy innovations that can drive change in the quality of the curriculum for students, the options students have to choose their school or program of study, the signals that colleges send to high schools and their students about what it takes to be "college ready," and the accountability and financing systems that have tended to reward colleges for enrollments rather than student outcomes.

The prescriptions in these chapters are sometimes complementary, sometimes contradictory. They reflect, however, the rich diversity of policy approaches and strategies that are being advanced and promoted by some of the nation's leading experts. Together, they comprise a provocative and ambitious agenda that responds to the call to "double the numbers" of low-income young people who successfully move through the secondary and postsecondary segments of the education pipeline.

*High schools:* Several authors focus primarily on the high school experience.

Patte Barth and Kati Haycock of The Education Trust argue that the best way for states to raise achievement for all high school students is to require a college-prep-level core curriculum for all high school students, as Texas and several other states now do. They see a fairly standardized but rigorous curriculum as the most powerful way to ensure that students in low-performing schools get the same opportunities as students in wealthier and more effective schools.

Joe Nathan of the University of Minnesota, a long-time advocate of school choice and competition as policy levers to drive improved student outcomes, presents a case for expanding the number of charter schools and for states to promote dual enrollment programs. Based on his experience in Minnesota, Nathan argues that well-designed charter school and dual enrollment programs bring healthy competition into the education arena and create incentives for quality improvement both within and outside existing school districts.

Cornell University economist John Bishop promotes merit scholarships tied specifically to state learning assessments as a way to better align financial aid policies with state K-12 achievement goals. He favorably contrasts the Michigan scholarship incentive, which is tied to performance on the statewide high school assessment rather than on grades, with similar scholarship programs in other states.

*Linkage between K-12 and postsecondary systems:* A second group of authors targets the inefficiencies in our country's links between K-12 education and higher education. They propose policy innovations and changes that can reduce leakage in the pipeline at the transition point between high school and postsecondary learning.

Marc Tucker, president of the National Center on Education and the Economy, argues for a dramatic restructuring of segments of the U.S. educational system along the lines of some European systems. He advocates a system of clear expectations and gateway exams, starting after completion of a core K-10 curriculum, and moving through varied academic and technical learning options that can lead either to quality employment or to further education.

Robert Schwartz, former president of Achieve, Inc., and long-time champion of raising standards in K-12 education, picks up on the theme of multiple pathways, suggesting that the "college for all" movement limits the emergence of additional routes to postsecondary success that might hold promise for many youth who are ill-served by existing institutions and curricula. Schwartz proposes a set of new pathways to postsecondary success and good jobs that can augment the current narrow set of options. He suggests a way to balance the goal of high standards for all with the equally important goal of more varied choices and options for young people.

Michael Kirst and Andrea Venezia of Stanford University's Bridge Project take a different tack. Rather than propose an ambitious restructuring of the various segments of the education pipeline, they advocate incremental steps that states can take to better link secondary and postsecondary systems and institutions, particularly through better signaling of college expectations and requirements to high schools, their staff, and their students. Sobered by research in five states on current policies to link K-12 and postsecondary institutions, Kirst and Venezia argue that even these modest policy changes will be difficult to achieve.

*Postsecondary institutions:* A third set of policy proposals addresses the disappointing performance of many public higher education systems in retaining and graduating those who enroll. These chapters focus on policy strategies that change the incentives guiding colleges and universities in their priority-setting and behavior.

Peter Ewell of the National Center for Higher Education Management Systems suggests how states might revamp accountability systems to promote student learning in, and graduation from, colleges and universities. He proposes a state-level accountability system that emphasizes learning gains and standards for achievement, a diverse set of quality assurance mechanisms aligned with the standards and benchmarks, a set of system- and institution-level measures to monitor progress and steer behavior, and an alternative credentialing system that can assess learning gained through work, home study, community participation, and other sources.

David Longanecker, executive director of the Western Interstate Commission for Higher Education and a former federal education official, argues for more aggressive use of performance funding by states in order to influence the behavior of public colleges and universities toward doubling the numbers. We should pay for what we want, he explains, emphasizing the need to make college affordable, reward retention and completion, and allocate funding in ways that enable institutions to provide quality educational services to the most difficult to serve students, who cost more to serve than better prepared students.

Finally, Arthur Hauptman proposes changes in federal financial aid policies and state institutional funding formulas in order to promote and reward not just enrollment but also attainment and achievement in postsecondary institutions. He advocates a return to the twin goals of the 1965 Higher Education Act: access and completion. Hauptman recommends both state and federal policy changes, focusing on revisions of state funding formulas to reward colleges that do a good job of retaining and graduating lower-income students, and on changes in federal Pell Grant policy that would pay colleges and universities for the number of grant recipients who stay in their programs, advance, and graduate.

*Is college-going for all the appropriate goal for the American high school? Or do colleges already exercise disproportionate influence on high school curricula, constraining program options in many schools? Robert Schwartz proposes a way to reconcile high standards with a diversity of school programs so that all students can reach college-level literacy and numeracy levels by high school graduation, without sacrificing the kind of programmatic diversity and choice that are critical to high school students' sense of identification with their school and motivation to learn. This would involve creating additional pathways to postsecondary credentials and giving young people access to individual education accounts to finance their chosen pathway.*

# 1. Multiple Pathways — and How to Get There[1]

## By Robert B. Schwartz

The standards movement has firmly established the proposition that states and school districts should be held accountable for assuring that all students leave high school with a solid foundation of academic knowledge and skills. While there is still considerable variation and fuzziness in what we mean by the latter phrase, the increasingly common translation is "all students ready for college." Given that upwards of 90 percent of high school students now say that they intend to go to college, and 75 percent of high school graduates actually enroll in college, should we now declare college preparation as the universal, overarching goal of high school education and college enrollment as the intended outcome for all high school graduates?

Certainly there are powerful arguments for moving in this direction. As Diane Ravitch (2000) documents so powerfully, the consequence of not expecting all students to master a rigorous academic curriculum has been to deny equal educational and economic opportunity to generations of low-income and minority youngsters. It is no accident that the standards movement has to date made very little progress in penetrating our high schools, for the core idea of the movement — common, high expectations for all students — runs counter to the culture and traditions of the comprehensive American high school. For most of the last century, our high schools have been quintessential sorting and selecting machines, separating those deemed to be "college material" from those deemed fit only for office or manual work, and providing each group a very different level of education. In the much-admired suburban high school I attended a half-century ago, there were four tracks: college prep, general, business, and vocational. Although the community was racially homogenous, it was ethnically diverse, and I can still remember my surprise that virtually all of my friends from my heavily Italian and Irish junior high school disappeared from view during the school day and reemerged only after school on the athletic field. Fifty years later, tracking is still a reality in most American high schools, and it is no accident that college-going rates continue to vary widely by race and parental income.

Given this history, why not once and for all attempt to abolish tracking, insist that all students be provided a rigorous academic curriculum along the lines called for 20 years ago in *A Nation at Risk*, and declare it to be national policy that all young Americans are expected to go on to college? Given the substantial and growing income disparity between the college-educated and those with only high school diplomas, and the radically shrinking number of family-wage jobs available to those without some college education, why not send a clear and unambiguous message to all young people that college-going is the only acceptable outcome of a high school education?

Despite the logic of this succession of seemingly rhetorical questions, I am not persuaded that college-going for all is the appropriate goal for the American high school. In fact, I would argue that one of the major problems our high schools face is that we have allowed our higher education system to exercise disproportionate influence on the high school curriculum, unduly constraining the programmatic options offered by many (if not most) schools.

## The Nature of the Problem

Let me begin my argument by asserting my own definition of the mission of the American high school. In my view, the purpose of high school is to equip all young people with the skills and knowledge necessary for work, citizenship, and further learning. The "further learning" goal takes as a given that in our rapidly changing economy the ability to keep on acquiring new skills and knowledge will be an essential requirement for economic self-sufficiency, but it does not assume that such knowledge and skills can only be acquired in a formal higher education institution. I am very comfortable with the educational goal articulated by Jobs for the Future: namely, that all young people obtain a postsecondary education credential by age 26. Again, I like this goal because it does not assume that our colleges and universities are the sole source of such credentials; rather, it allows for a broad enough definition of "postsecondary education" to acknowledge that employers, employer associations, trade unions, and a wide range of community-based organizations can also credential knowledge and skills.

At one level, my argument may seem to be semantic, turning on the distinction between "college" and "postsecondary education," but in my view these two terms carry very different implications when they are embedded in mission statements of American high schools.

For most Americans, especially opinion leaders and policy setters, "college" means a four-year college or university, for this is the goal they aspire to for their own children. Unfortunately, one of the most stubbornly persistent facts of American education has been the proportion of young adults who actually manage to obtain a baccalaureate degree. Despite the figures I cited about the proportion of high school graduates now enrolling in college, a proportion that has been steadily rising over the past two decades, only about one young American in four graduates from a four-year college.[2] More than twice that many enter, but only half obtain a degree within six years. It is with these facts in mind that I challenge the excessive influence of higher education on the high school curriculum: a sector that is effectively serving only a quarter of the population ought not to be the controlling voice in determining what gets taught to whom.

If we are serious about "doubling the numbers" of young people with a meaningful postsecondary credential, we first need to come to agreement on the nature of the problem. For many people in higher education, the problem seems obvious: too many people show up on the doorstep of college inadequately prepared to do college-level work. The short-term response to this problem is the huge college remediation industry, but there is general agreement that much of our investment in remediation is wasteful and inefficient, and the returns (as measured by college completion) to these investments are less than robust. The longer-term response, of course, is to strengthen the quality of secondary education; hence, the interest in directing virtually all students into a rigorous sequence of college preparatory courses.

A second possible explanation for the appallingly high college dropout rate is the college experience itself. This explanation could encompass a wide variety of variables: weak teaching, especially in large introductory courses; inadequate advising and student support services; insufficient financial aid.

This analysis shades into a third possible explanation: bored, disengaged, unmotivated students, not sure why they are in college in the first place, there largely by default because of the absence of other socially legitimate alternatives.

If one is going to fashion a credible strategy to "double the numbers," one needs to address at least those three pieces of the problem while not losing sight of the young people who are most at risk in our current arrangement: namely, the 30 percent who drop out before completing high school.

## Four New Pathways

If the goal, then, is to double the numbers of those obtaining a postsecondary credential, but not necessarily a college degree, by age 26, where do we start? This summer I was fortunate to participate in a five-day workshop on strengthening the pathways from high school to postsecondary education sponsored by the Aspen Institute's Program on Education, and the ideas I am about to outline evolved out of the discussions of my Aspen small group.[3] We began with two big ideas. First, there should be a clearly demarcated set of new pathways that lead from the early high school years to a postsecondary credential, with each pathway providing built-in supports for young people. These pathways should be on equal footing with the pathway to a two- or four-year college. And second, all students, upon graduating from high school, should have access to an individualized education-and-training account to support their participation in their chosen pathway.

We envisioned four broad pathways in addition to the direct-to-college pathway:

- A *"blended institutions" pathway*, which would blur the lines between secondary and postsecondary education and incorporate such innovations as early college high schools, middle college, and various dual-enrollment arrangements;
- A *"2+2" model*, incorporating agreements among high schools, colleges, and employers, and leading to a technology-based credential;
- A *work-based, employer- or union-led model*, in which the course development and credentialing is designed and delivered principally at the workplace, not at an educational institution; and
- A *service model*, encompassing military service as well as AmeriCorps-type projects, in which there is training, leadership development, and a postprogram stipend to be used for further education.

All of these models exist today in some form and serve some young people well. What does not exist is a financing scheme that would put these pathways on a relatively even footing with the dominant school-to-college pathway or a regulatory structure to assure quality control across the models and promote competition, choice, and accountability for results. It was these design issues that our Aspen group spent most of its time wrestling with.

The multiple pathways idea, even in its nascent form, provides a conceptual framework not only for rethinking the programmatic and organizational design of high schools but also for developing a credible strategy for doubling the numbers of young adults with a meaningful postsecondary credential. It suggests a way to give the preparation for work and citizenship goals of high schools more legitimacy while sending a strong message that all pathways require preparation for further learning.

## A Reconciliation Strategy

How might high schools be restructured in accordance with a multiple pathways framework? Much of the innovation underway in urban districts involving the creation of small schools and the redesign of larger schools with autonomous academies or small learning communities is already moving in the multiple pathways direction. If there is a common programmatic denominator across the small high schools movement, it is the provision of learning opportunities in community settings that enable young people to test themselves in more adult roles, explore possible career options, and understand how academic concepts and skills can be applied in real-world situations. To provide such learning opportunities at scale, and to sustain them over time, requires the development of long-term partnerships between high schools and other institutions in the community — employers, higher education institutions, community-based organizations — partnerships that in some cases may evolve into pathways that carry students across the secondary-postsecondary divide.

Despite the explosive growth in recent years of the small schools movement — a movement fueled in part by very substantial investments from the Bill & Melinda Gates Foundation and the Carnegie Corporation of New York — there is a strong countervailing movement constraining the willingness of school district leaders to move in this direction. Yet there is no logical reason why the standards movement and the small schools movement need be in opposition; indeed, in my view each needs the other to fully accomplish its purposes. But in too many states and school districts, the goal of equipping all students with a solid foundation of academic knowledge and skills is leading to an undue narrowing of curricular choices and a reduction in the kinds of learning opportunities for academically at-risk students that are most likely to engage and motivate them to take schooling seriously.

This is a painful acknowledgment from someone who considers himself a charter member of the standards movement, for in my view its principal goal is to help schools dramatically increase the achievement levels of those students whom they have historically served least well. But if the standards movement in fact leads to a one-size-fits-all standardization of the high school curriculum, the predictable consequences, I fear, will be continuing high dropout rates in our high schools and continuing low graduation rates in our colleges and universities.

How might the goals of the standards movement be reconciled with the creation of a more diverse secondary school system, and with the creation of a more robust set of pathways leading from high school to a meaningful postsecondary credential?

The first, and most critical, piece of a reconciliation strategy is to agree on the knowledge and skills that are absolutely essential for every high school graduate to possess in order to proceed successfully from high school into higher education or an employment-based pathway. Fortunately, the vast majority of states have limited their definition of absolutely essential skills to reading, writing, and mathematics, and these are the skills that No Child Left Behind requires states to test annually in grades 3-8, and at least once in high school.[4] Until now, however, there has been no way of assuring that the reading, writing, and math skills states are assessing in high school bear any relationship to the skills colleges and employers define as essential for success in their respective settings. Happily, this problem is now being addressed by the American Diploma Project (ADP), a joint effort of three respected national policy organizations — Achieve, The Education Trust, and the Thomas B. Fordham Foundation — and five states — Indiana, Kentucky, Massachusetts, Nevada, and Texas. With support from the William and Flora Hewlett Foundation, ADP has for the past two years worked with higher education leaders in its partner states and with a national cross-section of employers to craft a set of benchmark high school exit standards in reading, writing, and math that are firmly anchored in the entry-level expectations of higher education and high-performance workplaces. These benchmarks are about to be released. If they are embraced not only by the five partner states but also by other states and national higher education and employer associations, they could have a profoundly liberating effect on high schools.[5]

If the ADP definition of the essential knowledge and skills were to be broadly accepted by colleges and employers, and if states were to align their high school exit tests with the benchmarks, it would free up high schools in two ways. First, at least for the reading and writing benchmarks, it would enable school districts to spread the responsibility for the development of these skills across all teachers at all grade levels. While there would inevitably still be a need in most urban high schools for some English courses specifically focused on helping struggling students meet these benchmarks, the English curriculum for most students need not be artificially constrained by these requirements. Math is obviously a different matter, with the likely outcome of the ADP benchmarks being to require all students to take a prescribed sequence of courses at least through Algebra II, but the overall effect of agreement by colleges and employers on the certification of a limited set of reading, writing, and math skills as the essential prerequisites for admission or entry-level hiring would be to give high schools greater latitude in figuring out how to help all of their students acquire these skills.

## Organizational Strategies

I believe there are a variety of ways to organize high schools, large or small, around the interests of students to provide more programmatic diversity and choice while avoiding the trap of tracking. The program-major approach pioneered in Oregon represents one such model. Under this approach, all students choose a "major" from six or eight very broad thematic or career clusters (e.g., arts and humanities, technology, health and human services, environmental studies). The clusters are designed to enable students to build a program of studies around their interests, and through internships and other service- or work-based learning opportunities to gain some exposure to career options in the cluster. All clusters provide courses in the core academic subjects, but the content (e.g., the literature selections in English, the problems in math) is to some degree customized to fit the interests of the cluster. Obviously, the technology and health clusters would likely be heavier on math and science than the arts cluster, for example, but all students in all clusters would gain at least some exposure to all the core subjects, and all clusters would take responsibility for helping their students meet the ADP exit standards.

A second organizational strategy is best exemplified by the Talent Development High School model developed by researchers at Johns Hopkins University. Under this model, large urban high schools are organized into smaller theme- or career-based academies. Typically, there is a separate ninth-grade academy in which the focus is on enabling students to make more informed choices by introducing them to high school and strengthening their study skills, delivering intensive literacy and math instruction to those who are substantially below grade level, and providing short rotations through each of the theme-based academies.

As in the program majors model, the goal is not to prematurely slot students into career paths but to use their interests, and the applied learning opportunities offered in the field, as motivators to help them develop core academic skills and knowledge. Both of these models avoid the trap of separating students into the college-bound and the work-bound: all students get some exposure to careers, and all clusters and academies prepare students for postsecondary education as well as employment.

A third approach, perhaps most fully developed in New York City, is to create a portfolio of theme-oriented small schools. There are now small high schools in New York and some other cities organized around virtually every major profession — law, medicine, architecture, teaching, journalism — as well as such technical and vocational fields as aviation and culinary arts.

New York also happens to be the place with the sharpest collision between the small schools movement and the standards movement, for New York is one of the few states to require all high school students to pass exit tests not only in English and math but in three other academic subjects as well. Given New York State's long history of operating a two-tier high school system, with Regents exams and a Regents diploma for the college-bound and a general diploma for everyone else, the requirement that all students must now take and pass Regents exams was obviously designed to create a much more equitable system, but an unintended consequence has been to significantly constrain the curricular offerings of some of the city's most innovative and successful small schools.

In my view, other states would be well advised to avoid this problem by limiting their high-stakes high school exit tests to the ADP-recommended subjects (reading, writing, math). If states want to assure rigor and quality control in other academic subjects, as I believe they should, this can be accomplished through the development of end-of-course tests. Such tests can be designed as medium stakes — they can count as a fixed percentage of the final grade and results can be placed on students' transcripts. States can also encourage consortia of small schools to come forward with proposals for assessing interdisciplinary and other innovative courses for which there are no state-developed exams. If colleges and universities come to have confidence in the predictive validity of ADP-aligned high school exit tests, and graduates of the strongest small schools and theme-based academies build a solid track record in postsecondary education, at least some colleges and universities may begin to move away from course-based admissions requirements, as Oregon institutions are doing, in favor of a more competency-based system.

## An Incentive to Graduate

To return to the multiple pathways vision that I and my colleagues conjured up in the rarefied air of Aspen, the "push" to create a more diverse secondary school system would be enormously aided by the "pull" of a postsecondary system that allowed for and legitimized a variety of routes to a meaningful postsecondary credential, including some that were work-based and service-based. *In my view, the single most important policy step state and federal governments could take to realize the goal of doubling the numbers would be to create individual education-and-training accounts to support the quest for a meaningful postsecondary credential for all high school graduates.*

Among other things, this change, in combination with the liberalizing reforms I am advocating for the organization of high schools, would almost certainly dramatically increase the high school graduation rate. Students would now have a financial incentive to stay the course and a much wider array of programs and pathways from which to choose.

This is not the occasion to elaborate in detail the case for creating individual education and training accounts, but a few explanatory comments are in order. The individual accounts I advocate here would be available to all high school graduates, although they would be weighted for need using some family-income criteria. They could be used not just at accredited institutions of higher education, but at a broader range of learning providers that grant certificates with demonstrated currency in the labor market. This would require some state regulatory body to certify providers on the basis of their track record in placing graduates in jobs (and to exercise some other quality controls). Accounts would be a mechanism for pooling existing state and federal funds for postsecondary education or training (and might also include tax-preferred contributions by individuals or their families). The amount of the public contribution to the account would be sufficient to cover most or all of the costs of public higher education or short-duration training programs, but it would leave essentially unchanged the public funds that go to financing private four-year colleges and universities.

There are two compelling reasons for believing that the policy change suggested here could make a major contribution toward the goal of doubling the number of young adults who obtain a meaningful postsecondary credential. The first reason, as suggested above, has to do with the impact on those who are likeliest to drop out. While the dropout problem has a multiplicity of causes and no single policy intervention can provide a "magic bullet" solution, one common causal factor is the perception that no one else cares whether the young person stays in school or leaves. Perhaps the most powerful rationale for the creation of smaller high schools is that it is much easier to create an environment in which all kids are known and feel valued in a community of 300 than in a crowd of 3,000. The creation of individual education-and-training accounts would send a message to young people on the margins that the larger society needs them, values them, and is therefore prepared to invest in their future. The fact that young people themselves would control the decisions about how and where to redeem their vouchers (i.e., by choosing the education or training setting they deem likeliest to provide the skills and support they need) also sends an important signal about trust.

This set of principles is hardly new to federal policy, for they are largely embedded in the Pell Grant program. Individual education-and-training accounts, however, would universalize these principles, widen the purposes for which such funds could be used, and eliminate the gross inequity in governmental support between low-income young people who enroll in college and those who don't.

The second reason for believing that the creation of individual education-and-training accounts could radically affect the bottom-line numbers of young adults who succeed in obtaining meaningful postsecondary credentials is the likely impact of this policy change on institutional behavior, especially the behavior of four-year colleges and universities. Here a complex set of design and regulatory issues would need to be addressed, but the core notion is to inject significantly more market-based choice and competition into the system and to greatly strengthen institutional accountability for student success.

## A Risk Worth Taking

Under the system our Aspen group envisioned, colleges and universities would have powerful incentives to provide the supports necessary to help at-risk students succeed and graduate, and young people would have access to better information and data about institutional performance to guide their enrollment choices. With the creation of the four additional pathways to a meaningful postsecondary credential, and the resources to support successful participation in these pathways, students would have credible, socially sanctioned alternatives to the traditional college pathway, and colleges could no longer assume a captive market.

There are clearly significant risks associated with the strategy I am advocating. For high school policy, the big risk is that "multiple pathways" will devolve into just another form of tracking,[6] with prestige and resources tilted toward those pathways that are likeliest to attract the strongest students. A second risk is that the supply of educationally rich work- or service-based learning opportunities will be inadequate to meet the demand, further limiting the likelihood of achieving parity across pathways, a legitimate concern, given the experience to date of the school-to-work movement. A third risk, of course, is that the idea of individual education-and-training accounts will never get off the ground. Even if this idea could be accomplished largely through the reallocation of existing education, training, and work force development funds without a significant infusion of new money, the political resistance to such reallocation, especially from the higher education community, would likely be sufficient to torpedo such a proposal.

Without such a radical rethinking and restructuring, how likely is it that the doubling-the-numbers goal can be realized? Does anyone really believe that by herding all students into a "college-prep" curriculum we are going to motivate hitherto disengaged students into caring about academic achievement or enable underprepared teachers to teach such students to high standards? More important, does anyone believe that, absent major changes in the incentive and accountability systems operating in higher education, even better prepared students will graduate in significantly higher numbers? I believe incremental progress is possible in inching up the college graduation rates on the policy path we are now on, but the notion that we can leap from enabling one in three young adults to obtain a baccalaureate or associate's degree to two in three strikes me as wishful thinking. Achieving such a policy goal will require bolder action, whatever the risks.

---

1. An earlier version of this argument appeared in my contribution to *Shaping the Future of American Youth: Youth Policy in the 21st Century* (Lewis, 2003).

2. The most recent numbers I've seen indicate that in 1999 28 percent of 25- to 34-year-olds had a degree from a four-year institution, with another 8 percent having a two-year degree. The proposals outlined here would likely increase significantly the percentage of two-year degree holders.

3. The other members of the Aspen group were Michael Cohen, Chester Finn, Jr., Nancy Hoffman, Stan Jones, Nancy Pelz-Paget, Melissa Roderick, Rochelle Nichols Solomon, and Stefanie Sanford (chair). Needless to say, they should not be held responsible for the uses to which I have put their ideas.

4. Beginning in 2007–2008, states will also be required to administer annual assessments in science at three different grade levels.

5. For more information on ADP, see "Do American High School Diplomas Guarantee Postsecondary Success?" on page 145.

6. One possible safeguard would be for states to establish a long-term goal of having each pathway reflect the racial and economic demographics of the youth population, and to require schools, colleges, and other providers to report annually on progress toward that goal.

*The only way to ensure that all high school students graduate ready to succeed in college and careers is to require the same high-quality college preparatory curriculum for all students. Although this strategy runs the risk of limiting the proliferation of creative-learning programs at the high school level, Patte Barth and Kati Haycock argue that the benefits of this new, common, high-standards curriculum, particularly for low-achieving students in poorly performing schools, outweigh the risks of reducing program options for older adolescents.*

# 2. A Core Curriculum for All Students

## By Patte Barth and Kati Haycock[1]

Inexorably, the aspirations of American high school students rise: more and more young people want education and training beyond high school. Indeed, nearly three-quarters of our high school graduates now go on to two- or four-year institutions within two years, and others follow within a few more years. This is good news, because today's economy makes postsecondary education or training essential to anybody who wants a decent foothold.

Unfortunately, we have a way to go before our high schools and colleges meet the rising aspirations for skills and knowledge. The now-familiar statistics are sobering:

- Although elementary schools have grown more effective over the past two decades, the value added by secondary schools has declined.
- While achievement problems are by no means unique to low-income and minority students, their problems are much more severe. At the end of high school, African American and Latino students have skills that are indistinguishable from white students at the end of middle school.
- About half of all newly enrolled college students must take some form of remediation; nearly one-third never make it to the sophomore year of college.

- Only about half of the students who enter college complete a postsecondary degree within six years. The numbers aren't pretty for any student group, but they are worst for students who are black, Latino, or from low-income households.

The single most important thing we can do to help students succeed after high school is to provide a challenging high school curriculum. Why? Because the biggest contributor to success in college isn't a student's SAT or ACT score, nor is it GPA or rank in class. Rather, the single best predictor of college success is the quality and intensity of a student's high school curriculum.

The relationship of high school course-taking to college success is clearest in mathematics. Research from the U.S. Department of Education shows that high school students who complete math higher than Algebra II (e.g., trigonometry or pre-calculus) earn a college degree at twice the rate of those whose high school math curriculum was less rigorous (Adelman, 1999).

Differences in high school course-taking across subjects may explain much of the lower college completion rates of African American and Latino college freshmen. The variation in overall graduation rates for college freshmen from different population groups is alarming. But most of those differences disappear among students who have completed a robust college-prep curriculum (see Chart 1).

## Benefits beyond College Success

College preparatory courses do not benefit just students who know they are college-bound. A growing body of evidence shows that such a curriculum has benefits for virtually all kids.

*All* kids? Many Americans, including many educators, doubt that all young people are capable of learning subjects like algebra. All Japanese kids, maybe. Even all Russian kids. But for some reason, not our students.

These views are dead wrong. All students benefit from taking high-level courses, regardless of their academic record prior to enrollment.

1. *Students of all abilities learn more in college-prep courses.*
Researchers have looked closely at what happens with different types of students when enrolled in different high school curricula. Their analysis, sum-

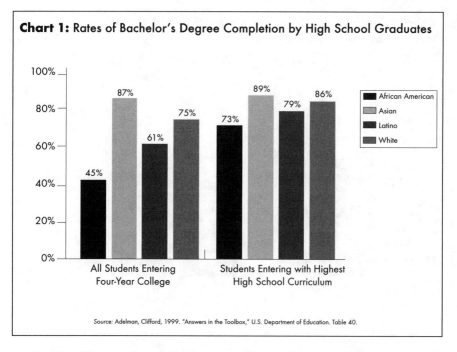

**Chart 1:** Rates of Bachelor's Degree Completion by High School Graduates

Legend:
- African American
- Asian
- Latino
- White

All Students Entering Four-Year College: 45%, 87%, 61%, 75%

Students Entering with Highest High School Curriculum: 73%, 89%, 79%, 86%

Source: Adelman, Clifford, 1999. "Answers in the Toolbox," U.S. Department of Education. Table 40.

marized in Chart 2, found that even students who enter high school in the lowest quartile of performance post higher gains in college-prep courses than in the vocational courses they typically enroll in.

These findings are mirrored in the experience of the Southern Regional Education Board's High Schools That Work Initiative (HSTW), a school-wide reform model created primarily to improve achievement among vocational students. When efforts to raise standards in vocational courses did not produce desired across-the-board gains, participating schools were encouraged to take these so-called "work-bound" students and place them into college-prep courses for part of the day. HSTW schools that enroll large numbers of such students in high-level courses are raising student achievement and simultaneously increasing the overall percentage of program completers — even though vocational track students have been traditionally among the lowest achieving and at the highest risk of failing (Frome, 2001).

*2. Students are more likely to pass high-level courses than low-level ones.*
Teachers often hesitate to place low-achieving students into tough courses

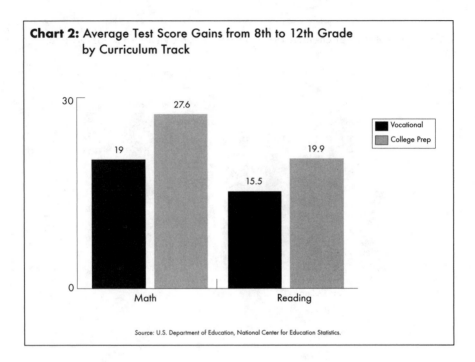

**Chart 2:** Average Test Score Gains from 8th to 12th Grade by Curriculum Track

Source: U.S. Department of Education, National Center for Education Statistics.

for fear it will set them up for failure. Yet we're learning that low-achieving students are typically no more likely to fail more difficult classes than they are in the watered-down ones where we often warehouse them. Indeed, when bottom-quartile students are placed in a low-level English course, nearly half — 47 percent — fail. Put the same students in a college-prep English course, and failure rates decline by about half (see Chart 3).

Skeptics argue that if all students were placed in a high-level curriculum, course failure rates would skyrocket. But this did not happen when the El Paso area school districts opened their college-prep tracks to more students. Throughout the 1990s, El Paso high schools focused on expanding student enrollments in rigorous courses. Since then, El Paso has shown that it is quite possible both to increase enrollment in college-prep courses and simultaneously increase the number of students passing these courses (see Chart 4).

Skeptics also worry that a high-level curriculum will force more students to drop out. This does not seem to be happening in El Paso. A recent

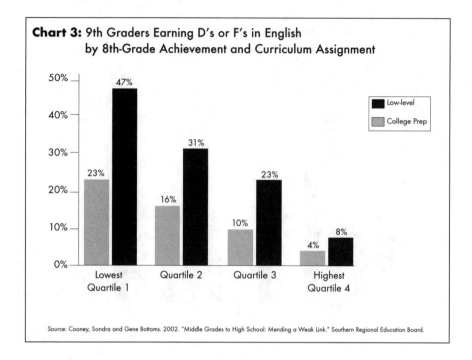

**Chart 3:** 9th Graders Earning D's or F's in English by 8th-Grade Achievement and Curriculum Assignment

Source: Cooney, Sondra and Gene Bottoms. 2002. "Middle Grades to High School: Mending a Weak Link." Southern Regional Education Board.

national study reports that graduation rates in this high-poverty high-Latino district are 14th highest among the nation's 50 largest school districts — a group that includes such affluent suburban communities as Fairfax County, Virginia, and Montgomery County, Maryland (Greene & Winters, 2002).

The experience in the San Jose, California, school district has been similar. San Jose changed its placement policy in 1997 to require all students to complete the curriculum required for admission into California's two public university systems. In 2002, the first students under the new policy graduated with impressive results. San Jose students' progress in reading and math outpaced the state average, with African Americans and Latinos posting the greatest gains. Between 1998 and 2002, test scores for African American 11th graders in San Jose rose seven times as much as their peers statewide. Most important, dropout rates did not increase, even as the more rigorous and demanding curriculum became the default.[2]

*3. Students are likely to be better prepared for work, too.*

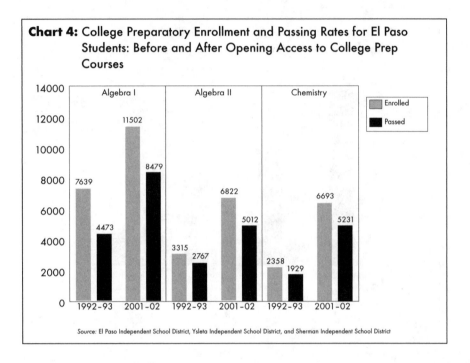

**Chart 4:** College Preparatory Enrollment and Passing Rates for El Paso Students: Before and After Opening Access to College Prep Courses

Source: El Paso Independent School District, Ysleta Independent School District, and Sherman Independent School District

A college-prep curriculum also contributes to another important goal for many students: success in finding and keeping a well-paying job.

In today's economy, the skills and academic abilities needed to find and succeed in a well-paying job are merging with those needed to succeed in college.

Manufacturing, for example, has for many years been the occupational haven for youth who leave high school without a diploma. In 1973, 51 percent of factory jobs were held by dropouts; by the year 2000, only 19 percent were. The proportion of factory jobs held by individuals with at least some college *tripled* and their wages held steady or dropped only slightly, while the real wages of high school graduates and dropouts in manufacturing fell (Carnevale & Desrochers, 2002).

Good jobs in manufacturing can pay over $40,000 a year and tend to require four to five years of postsecondary education or apprenticeship. The skills required to get into these programs often include mastery of algebra, geometry, trigonometry, chemistry, physics, or statistics.

It's not just in manufacturing, either. In unpublished research conducted for the American Diploma Project, the National Alliance of Business surveyed officials from 22 fields about the high school–level skills they believe are most useful for their employees to bring to the job. The employers unanimously cited the need for strong reading ability, mathematical reasoning, and problem-solving skills. Indeed, the list generated by employers looked almost exactly like the lists subsequently generated by college faculty from across the country.

## Curricular Misalignment: The Norm, Not the Exception

A college-preparatory curriculum has clear benefits to efforts to give certain students real choices at the conclusion of high school. Nonetheless, large numbers of American high school graduates — including many bound for college — do not complete such a curriculum. Why is that?

For starters, many college-bound students simply don't know which high school courses are necessary not just to enter college but also to begin credit-bearing courses. According to a recent report from Stanford University's Bridge Project, one of the most common student misconceptions about college readiness is that meeting their high school graduation requirements prepares them for college. Across the six states in this study, fewer than 12 percent of students surveyed knew the curricular requirements for admission to their public postsecondary institutions (Venezia, Kirst, & Antonio, 2003).

Even parents and school counselors are often misled into thinking that courses needed for admission are the same as college *readiness*. This can be a particular problem in two-year and other open-access colleges. While these colleges may admit anyone with a high school diploma, these new freshmen will find themselves still taking high school–level courses if they fail to pass placement exams. Only the campus will have changed.

Higher education has not been as helpful as it should be. Rather than coming to statewide agreement on which courses students should take in high school to be ready for college, many states leave this decision to individual institutions, leaving students to figure out what each institution wants.

State requirements for the high school diploma are often no more helpful. Eight states leave course requirements entirely to local school districts.

Many more specify the number of courses necessary in a particular subject area, but not their content. When K-12 and postsecondary systems are clear in defining content standards, those definitions almost never match. In only one state — Oklahoma — is there cross-sector agreement on both number and topics.

In a few states, course requirements for high school graduation exceed those for college entry. But the effect in most states is that the curriculum required for graduation — sometimes including even the curriculum labeled "college prep" — falls short of what students need to succeed in two- or four-year institutions (Somerville & Yi, 2002).

For new high school graduates this means that their high school diploma is no guarantee they meet postsecondary education's course requirements — or have the skills they need to get a good job.

## Bold Action in the States

The idea of aligning requirements for high school graduation with those for entering postsecondary institutions is beginning to take hold not just in leading school districts — for example, San Jose, El Paso, and Ysleta (near El Paso) — but at the state level, too.

Texas has taken a major step toward aligning K-12 and higher education by making college-prep courses the recommended curriculum for all students. Beginning with the class entering ninth grade in 2004, students will automatically be enrolled in this 24-unit curriculum unless they and their parents explicitly choose for them not to be.

Policymakers in Indiana are poised to do much the same thing. In 1994, Indiana's Education Roundtable, which works across the K-12, higher education, and business sectors, put forth a plan to raise educational standards in the state. In response, the legislature established the college-prep sequence of courses, called Core 40, as the recommended curriculum for all high school students. However, even though students were required to begin the sequence, they weren't necessarily expected to complete it.

The Education Roundtable is now promoting Core 40 as the required curriculum for high school graduation. It further recommends that the Core 40 assessments be aligned not only with college admissions criteria, but also with standards for college placement. As a further incentive to students,

Core 40 completion could be tied to state financial aid eligibility.

Making the college curriculum the "default" curriculum is the very least all districts and states should do: more than any other step, this change immediately signals society's expectation that all young people can and should be prepared not for college or for work but for both. Guidance counselors and savvy parents should not be the only ones who know which courses will prepare students for college.

## Why Not Standards Instead of More Course Requirements?

States and districts across the country have invested considerable time, effort, and resources in developing a system of K-12 standards and assessments, in part to get away from the tyranny of the Carnegie unit. Are we now advocating a return to the not-so-good ol' days of promotion by seat time, or worse, the imposition of dual requirements that will literally strangle high school students and their teachers?

No such thing.

We recognize the implicit dangers of course requirements. Schools and districts might try to change course names rather than course content, as in the past. Requiring a core curriculum for most of students' four years in high school might also discourage innovative learning programs and dampen enthusiasm for alternative curricula that might also be high level.

But at the moment, high schools are organized around courses, and states and districts have leverage over how courses are included in graduation requirements. Moreover, abundant research shows that certain courses have a strong relationship to later success in the workplace and in college, and that students who take a course called "Algebra" are better off than if they had taken "Consumer Mathematics."

Still, not all "Algebra" is created equal. States, districts, and schools have a lot of work to do to help teachers of courses with the same names make sure they are teaching to the same standard — including providing model lessons, sample assignments and student work, and benchmark assessments.

We believe that requiring a rigorous common curriculum is the best way states and districts can begin to provide all students the education they need and deserve. Eventually, we hope there will be multiple ways for students to access and engage with the same content. In the meantime, these courses are better than their watered-down alternatives.

## Break the Logjam

A strong "default" curriculum for all students is an important next step for most states and districts, but many other steps must also be taken before the curriculum is perfectly aligned and working well for every young person. And K-12 cannot do all the heavy lifting.

Higher education needs to take a long overdue look at admissions and placement policies. Not only are these often inconsistent with high school graduation requirements, they are also inconsistent among postsecondary institutions, and even between admissions and placement into college-level work in the same institution.

Clearly, a consensus about what "college ready" means is needed. And because this curriculum will be the standard for all secondary students, the content needs to be justified with better reasons than "that's the way it's always been done." Research shows, for example, that Algebra II in high school is a strong predictor of college success and beyond. What about other mathematics, notably probability and statistics? This strand of math is conspicuous by its absence from admissions and placement tests, but it is necessary for work and citizenship in addition to other disciplinary studies. What level of reading and writing skills are likewise predictive?

Business also has a responsibility to be thoughtful and explicit about the skills that are valuable in the workplace. Business organizations in many states are actively involved in education reform. As in Texas and Indiana, their advocacy can do a lot to promote policy change.

Implementing the new common curriculum will raise another set of issues. Schools will need enough teachers who have qualified in their subjects and who have strategies for helping all students master high-level content.[3] Also, schools will need new models for structuring time and support for students and teachers alike. And they will need aligned assessments for both individual diagnostic use in the classroom and for school accountability.

Above all, schools will need to break the logjam of outdated beliefs that defines the present high school diploma.

The knowledge and skills that today's young people need to succeed in the 21st century far exceed those that were enough for their counterparts a mere generation ago. The only prediction we can confidently make about future jobs is that they will change — and change yet again. Even those youngsters who go directly to work after high school will likely find themselves needing more training and education at some point in their working lives. So our eyes — and our energies — must be focused on ensuring that they leave high school with the foundation they need to access that additional learning, as well as to participate fully in family and civic life. A common college-prep curriculum is the shortest path toward meeting that goal.

---

1. Parts of this paper previously appeared in "A New Core Curriculum for All," *Thinking K-16*, Winter 2003, published by The Education Trust, Washington, DC.

2. Calculations by The Education Trust-West, based on 2002 data from the California Department of Education.

3. For this to work, higher education absolutely must increase production of teachers in certain shortage areas.

*European education systems have a lot to teach in terms of the coherence, flexibility, and efficiency of the transition from one level of education to the next. These systems are characterized by a common curriculum through grade nine or ten, a national school-leaving exam that doubles as a university entrance exam, and an occupational learning pathway that leads to high-paying, high-prestige jobs. Marc Tucker argues that we can learn from these systems' emphasis on clear and universal standards that serve as fixed gateways from one level of education to another, their multiple routes for preparing to pass through each gateway, and their treatment of the upper years of high school as a distinct, more adult level of education, closer to our community and technical colleges.*

# 3. High School and Beyond: The System Is the Problem — and the Solution[1]

## By Marc S. Tucker

High school is the Waterloo of the current round of school reform. There are many signs that the standards and accountability movement is having a substantial effect on the performance of elementary schools, even those that have a history of poor performance. And there are grounds for hope that real progress will be made in the middle schools. But high schools are another matter. Virtually everyone familiar with this landscape believes that our high schools are the most deeply troubled and most difficult to change of our elementary and secondary education institutions.

While it is still possible for young people to leave high school with an eighth-grade level of literacy or less and get a low-skill job that pays a little more than the minimum wage, it is not possible for that young person to support a family on that wage or with that kind of education. More and more, a young person who leaves high school unable to earn at least a two-year college degree faces a life of constant economic struggle. And in any cohort of ninth graders, only 25 percent will stay long enough to earn some sort of postsecondary qualification.

The reason only 25 percent make it is not a mystery. As many as half of all students who leave high school with or without a diploma probably have no more than an eighth-grade level of literacy. It is easy enough for high school graduates to get into our open enrollment institutions. The problem is getting out with a degree that means something.

The problem does not lie solely in our high schools. The incentives that operate on our postsecondary institutions cause them to take anyone who can add to the full-time equivalent totals that determine state reimbursements. They will take anyone who meets the minimum qualifications if the alternative is releasing their staff and shutting down their classrooms.

Employer decisionmaking parallels the postsecondary situation. There is a two-tier employment system in the United States. Large employers offering good careers will not hire young people who have just graduated high school. The jobs available to freshly minted high school graduates tend to be with small employers or franchisees of large retailing or food-service companies, where pay and benefits tend to be very low. While the more desirable employers have explicit hiring criteria, those in the lowest tier, like the open-enrollment institutions, take the best they can get.

The message to high schools and students is that virtually any student who can stagger to the finish line of high school can get a job or go to college and therefore has a glorious future awaiting them, even though their actual skill level may be well below that of a substantial fraction of the basic school graduates of many developing countries.

I have just described what can only be considered a growing national disaster. More and more students will find themselves unable to hold their economic heads above water. Employers will suffer ever greater shortages of qualified technical personnel. Those employers that can do so will go offshore to get what they need. Others will invest in labor-saving technology or go out of business.

If we are to avoid this disaster, we need a new system for bridging the end of compulsory education and the beginning of work and further education.

By way of explaining what I mean by a system, I will quickly sketch the way a number of other advanced industrialized nations organize education for the years in which our students attend high school. The easiest way to identify the weaknesses of our present system — and point the way to a better alternative — is to contrast it with systems that are producing better results.

In the countries I have in mind, all students take more or less the same curriculum for their first nine or ten years, set to the same standards, and then go their separate ways. The stereotypical view of the European system is that the decisions made at the end of basic schooling are irrevocable for life. That was true at one time but is no longer. In Denmark, for example, students who elect gymnasium (the route to university) for their upper-secondary path increasingly make a lateral move afterward to pick up a vocational credential. Governments are making it easier for students who start in the upper-secondary vocational curriculum to add enough demanding academic courses to qualify them to take the university exams. Denmark has created a technical gymnasium program that is just as demanding as the traditional gymnasium but is composed of specialized courses, many of which are built around problems and projects. Graduates of this program are highly valued by both the universities and top-tier employers.

These countries are responding to the same pressures we are — the drying up of low-skill jobs and the resulting political pressure to provide postsecondary education to virtually everyone — but their responses have some very important advantages.

*First, many of these countries have done a much better job than we have in the first nine or ten years of the education process.* The effects are most visible in the bottom half of the distribution, where their students typically achieve at far higher levels than ours. That means that they are better prepared for gymnasium and for a vocational education that requires serious intellectual effort. Many factors explain their success, including common expectations for all students set by their standards and examination systems; a standard curriculum that all students take through what we think of as the lower division of high school (10th grade); schools that are typically much smaller than ours, especially for the upper grades; and interscholastic sports organized and managed by municipalities, not school systems.

*Second, most of these countries have a national school-leaving exam that also serves as a university entrance exam.* There are few private universities, so it is very clear how well a student has to do to go to university, thereby providing a powerful motivation to achieve.

*Third, these nations have a much stronger tradition of vocational education, typically accompanied by a national system of occupational skills standards and strong employer participation.* In most of northern Europe, students who do not meet the skills standards simply cannot get a job in their chosen occupation, so high school–age students planning to enter the work force have strong incentives to take tough courses and work hard in school. Employers help train the students for their chosen occupations, assess them against the standards, and, in many other ways, ease the transition from school to work.

One other feature of these other systems is important to note. When students go from gymnasium or its equivalent to university, they enter professional school, not the equivalent of the American college. Gymnasium typically begins in the 10th or 11th year of schooling and lasts three years. University typically begins in the 13th or 14th year. From the standpoint of system efficiency, these other nations have created a system that produces the same or better outcomes while saving the cost of one to three years of expensive university education.

Systems so constructed have many advantages. They are, among other things 1) effective in terms of producing a total population that is as highly skilled as that of any other nation and, no less important, able to learn quickly what they need to adjust quickly to changes as they come; 2) flexible, in terms of enabling people to pursue enormously varied objectives and to change their minds along the way; and 3) efficient, in terms of the time and money needed to produce a person with a given qualification.

Certain other features are worth noting.

*First, these systems depend on clearly demarcated levels and clear, universal standards that serve as gateways for moving from one part of the system to another,* in particular from lower-secondary to upper-secondary education, from upper-secondary education to university, and from upper-secondary vocational education into the labor market. This provides strong incentives for students at every level to take tough courses and study hard in order to reach their goals, which can only be won by successfully passing through these gates.

*Second, these systems invest heavily in assessment,* which is typically done by having real people examine the students' extended work product and comparing it to the standards. Very few of these countries use the standardized, norm-referenced, machine-scored tests that are so popular in this country.

*Third, the high schools in these countries are much smaller than those in the United States at the lower division level.* Teachers frequently follow students through the grades, getting to know both students and their families much better than is the case in the United States.

*Fourth, the institutions offering programs at a level comparable to the upper division of high school (11th and 12th grades) here have the feel, not of our high schools but of our community and technical colleges.* Students are treated much more like adults; the place feels much less custodial.

*Fifth, these countries are paying more and more attention to guidance,* finding ways to help students understand their options and identify those that suit them.

*Sixth, although these systems are dynamic, they are not an endless amorphous experiment.* The governments that use systems of this sort believe it is important to have structures that guarantee similar opportunities for students throughout the nation, structures that are simple and stable enough to be understood and negotiated by everyone, everywhere.

## Establishing a Gateway System

I want to explore more thoroughly the concept of clear gateways and many flexible paths between those gateways. The European pattern, as I said above, calls for nine or ten years of basic education set to common standards. During their basic education, students take a common required curriculum with very few choices, culminating in a set of examinations set by the ministry of education. Students can then choose among a variety of academic and vocational courses and programs, and they can mix and match those options. The range of initial choices is constrained by the grades students received in their exams and basic education courses, but, increasingly, students who do not do well in basic school can, with enough hard work, still get to university. The standards for getting into the next stage of education and for getting an entry-level job in these systems are very clear, and they are not waived. Typically, there are multiple pathways available for getting to the next destination, with a wide variety of safety-net programs and institutions that provide alternative routes to the established gateways for those who failed in the regular programs. But the standards that must be met to get through the gateways are clear and inflexible.

It is this combination of fixed gateways, clear standards, and multiple pathways for getting to those standards that makes these systems work as well as they do. The gateways align the different levels of the system: everyone at a given level knows what students entering that level know and can do. There is no "remediation," because one does not move up to a higher level until meeting the standards required to do so. Programs for students who have not succeeded at a given level help them get to the point at which they can meet the standard for entering the next stage of their education, but those programs do not confer credit for the next stage.

I would like to offer a modest proposal for an American adaptation of this international system. This proposal is intended to enable us to achieve greater quality, flexibility, and efficiency. We should not copy the system of any other nation and probably could not, even if we wanted to. But when you have fallen a long way behind the leaders, it is not out of order to look at how the leaders get results.

The principles that underlie the following proposal are those that the National Center on Education and the Economy used to develop our "America's Choice" high school design, but they could just as easily become the basis for a state's formal grade 9-16 education policy.

*STEP ONE: Establish the first Gateway: a state standard for entrance to the state college system without remediation, and establish this as a standard that all high school students must meet as a condition for advancing to the upper division of high school.*

Meeting this standard would certify that the person has the reading, writing, and mathematics skills needed to do college-level work. States would issue a certificate to high school students who meet this standard.

The expectation would be that this standard would be met by the time a student is 16 years old or at the end of the tenth grade. Some students would take longer, but all students would have to meet it to be admitted to a two-year or four-year state college. Setting this standard is not based on the assumption that everyone will go to college but rather that, in the current economic environment, it is the obligation of government to provide everyone with the skills they need to do so.

*STEP TWO: Develop assessments to judge when students have met the standard stipulated for the first Gateway.*

This is no small step. We would model the new assessments on the Cambridge University examination system, which uses multiple modes of assessment that include course syllabi, end-of-course exams, end-of-course-sequence exams, and a scoring system that takes into account not only the scores on those exams but also scores based on teacher grades on teacher-assigned tasks that are checked by professional assessors. The Cambridge tests do not cost as much as the $75 per student per exam for Advanced Placement tests, but they are much more expensive than the typical state high-stakes, tenth-grade test.

*STEP THREE: Create the conditions that make it possible for high schools to get all their students to the new college-ready standard.*

A brief sketch of this incredibly complex issue emphasizes three priorities:

- *Create policies and provide the funds needed to convert large high schools into much smaller institutions, on the order of 400 students each.* Where new buildings cannot be created, convert existing ones into buildings where separate small schools co-locate.
- *Create a "standard state curriculum" for the lower division.* Syllabi would specify the content and sequencing of about three-quarters of the total course load for the lower division of high school, complete with end-of-course exams. Successful completion of these courses would normally mean that a student could expect to meet the standard for the exams on which the first Gateway certificate would be based. The rest of the time in the freshman and sophomore years would be available for electives or for double-period courses in the core subjects needed by students who enter high school two or more grade levels behind. There will be no general track, no vocational track, no career academies (i.e., a program with a career education focus), and no distractions. These programs may employ any pedagogy they choose, but they exist for one purpose only:

to get their students through the first Gateway.

- *Require low-performing high schools to use a comprehensive school design that has a record of raising achievement in low-performing schools.* These schools are typically in chaos and suffer from poor leadership. They require the kind of extensive support and cohesive program that only a comprehensive school design can provide. Because astonishingly little research exists on the problems of low-performing high school students, and even less on developing an effective curriculum for them, the states and the federal government need to greatly increase the level of effort on this front.

*STEP FOUR: Establish the options available to students who successfully pass through the first Gateway.*

The next step is to carefully define the options that are available to students who reach the new certificate standard. At the National Center on Education and the Economy, where we have been working on this problem for 12 years, we are convinced that the next step for all students should be the beginning of some form of college. If the standard that the student has met qualifies that student for college-level work, why not send that student to college?

But students need not leave high school to embark on college, although they should have that option. Here's what I mean.

Students who get their certificate and want to pursue a program leading to a two-year technical degree or certificate ought to go straight to a community or technical college offering such a program. Very few high schools in the United States can afford the equipment and the faculty needed for technical programs — from welding and auto mechanics to software systems management, hotel and restaurant management, cardiovascular technology, and graphics and design. Community and technical colleges should house these programs, and that is where students who want to pursue such programs should go.

States that go down this path may have to strengthen the incentives operating on their community colleges to offer strong two-year technical programs, since current financial and status incentives lead many colleges to favor general education over technical programs. Or states might choose to create a separate system of technical colleges, if they have not done so already.

What about the students who do not choose to leave their high school to pursue a technical program at the local community or technical college?

These students should have as broad a range of options as possible for going to college in high school. The variety and nature of the options will depend on the size and location of the school and the preferences of the community. The International Baccalaureate program, conceived as the embodiment of a European gymnasium program set to a high European standard, is one example. Even the most selective American colleges admit IB diploma holders as college sophomores. Another alternative would be a demanding program based on the admission requirements of the highest level of the state university system and including a substantial number of Advanced Placement courses. A third would, like the curriculum now being developed at NCEE, employ a pedagogy rich in problems and projects but set to a high academic standard. Some high schools may be able to offer only one such option. Others might offer many. Most options will take advantage of faculty resident in the school, but others might be virtual.

In this conception of a new system, high schools and community colleges will compete for students. The public and the students will benefit greatly from such competition. This can only improve course offerings and moderate costs.

High schools will have to give their upper-division high schools the look and feel of college, not custodial institutions. Both the public and students will benefit enormously from cutting out what is now a largely wasted senior year in high school.

College can begin right after the sophomore year, not the senior year, for those who want that option. Those who want more time to prepare for a very competitive college can stay in high school.

There would not be a standard state curriculum at this tier of the system, but there would not be a free-for-all either. The range of course and program offerings would be framed by the next set of Gateways.

*STEP FIVE: Establish the second Gateway: the standard required for transfer into the upper division of the equivalent of the baccalaureate-granting lower tier of the state college system. Create the examinations needed to determine whether this standard has been met.*

This second set of Gateway examinations would be available to high school upper-division students and lower-division college students who might want to transfer into the state four-year college system at the end of their program. Meeting the standard set for this Gateway would guarantee transfer into the state system. The state would require all upper-division high schools and community colleges to offer programs that, as a minimum, provided the skills and knowledge needed to meet this Gateway standard. The standard would be set not in terms of courses taken and time spent but in terms of performance to be demonstrated on an examination, leaving room for creativity and variation with respect to course and program design. Individual postsecondary institutions and programs within those institutions could impose additional requirements, but the core performance requirements in the public institutions would be known by everyone and common across the board.

I do not mean to suggest that only conventional high schools and community colleges would prepare people for this second set of Gateway exams. To visit Denmark is to encounter a dizzying array of formal and informal institutions dedicated to getting people of all ages and conditions ready for one or another of the gateways. If policy focuses on defining the gateways, creating appropriate performance measures, and providing flexible funding for people in a great variety of situations, so that many different institutional types can offer the services needed to get to a particular gateway, then the taxpayer and the student will enjoy a system that runs more efficiently and provides many more pathways for people in every circumstance.

*STEP SIX: Establish the third set of Gateways: skill standards for the technical degree programs to be offered in two-year postsecondary institutions.*

What is missing and badly needed in the community and technical college system are standards for the technical occupations and assessments to gauge when those standards have been met. The National Skill Standards Board, chartered to develop such a system, may not do so before it sunsets. Some states are working on the task, but state standards are no substitute for a national system.

The states, working separately and together, need to redouble their efforts to establish clear performance standards for the technical occupations, not courses-taken and time-in-the-seat standards. Employers, representatives of labor, and educators need to collaborate in setting the standards, and there must be a fair way to assess them. Examples of such systems abound in other nations.

*STEP SEVEN: Create mechanisms to align education finance with the new organizational structure.*

If community colleges and new upper-division high schools are to compete on an equal footing, their general-education programs will have to be financed on the same basis. They should be financed based on student enrollment, but institutional compensation for each full-time equivalent student should be calculated based on the cost of offering different courses, so incentives do not favor cheaper general-education courses over technical offerings.

Implementation of the system I have described could become the occasion for the state's providing a free education for all state residents through the first two years of college. I say that because, by collapsing the last two years of high school and the first two years of college for many students, this system will save the state enormous sums of money.

One other point about finance. Great Britain has found a way to deal with their shameful dropout statistics in higher education. They give their further education colleges (similar to our community colleges) a sign-up fee when a student matriculates and a certain amount each year thereafter, but most compensation does not come to the college until the student has received his or her degree. While mobility among college students is greater in the United States, I still believe it would be possible and useful to adapt the British system by deferring some of the compensation to the postsecondary institutions the student attends until a degree is awarded, whether the student attends only one such institution or several.

## Into the Political Arena

Some additional comments are in order.

*Accountability.* The lower-division high schools would be accountable for getting all their students through the first Gateway. That is a very focused accountability standard. Community college general-education programs and upper-division high schools would be held accountable, at a minimum, for the proportion of students meeting the second Gateway standard. This standard is just as focused as the first. Community and technical colleges offering two- to five-year technical programs in areas for which standards have been established would be held accountable for the proportion of their candidates who actually meet the standards in their field.

*Governance.* States that have separate governance mechanisms for community colleges, state colleges, state universities, state vocational education and training, and public schools will find it very hard to pull off the kind of system integration that I am advocating unless they establish some superordinant mechanism to coordinate policymaking. New Zealand, some years ago, established a governmental unit separate from all the entities just named to establish the standards and measures used to build all the key gateways in their system. That is an extreme measure, but it illustrates the lengths to which New Zealand was willing to go to build a coherent system.

*The high school diploma.* Under this proposal, the high school diploma is not a gateway, but the diploma will continue to be important. Up to now, the diploma has served as a measure of the student's persistence and determination. Employers and higher education institutions have valued it on those grounds, knowing that students who have what it takes to persist are more likely to do well after high school than those who do not. The state should continue to authorize high schools to issue the diploma to people who complete a prescribed program of studies with passing grades. Most employers and four-year higher education institutions will require that candidates both have the diploma and meet the requirements for the first Gateway certificate. In many cases, the diploma will not be awarded until the candidate has completed both the lower and upper divisions of high school or the lower-division program and a two-year college program.

*Politics of changing the system as it currently exists.* Why would community colleges want to educate high school students? Why would high schools be willing to give up students to the community colleges? How can the state get the higher education community to work with the schools to establish the criteria and set the exams for the first gateway certificate? How can the state get employers, representatives of labor, and educators to agree on occupational standards that will be used to set the curriculum for the provider institutions and judge their performance? How can the state merge two quite different funding schemes for the schools and for the colleges into one equitable system?

These are only some of the issues that will have to addressed in the political arena to make this system work. Because the situation on the ground differs so greatly from state to state, it would be foolish to offer pat solutions to these problems. Having said that, it would irresponsible to make no suggestions as to the direction of possible solutions.

Take the matter of high schools being willing to give up some of their students to the postsecondary sector. This actually happened some years ago in Minnesota, where the state made it possible for high school students to enroll in any higher education institution that would admit them before high school graduation, and to take their daily average attendance money with them. Many states now permit high school students to take courses in community colleges while still enrolled in their high school program. Some make it possible for students to leave their high school before graduating to enroll in their community college as a degree candidate, sometimes getting their high school diploma and two-year degree at the same time. There is ample precedent for the kind of policy structure proposed here.

Community colleges are the most entrepreneurial of our educational institutions. I think it quite likely that they would be happy to enroll degree candidates coming out of the sophomore year of high school, and they would probably be happy to strengthen their technical offerings if the additional costs of these programs were taken into account in the policies that govern reimbursements by the state.

The proposal on the table assumes that the higher education system would no longer be permitted to offer remedial courses for credit. While nothing would prevent them from offering noncredit safety-net programs, this prohibition would probably result in a net decline in enrollment and would therefore produce substantial opposition. Such policies, however, are being instituted in some parts of the country, which is proof that it is possible to do so.

In the longer run, of course, the policies suggested here are likely to result in larger enrollments throughout higher education, because demand will steadily rise and the current failure rates should be sharply curtailed. But long-run benefits are of little interest to political leaders who could be defeated in the short run on the basis of positions they take today.

One last point. I regret if the breezy air of this paper suggests that I believe the agenda laid out here can be easily accomplished. I do not. It is very difficult to establish a sound skill-standards system and to organize an upper-secondary vocational system that is matched to the standards and at the same time nimble enough to be responsive to rapid technological developments and changes in work organization. The task of creating a lower-division high school program that actually enables the vast majority of students to reach the first Gateway standard in two years is an immense challenge.

It is not easy. But it is both possible and necessary.

We know that it is possible because other nations have done it and many of the pieces have been enacted somewhere in the United States. We know that it is necessary because our analysis of the economy leads to no other conclusion.

---

1. Jobs for the Future commissioned this paper for discussion at two meetings in October 2002, sponsored by the Bill & Melinda Gates Foundation and co-sponsored by Aspen Institute, Jobs for the Future, the National Conference of State Legislatures, and the National Governors Association.

*If students are to be college ready when they graduate from high school, colleges must do a better job of signaling to high school students, teachers, and counselors what college-level work requires. Rather than proposing a common college-prep curriculum or a highly structured set of standardized gateways, Michael Kirst and Andrea Venezia emphasize ways for states to improve the alignment of college expectations and high school curricula and graduation standards. They emphasize better information, clearer signals and feedback from colleges to high schools, more logical alignment of assessments, and greater attention to what students need to succeed in the broad-access colleges that serve the vast majority of students.*

# 4. The Case for Improving Connections between K-12 Schools and Colleges

## By Michael W. Kirst and Andrea Venezia

Stanford University's Bridge Project, a six-year national study, sought to analyze the policies for high school exit and college entrance to learn if they had different standards — if they were asking students to know and use different concepts and skills between graduating from high school and entering college. Researchers wanted to understand what students, parents, and K-12 educators know about college admission and course placement policies, and if they have the resources they need to make informed decisions.

The project focused on signals and incentives that enhance the college knowledge of prospective students in secondary schools and help them gain admission to colleges, be placed into college-level courses upon entry, and complete their desired education. Such signals are especially important for students who are currently not exposed to high-level K-12 curricula or who do not receive information about college in a consistent manner from their parents, counselors, siblings, or teachers.[1]

We found that current state policies have created a layer of inequalities through unnecessary and detrimental barriers between high school and college, barriers that are undermining student aspirations, particularly at broad-access institutions. The current fractured systems send students, their parents, and K-12 educators conflicting and vague messages about what students need to know and be able to do to enter and succeed in college.

America's high school students have higher educational aspirations than ever before, aspirations that cut across racial and ethnic lines with scant differences (Education Trust, 1999). Parents, educators, policymakers, business leaders, community members, and researchers have told students that they need to go to college to succeed in our society, and students have heard that message. Eighty-eight percent of eighth graders expect to participate in some form of postsecondary education, and about 70 percent of high school graduates actually do go to college within two years of graduating (National Center for Education Statistics, 1996). Yet their aspirations are being undermined by disconnected educational systems and other barriers. Not all students can prepare well for postsecondary education, many do not know which courses they should take, and others are in schools that do not offer all the appropriate courses.

Inadequate and inequitable preparation for college translates into high remediation rates and low persistence rates at postsecondary institutions throughout the country. For example, 40 percent of students in four-year institutions take some remedial education, as do 63 percent at two-year institutions (U.S. Department of Education, 2001). Remediation problems are the greatest in the "broad-access postsecondary institutions" that admit almost every student who applies. Broad-access institutions comprise about 85 percent of all postsecondary schools and educate about 80 percent of the nation's first-year college students.[2]

At broad-access institutions, the placement exams students take when they enter college are the critical academic standard. These are the pathway to college-level credit courses, and although they are not a perfect proxy for what students need to know and do to take college-level courses — many college faculty members use their own classroom-specific exams — they are the best we have. High school students need to understand what will be expected of them in order to succeed in college-level work. Currently, they do not receive enough consistent, high-quality information about college standards or how to prepare for them.

Moreover, most media and public attention focuses on postsecondary admission, not on postsecondary success. This is particularly problematic for students who are traditionally underrepresented in postsecondary education, such as first-generation college-goers, students of color, and economically disadvantaged students. High schools often lack counselors who focus solely on college-related issues; many teachers of non-honors courses do not view their role as helping students prepare for college; and college preparation is a daunting and confusing process, even for students with many resources.

## Bridge Project Findings

The table summarizes the Bridge Project's findings of many students' misconceptions, from overestimates of the cost of college to the difficulties of succeeding in college once they are admitted.

Other major Bridge Project findings include:

*Inequalities exist in access to quality information about college options.* Such inequality has been documented by numerous studies. Because almost all students plan to attend college, and most at least start college, it makes sense to help all students learn about their postsecondary options and prepare for college. However, there are deep inequalities in areas such as college counseling, college-preparation course offerings, and connections with local postsecondary institutions.[3] There is also an unequal distribution of such resources as college centers on high school campuses, opportunities to visit

TABLE 1

| STUDENT MISCONCEPTIONS ABOUT PREPARING FOR AND ATTENDING COLLEGE | |
| --- | --- |
| *Many students believe:* | *In truth:* |
| I can't afford college. | Students and parents regularly overestimate the cost of college. |
| I have to be a stellar athlete or student to get financial aid. | Most students receive some form of financial aid. |

| | |
|---|---|
| Meeting high school graduation requirements will prepare me for college. | Adequate preparation for college usually requires a more demanding curriculum than is reflected in minimum requirements for high school graduation, sometimes even if that curriculum is termed "college preparation." |
| Getting into college is the hardest part. | For the majority of students, the hardest part is completing college. |
| Community colleges don't have academic standards. | Students usually must take placement tests at community colleges in order to qualify for college-level work. |
| My senior year in high school doesn't matter. | The classes students take in their senior year will often determine the classes they are able to take in college and how well prepared they are for those classes. |
| I don't have to worry about my grades, or the kind of classes I take, until my sophomore year. | Many colleges look at sophomore-year grades and, in order to enroll in college-level courses, students need to prepare well for college. This means taking a well-thought-out series of courses starting no later than 9th or 10th grade. |
| I can't start thinking about financial aid until I know where I'm going to college. | Students need to file a federal aid form prior to the time most colleges send out their acceptance letters. This applies to students who attend community colleges, too, even though they can apply and enroll in the fall of the year they wish to attend. |
| I can take whatever classes I want when I get to college. | Most colleges and universities require entering students to take placement exams in core subject areas. Those tests will determine the classes students can take. |

colleges, and visits from college recruiters on high school campuses. Students in accelerated curricular tracks in high school receive clearer signals about college preparation than do their peers in other tracks. Many students in middle- and lower-level high school courses are not reached by postsecondary education outreach efforts or by college counseling staff in their high schools. Many economically disadvantaged parents lack experience and information concerning college preparation.

In Illinois, Maryland, and Oregon, 42 percent, 44 percent, and 47 percent, respectively, of economically disadvantaged parents stated that they had received college information, as compared with 74 percent, 71 percent, and 66 percent of their more economically well-off counterparts.

Current data systems are not set up for easy and high-value uses across K-12 and higher education systems. Most states can neither identify students' needs as they transition from one education system to another nor assess outcomes from K-16 reforms. They have no K-16 data systems that would make this possible. In some states, such as Illinois, Texas, Oregon, and Maryland, data from postsecondary institutions are shared with high schools. However, none of the K-12 educators interviewed by the Bridge Project who knew about those data reported using them for any purpose.

There are no models of effective state K-16 accountability systems. No one is held accountable for K-16 outcomes, such as remediation, preparation, and completion of degrees or vocational certificates.

*State K-12 and higher education curricula are poorly aligned.* Many high school graduation standards do not meet the demands of college-entrance or -placement requirements, but that fact is often left unpublicized by high schools or colleges. Out of the six states studied by the Bridge Project, only Texas had legislated curricular alignment across the systems, making the college-prep curriculum the default curriculum for all public high schools beginning in 2005. Most states have large gaps between high school and college standards. Table 2 illustrates California's curricular disconnects.

*Student knowledge of college curricular requirements is sporadic and vague.* Few students surveyed knew all the course requirements for the institutions studied. This ranged from one percent of students in California to 11 percent in Maryland. Students do appear to have considerable partial knowledge of curricular requirements: slightly more than half of the students knew three or more course requirements.

Teachers play a major role in helping students prepare for college, yet they do not have the resources they need to give students accurate information. Teachers often took a greater role in helping students prepare for college than did counselors, but teachers lack connections with postsecondary institutions and up-to-date admission and placement information. Also, the teachers who were most active in helping students prepare for college were

**TABLE 2**

| CALIFORNIA'S HIGH SCHOOL GRADUATION AND UNIVERSITY ENTRANCE COURSE REQUIREMENTS | | |
|---|---|---|
| | *Required by Four-Year Public Universities* | *Minimum High School Requirements* |
| *English* | 4 years college-prep classes | 3 years |
| *Mathematics* | 3 years college-prep classes required (topics through Algebra II), 4 years recommended | 2 years (topics through Algebra I) |
| *Science* | 2 years with a lab required, 3 recommended (biology, chemistry, physics) | 2 years (including biological and physical sciences) |
| *History/Social Science* | 2 years U.S. history, American government, world history, and cultures | 3 years |
| *Language* | 2 years required, 3 recommended | none |
| *Visual and Performing Arts* | 1 year | 1 year of visual or performing arts or second language |
| *Electives* | 1 year (academic course or non-introductory arts course) | 2 years of physical education and other coursework locally specified |

usually teachers of honors and college-prep courses.

*Students are generally unaware of the existence and content of postsecondary course placement exams.* Across all six states in the study, fewer than half of the sampled students knew the specific placement testing policies for the institutions in the study. Placement exam standards have not been connected to the K-12 standards movement that has swept the country. Indeed, the entire K-12 standards movement has lacked participation and buy-in from postsecondary policymakers, because standards policies are made in separate K-12 and postsecondary education orbits that rarely intersect. Public information on the content of placement exams is scant and poorly publicized to prospective students and secondary schools. The content and cognitive demands of placement exams are an unknown research area when compared to the SAT or ACT research base. Students, particularly at broad-access institutions, are admitted under one standard but placed in credit courses or remediation on another standard that is often much higher (e.g., math at or above Algebra II). Secondary school students often wrongly believe that their high school graduation requirements are sufficient for postsecondary credit-level work and rarely know about the standards and consequences related to placement exams.

Bridge Project research found that high school assessments often stress different knowledge and skills than do college entrance and placement requirements. Similarly, the coursework between high school and college is not connected; students graduate from high school under one set of standards, and three months later they are required to meet a whole new set of standards in college. Research conducted by RAND for the Bridge Project found, for example, that approximately 33 percent of the items on any state high school assessment were framed within realistic situations, and as many as 92 percent of the items were contextualized. In contrast, the placement tests and college entrance exams assessed examinees primarily with abstract questions. Also, many states are using writing samples in their K-12 assessments. By contrast, ACT and SAT I use multiple-choice formats to test writing skills (although the College Board is planning to add a writing component to the SAT I). With the exception of the COMPASS Numerical Skills test, no more than 25 percent of the items on the placement exams and college entrance assessments were presented in realistic settings, and as few as 5 percent of the items were contextualized (Le & Robyn, 2001). Other studies have come to similar conclusions. For example, The Education Trust has shown that placement standards in mathematics often include Algebra II, while admission tests rarely exceed Algebra I (Education Trust, 1999).

A statement by an Oregon community college student interviewed by Bridge Project researchers captures some of the lack of information about K-16 tests: "So I did my orientation, and they told me something about [placement] testing. I was like, what? You have to do a test? . . . Nobody told me about them when I graduated from high school."

## Primary Recommendations

It is predictable that these problems exist, given the disconnection between K-12 and postsecondary education, the scarcity of data to analyze problems and needs across the sectors, the few K-16 accountability mechanisms that exist, and other related weaknesses of collaboration between K-12 and higher education. Yet, given these challenges, what should policymakers and education leaders strive to change? Our research found that the following three actions are most promising for immediate reform:

*1. Provide all students, their parents, and educators with accurate, high-quality information about and access to courses that will help prepare students for college-level standards.*

Access to college is crucial, but so is access to high-quality college-preparation curricula and to information that will help students plan well for college. Adelman (1999) demonstrated that the content of the courses high school students take is the main predictor of college success. Currently, in many middle and high schools, access to college-preparatory information and curricula is not available to all students.

*2. Focus on the institutions that serve the majority of students.*

Shift media, policy, and research attention to include broad-access colleges and universities attended by the vast majority of students (approximately 80%). Broad-access colleges need the financial and policy attention of federal, state, and other leaders. Increasing the rates of student success at these colleges is a sound public investment. It can have a tremendous impact on the civic and economic well-being of each state by improving people's economic security, increasing their civic participation, and increasing college completion rates for economically disadvantaged students and students of color.

*3. Create the awareness that getting into college is not the hardest part, but that the real challenge is earning a credential.*

Expand the focus of local, state, and federal programs from access to college to include success in college. Access to college is only half the picture. It is time to focus policy attention on improving college success rates. High school course content, academic counseling, college outreach, and other programming needs to reflect this so that students are clear about what it takes to succeed in college, including community college.

How can our nation achieve these ends? For a start, college stakeholders must be at the table when state K-12 standards are developed. Likewise, K-12 educators must be engaged as postsecondary admission and placement policies are under review. Reforms across the two education systems will be difficult if not impossible to implement without meaningful communication and policymaking between the levels.

## Additional Recommendations

States, K-12 schools and districts, postsecondary institutions and systems, and the federal government can take several other important steps to improve the transition from high school to college for all students. These include:

*Ensure that colleges and universities specify, and publicize, their academic standards so that students, their parents, and educators have accurate college-preparation information.* This effort must go beyond targeted outreach and fragmented categorical programs to universal programs for all students. In addition, states should disseminate materials in languages other than English, depending on the language groups in their states.

*Examine the relationship between the content of postsecondary placement exams and K-12 exit standards and assessments to determine if more compatibility is necessary and possible.* K-12 standards and assessments that are aligned with postsecondary education standards and assessments can provide clear signals and incentives, if the standards and assessments are high quality. Assessments should be diagnostic in nature and indicate to students the relationships between their scores and the level necessary for college preparation and course placement without remediation. Appropriate K-12 assessments could be used as an admission and placement factor by public postsecondary education institutions, although caution must be taken to ensure that more than one measure of student preparation is used, and that the stakes attached to K-12 assessments are not too high for students.

*Review postsecondary education placement exams for reliability, validity, efficacy, and the extent to which they promote teaching for understanding.* Data need to be maintained regarding the success of placement procedures and predictive validity for student performance in college courses.

*Allow students to take placement exams in high school so they can prepare academically for college and understand college-level expectations.* These assessments should be diagnostic so that students, their parents, and their teachers know how to improve students' preparation for college.

*Sequence undergraduate general-education requirements so that appropriate senior-year courses are linked to postsecondary general-education courses.* For students who are not well prepared for college, the senior year should be a time of intense academic preparation.[4] One example was provided by an administrator at Portland State University in Oregon, who was interviewed by Bridge Project researchers:

> The students that we counsel . . . they'll choose the co-admit program because it connects them to our university and provides on-site advising at the community college so that there's a seamless transition, or as near seamless as we can make it. It really is a nice program. They love it, and we love it because there are no surprises.

*Expand successful dual or concurrent enrollment programs between high schools and colleges so that they include all students, not just traditionally "college-bound" students.* Many such programs are solely for students who are considered college bound. Yet, all students could benefit from course offerings that blend high school and college faculty and subject areas.

*Collect, and connect, data from all education sectors.* States and regions should create common identifier numbers for students and track teacher performance during preparation and professional development programs. Data should be tied to a K-16 accountability system. Postsecondary institutions and K-12 schools need assistance in learning how to use data to inform curricular and instructional policies and practices.

*Provide technical support to states by having the federal government establish voluntary data collection standards.* Many state policymakers and analysts interviewed by the Bridge Project expressed the need for technical assistance to develop and use a K-16 data system.

*Expand federal grants to stimulate K-16 policymaking.* Specifically, federal competitive grants should be available for collaborative discussions between K-12 and postsecondary education, with requirements for examining and improving particular issues (such as the collection and use of data across the systems); and for K-16 collaboration that enables students to make a successful transition from one system to the next.

These recommendations will be easier to accomplish and more effective in their implementation if there is an overall organizational base for K-16 policymaking and oversight. While each state and region needs its own form of governance, they have many models upon which to draw. Most states implicitly discourage K-16 policymakers by having separate K-12 and higher education legislative committees and state agencies. These structural barriers inhibit joint policymaking and communication for issues such as funding, data sharing, student learning (curriculum, standards, and assessment), matriculation and transfer, teacher training and professional development, and accountability.

Having a K-16 entity will not ensure that innovative K-16 reforms follow. Only a concerted effort by policymakers, educators, parents, and students will do the job. Nor will implementing these recommendations magically eliminate the dozens of other reasons why students are not prepared adequately for college. But these are important steps toward developing a more equitable educational experience for all students and providing all students with the preparation they need to succeed in college.

---

1. Bridge Project researchers analyzed state and institutional policies in regions in California, Georgia, Illinois, Maryland, Oregon, and Texas. They surveyed nearly 2,000 students and parents from 23 schools about students' post–high school aspirations and their knowledge of issues related to student preparation for college, including tuition, admission criteria, and placement criteria. Researchers also talked with community college students about their college preparation activities and academic experiences in college, including course placement.

   In addition, researchers gathered information on state-level high school graduation and college entrance policies, and on placement policies, admissions requirements, and outreach and communication strategies from 18 selective and less-selective colleges and universities. They interviewed high school administrators, counselors, and teachers about high school coursework and college counseling for students. This research was conducted between 1997 and 2000, depending on the state. The project was supported by generous contributions from the Pew Charitable Trusts and the U.S. Department of Education.

2. Calculations are based on data from the Carnegie Foundation for the Advancement of Teaching (2001). Researchers checked the Carnegie classifications with College Board data concerning the percentage of applicants accepted by postsecondary institutions, and with data in Tom Mortenson, "Freshman-to-Sophomore Persistence Rates by Institutional Control, Academic Selectivity and Degree Level, 1983 to 1998," in *Postsecondary Education Opportunity*, Oskaloosa, Iowa (1998).

3. For example, for information and recommendations about Latino parents' knowledge of college preparation issues, see *College Knowledge: What Latino Parents Need to Know and Why They Don't Know It*, by the Tomás Rivera Policy Institute, *www.trpi.org*.

4. For additional information and recommendations regarding the senior year of high school, see "Overcoming the High School Senior Slump," by Michael W. Kirst at *http://bridgeproject.stanford.edu*.

*In the current fiscal environment facing states, strategies to improve high school outcomes, and therefore college success, will have to be fairly low-cost to the public sector. Joe Nathan suggests a few strategies that can leverage significant change with limited new investment. These are: 1) expand state programs that allow high school students to enroll in college courses and earn college credit; 2) promote small, accountable high schools, either as charters or run by local districts; and 3) require better information about high school performance and college remediation rates, then disseminate that information widely to schools, parents, policymakers, and the public.*

# 5. More High School Options, Better Information: Low-Cost Approaches to Getting More Youth Prepared for and into College

## By Joe Nathan

Raul became the first of his family to attend a college or university. His family's income was very low, but Minnesota's Post-Secondary Options program allowed him to spend part of his high school junior and senior years at a community college or four-year university. Raul earned enough college credits while still in high school to enter the state's major research university with almost enough credits to qualify as a junior.

Xiong attends a charter high school that is located on the campus of a community college. This has made it easy for her to take a number of college courses while still technically in high school. Equally important, being on a college campus has helped her see that she really does belong there, even though none of her older brothers or sisters or her parents ever attended a college or university.

These stories of real youngsters inspired this paper. Around the country there is growing experience and interest in helping young people negotiate the transition from high school to postsecondary learning by getting a jump on college while still in high school. Some of the most exciting initiatives include small school efforts — such as charter high schools or early college high schools. But these innovations are typically small and hard to bring about on a larger scale. What can states do to help promote innovation of this kind? In particular, what can states do in a fiscal environment where significant new investments are unlikely to be forthcoming?

From experience working with the National Governors Association; teaching in an award-winning, innovative urban K-12 public school now in its 33rd year; helping others create innovative district and charter high schools; and providing invited testimony in 22 state legislatures, I suggest three policies that states can adopt to increase the percentage of students attending colleges and universities and help stimulate improvement in existing public schools:

1. Develop, promote, and refine state programs that allow high school students to take college courses, full- or part-time, with state funds following the students.
2. Promote and encourage the development of small, accountable high schools, run either by districts or as part of a state's charter public school sector.
3. Require information-gathering regarding graduation rates, rates of remedial courses, and other information that policymakers, educators, families, and the broader public need in order to understand what's happening in schools and how well they are progressing.

Any recommendations in 2004 require fiscal realism. State education policymakers face major budget pressures and steadily increasing regulatory and public expectations of schools. My goal is to describe how state-level leaders can deal with these obstacles as they try to help more youngsters graduate from high school and enter some form of postsecondary education.

The cost of failing to serve a high-risk student well in public education is potentially quite high. Vanderbilt University professor Mark Cohen (1996) has estimated the monetary value of "saving" a high-risk youth at $1.5 to $2.0 million dollars, taking into account typical costs to society of dropping out, potentially using drugs, and potentially becoming involved in the criminal justice system. Each youngster who starts off on the wrong road but then is helped to graduate high school and continue his education produces enormous savings, along with greater contributions, to a community.

These powerful gains are important to society, but they do not count on state balance sheets. State leaders are more concerned about short-term costs and visible benefits. For decades, legislators and governors have been increasing state investments in K-12 (and higher) education. In some states, this helped produced some achievement and attainment gains. However, a significant achievement gap remains.

"Business as usual" will not achieve the improvements we seek. We cannot simply pour more dollars into existing ways of educating young people — or existing governance systems. This paper advocates a two-prong approach: 1) continue working to improve existing schools, and 2) use public school choice, innovation, and competition to help create new high-quality schools and education pathways that can also stimulate improvement in existing systems. The first approach is necessary because existing schools will be educating most of our young people for years to come. The second approach embodies democratic principles of freedom and choice, as well as our economy's successful encouragement of entrepreneurs. The second approach also can promote improvement and innovation in more cost-effective ways.

The policies and programs proposed here have demonstrated effectiveness, and they require little if any additional funding. More funds, spent wisely, can clearly have an impact. But with state policymakers struggling to retain current resources, much less add substantially to them, the priorities outlined below and funding strategies to support their expansion should be important foundations of a "double-the-numbers" strategy.

## Expand and Strengthen High School/University Dual-Enrollment Programs

A promising direction for innovation is the creation or expansion of state programs allowing high school students to take college courses on college campuses or at their high schools, with public dollars for tuition, books, and other fees following the student to the institution that delivers the instruction.

More than 40 states have some form of dual-enrollment program.

However, many states don't use the full power of this idea. This comes when families decide, with colleges or universities, when a student is ready to take college courses. The push from dual-enrollment or postsecondary option programs for improvement in high schools comes when the state, rather than school districts, decides that funds will follow students judged ready to take postsecondary courses. According to the Education Commission of the States (2001), many states give school districts the power to determine whether state funds will flow to colleges and universities, effectively limiting the potential of the dual-enrollment program to generate competition and stimulate reform.

In Minnesota and Washington, unlike many states, the legislature gives students and their families the authority to decide if they are ready to take college courses. If students meet certain entry requirements, postsecondary institutions that have room accept them into their courses, and state funds follow automatically from school districts to pay for tuition and books. In Minnesota the policy is called Post-Secondary Options. In 2000–2001, 7,100 high school students took courses on college campuses; another 9,700 took postsecondary courses offered at their high school. The Washington State program is called Running Start. About 14,000 Washington high school students took advantage of Running Start in 2000–2001. (For more information on Running Start, see "Dual Enrollment," page 205.)

Details vary between Minnesota and Washington. Minnesota allows students to attend any accredited postsecondary institution in the state (though students may not take a course focusing on religion). Washington's program was initially restricted to public community college courses, but that has since been changed to include four-year public state universities as well.

Participating higher education institutions are allowed to set entrance requirements. Some require students to take an entrance test or to have a certain grade point average in high school, but sometimes students with lower high school grade point averages have been among the strongest performers in college courses. These tend to be youth who urgently needed the challenge and freedom that being on a college campus provides.

Minnesota's experience suggests that states will get a more competitive response from existing high schools — more improvement in high school options and outcomes — if the proportionate state funds for each dual-enrollment course follow the student, and if school districts cannot veto a student's enrollment in a postsecondary course. That is, if a student takes a quarter of her education at a college, then a quarter of state funds normally sent to the high school should go to the college; if a student enrolls full time in a college, all the state funds should follow.

This funding mechanism makes each student's decision of significant economic value to the high school and the college. It differs, though, from the funding formula in many states. More typically, political compromise has resulted in both high schools and colleges receiving state funding for the participation of their students in dual-enrollment classes. This may make it easier to get a program started, but it also may make a program more difficult to sustain in the current fiscal environment and also weaken the economic incentives that the Minnesota funding policy provides to expand and improve high school offerings.

Since the Post-Secondary Options program was established in 1985, the growth in the number of Minnesota students taking Advanced Placement courses in high school has been much greater than for the United States as a whole (Figure 1). Many attribute this expansion to the competitive response of districts and their high schools to the dual-enrollment option.

Minnesota's experience also shows the value of states' empowering families and permitting students to enroll in any postsecondary courses that fulfill the high school graduation requirement. School districts often resist giving students permission to attend a college or university if state funds are following students. But district resistance can be overcome by giving the choice of enrolling to individual students and their families.

This certainly will be controversial. A Minnesota School Board Association lobbyist called the idea "the most devastating piece of legislation adopted in the past 20 or 30 years" when it was approved in 1985 (Wehrwein, 1985). However, a poll conducted in 2003 found that 80 percent of Minnesotans either strongly approved or approved of the law (Mason-Dixon Polling, 2003).

Research in Minnesota consistently finds very high levels of satisfaction among students who participate in these programs. In a Minnesota Legislative Auditor study, 95 percent of families whose children participated in Post-Secondary Options said they "definitely" or probably would

**FIGURE 1**

| PERCENT INCREASES IN THE NUMBER OF STUDENTS TAKING ADVANCED PLACEMENT TESTS AND THE NUMBER OF TESTS TAKEN, NATIONWIDE AND IN MINNESOTA | | | |
|---|---|---|---|
| | 1986 | 2001 | Increase |
| Number of students taking AP tests | | | |
| Nationwide | 231,378 | 844,741 | 365% |
| Minnesota | 1,970 | 14,839 | 753% |
| Number of AP tests taken | | | |
| Nationwide | 319, 224 | 1,414,387 | 443% |
| Minnesota | 2,483 | 23,015 | 927% |

*Source:* College Board, 2003

encourage their children to participate if they had to do it over again; 73 percent of participating students reported being "very satisfied" with their experiences (Office of Legislative Auditor, 1996). Another study asked more than 1,000 high school students, "If you were to do it over again, would you choose to participate in the program?" Eighty-four percent of students attending state universities replied "definitely yes," and 87 percent of students in community or technical colleges responded, "definitely yes" (Boyd, Hare, & Nathan, 2002).

This suggests that empowering high school youth to take all or part of their latter high school education at a college can help stimulate improvements in high school. Some students are ready for the challenge and greater freedom of college programs.

Over the last 15 years, the "middle college" movement has created a new form of dual enrollment via the placement of some innovative high schools on college campuses. Middle colleges frequently target students from low-income families who may be performing below their potential in school. For example, the Arizona School of Agriculture and Equine Science, a charter high school, is located on the campus of South Mountain

Community College. Most of its students, many from low-income families, take at least some courses from college instructors. Moreover, high school students can use community college facilities, such as computer labs, the library, laboratories, and physical fitness facilities. Some of the students complete their programs with a high school diploma and an associate's degree from the college. Both high school and college administrators report that the collaboration is working well (Nathan & Febey, 2001). Other examples of schools designed in a way that offers college courses to high school–age youth are emerging around the nation, for example, in Portland, Oregon, New York City, and Long Island City, New York (Steinberg, Almeid, Allen, & Goldberger, 2003).

## Develop Small, Focused, Accountable High Schools through Charter and Other Mechanisms

A second priority for policymakers ought to be to encourage the creation of small, accountable public high schools. Research on the positive outcomes of small high schools is clear and encouraging. One federal summary noted that, among students from similar backgrounds, those who had attended small schools had, in general, higher test scores, higher graduation and satisfaction rates, and lower rates of absence, truancy, and misbehavior. The study noted that these findings have been "confirmed with a level of confidence rare in the annals of educational research" (Raywid, 1999).

Some fear that smaller high schools will be more expensive. However, research in New York City found that the cost per graduate of small high schools was below that of large high schools (Stiefel, Latarola, Fruchter, & Berne, 1998).

A vast array of such schools have an outstanding record of preparing and helping arrange for entrance into college by low-income students, often from families that do not speak English. Examples include Fenway High School in Boston, Frederick Douglass in Harlem, El Puente Academy in Brooklyn, Nova High School in Seattle, and Perspectives Charter School in Chicago (Nathan & Febey, 2001).

State officials can take several steps to promote the creation of small schools, some of which do not require significant new resources:

Examine state policies and procedures to determine whether they encourage creation of large high schools. South Carolina recently adopted legislation clarifying that it would no longer require a school to have a minimum amount of space, a common requirement that has led many districts and communities to create mega-schools in the past. Most states use facilities guidelines, developed more than 50 years ago by the Council of Educational Facilities, that call for large tracts of land for high schools (Lawrence, forthcoming). While states sometimes grant exemptions, many local officials do not realize that waivers are available. A forthcoming guide by the council does not suggest any firm guidelines on the amount of space needed for a high school. States should update their policies to eliminate any bias toward large high schools.

Encourage state agencies to examine whether they have land that can be donated or shared with those who wish to create small high schools. Examples of high schools on college campuses have already been noted. The Minnesota Zoo, a statewide agency, donated unused land on its campus to the local school district. The result was the School for Environmental Studies, a small high school that won a national award for its success.

Encourage statewide foundations to collaborate to promote creation of more small schools. With the encouragement of Ohio governor Bob Taft, the Cincinnati-based KnowledgeWorks Foundation leveraged $5 million into a total of $31.5 million with funding from the Bill & Melinda Gates and Ford Foundations, along with the Ohio and U.S. Departments of Education, to help create small high schools and transform existing large district schools into clusters of small schools of choice (personal communication, C. Hedges, September 29, 2003). States might encourage and even partner with foundations to establish "start-up" funds that help create new small, independent, accountable public high schools, such as those found in states with strong charter laws, or in district programs such as the Pilot School program in Boston or the New Visions Schools in New York City.

## Encourage Strong Chartered School Programs

Over 40 states have charter school legislation of some kind. But the charter concept requires that educators, parents, and community groups have the opportunity to create new or convert existing schools that are independent of local labor-management relationships, receive the same per-pupil dollars as other public schools, and have the opportunity to be authorized by one of several organizations — including school districts, nonprofit organizations, colleges and universities, and the state itself.

After studying the charter approach throughout the country, Eric Rofes (n.d.) concluded, "States which had policies that provided for the chartering of new schools only through the local district showed significantly less evidence of reform efforts from the development of charter schools than did states which allowed for multiple sponsors."

In 1990, education analyst Ted Kolderie urged that states withdraw the "exclusive franchise" previously given to school districts by creating a charter sector. Kolderie had encouraged Minnesota to create the Post-Secondary Options, and noted the improvements district schools made when faced with competition from colleges and universities. He urged that states take the next step by permitting, even encouraging, educators, parents, and community groups to create new, more accountable public schools (Kolderie, 1990).

Well-designed charter laws produced several important results. First, they have made it possible for a number of strong, independent, accountable charter high schools to be created. Second, they have helped provide more quality options for at-risk, minority, and low-income youth.

Despite the fears of some critics that charter schools would "cream" students, charter secondary schools enroll a higher percentage of low-income students and students from minority groups than do district-operated public schools. According to the U.S. Department of Education, 43.6 percent of charter high school students come from low-income families, compared to 28.4 percent of secondary students enrolled in district schools (Figure 2). Two-thirds of district secondary school students are white, compared with less than half of secondary charter school students.

In many states, charter schools receive less per-pupil funding than district schools. In most states, chartered schools do not receive public funds to help rent or buy school buildings. However, despite lower financial support than district-run schools, several recent studies show that students in charter schools are doing as well as or better than students in traditional schools. For example:

• A national study by Jay Greene and colleagues found that when students in schools serving a "general population" were compared with students in similar district schools, those in charters had greater achievement gains in reading and math (Greene, Forster, & Winters, 2003).

- A study conducted by the Rand Corporation found that newly created charter schools in California that provide students with instruction in the classroom (as opposed to virtual schools) have somewhat higher achievement than students in comparable schools (Rand, 2003).

- Research by the State University of New York found that charter schools it authorized are making significantly greater fourth- and eighth-grade language arts progress than district-operated charter schools (Charter School Institute, 2003).

Recent research by Eric Rofes has found that, in states with strong charter laws, including multiple forms of charter sponsorship, the growth of

**Figure 2**

| DEMOGRAPHICS OF U.S. DISTRICT AND CHARTER SCHOOLS | | |
|---|---|---|
| | District Public Schools* | Charter Public Schools* |
| Race/ethnicity of students | | |
| White | 66.6% | 48.9% |
| Black | 15.9% | 21.8% |
| Hispanic | 13.3% | 22.7% |
| Asian Pacific Islander | 3.9% | 3.1% |
| American Indian/ Alaska Native | 1.2% | 3.5% |
| Percent of students eligible for free or reduced-price lunch | | |
| Less than 50% | 71.6% | 56.4% |
| 50-100% | 28.4% | 43.6% |

\* Secondary and combined
Source: U.S. Department of Education, NCES, Schools and Staffing Survey, 1999–2000

charter public schools is encouraging improvement in existing schools. A number of district personnel interviewed by Rofes acknowledged, "sometimes begrudgingly, that charters had served to jump-start their reform efforts. While they initially opposed charters and the chartering had been accomplished outside their authority, these district leaders felt that district schools ultimately had benefited from the dynamics introduced by local charter schools" (Rofes, n.d.).

While the research is not, and probably never will be, definitive, there is substantial evidence that allowing educators, community groups, and parents to create new, accountable public schools using the charter approach provides many benefits to students, families, educators, and the broader education system (Center for Education Reform, 2003; Charter School Institute, 2003; Greene et al., 2003; Nathan, 1996; Rand, 2003; Rofes, n.d.).

State policymakers can take several steps to help promote a strong charter sector:

*Authorize multiple institutions, in addition to local school districts, to sponsor or authorize new, or convert existing, schools into chartered schools.* State laws should enable colleges and universities, other nonprofit organizations and institutions, and the state itself to sponsor and authorize new charter schools.

*Insist that schools in the charter sector receive the same per-pupil dollars as other public schools.* In many states, students attending charters generate fewer state dollars than they would if they attended district schools. This creates a competitive disadvantage for charter schools; states should stipulate that the full "per-pupil" dollars generated by charter students follow students to these schools.

Encourage state agencies to determine whether they have space that a small charter high school may be able to use or share. As with small schools that are not charters, the difficulty of finding appropriate and affordable facilities is a critical barrier to proliferation. State agencies can help charters and enhance their own efficiency if they can move surplus facilities or space into use as a charter school.

There are several other low-cost state strategies for addressing the challenge of facilities for new schools — charters and otherwise. In Florida, where the school population is rising quickly and new school construction is lagging behind demand, the state provides charter schools with funds to rent existing buildings. Minnesota's Lease Aid program provides charter high schools with $1,200 per student for leasing costs (particularly helpful since the state does not allow charter schools to own their own buildings). An interesting proposal for addressing facilities needs creatively would provide incentives for existing nonprofit institutions to collaborate with charters: if a nonprofit institution (e.g., a Boys and Girls Club, a museum) would enhance the charter's educational program at no extra cost to the state, through internships, hands-on projects, etc., then the state would provide some help with leasing space from that institution as an incentive to work together.

## Encourage Richer, More Accurate Data Gathering and Information-Sharing Programs

Good decisions come, in part, from accurate information. State policymakers, along with the general public, benefit when good information about student and school performance is available. The federal government's No Child Left Behind (NCLB) legislation requires states to collect and report certain data.

At a minimum, states wishing to promote better transitions to college, more effective high schools, and a more vibrant public charter sector should collect and disseminate the following information, some of which is required by NCLB. This is a relatively low-cost way for states to encourage improvement, and to provide vital information to the public to target improvement efforts.

*High school graduation rates:* Each public high school should be required to publish information on the percentage of ninth-grade students who graduate four years later. In many states, the true extent of dropout rates is masked by data that only reflect the percentage of students who entered the senior year of high school but then did not graduate. Unquestionably, some students transfer or move away, and cohort analyses must be done carefully or they can overstate dropout rates. However, when studies accurately track students from ninth grade on, as in a recent study by Jay Greene (2002) of the Manhattan Institute, more realistic — and lower — graduation rates become available. In addition, it is vital to disaggregate graduation data: Greene found 30 to 40 percent differences in some districts between the graduation rates of white and African American students. Some states report graduation rate by high schools. This will be required by NCLB and seems highly appropriate.

*Rates of remediation required by graduates of particular high schools:* Some research suggests that colleges and universities are spending as much as one billion dollars on developmental education and remediation (Steinberg et al., 2003). The University of Minnesota State College System found that, statewide, more than 30 percent of Minnesota students who graduated from a public high school and entered one of Minnesota's public universities had to take at least one remedial course. The research also disaggregated information school by school, enabling families and policymakers to understand what was happening to graduates.

*Evidence from the state's charter sector:* As state public charter school sectors grow and mature, state education authorities should require careful analysis and dissemination of both how the sector is evolving and how its schools are performing (consistent with the data required of all high schools). Useful data questions include:

- Is the state law actually promoting the creation of new charter schools?
- What are the demographics of students attending schools in the charter sector?
- Which of these schools are most effective (with outcome data disaggregated by income, race, and ethnicity)?
- How is the state using/promoting lessons learned from the most effective charter schools?
- What do directors of the most effective charter high schools say can be done to help strengthen these schools?

*Information for parents:* It is critical for families to have good information about the range of educational options available to them. This can be done via computer, public service announcements in various languages on radio and television stations, toll-free phone numbers, and sometimes through information shared at commercial businesses, such as fast-food franchises, grocery stores, etc. The strongest programs also provide multilingual people who are independent of any school system and can provide accurate, unbiased information to help families make decisions.

## Transforming Lives

Considerable experience and evidence are available to state policymakers who want to increase graduation rates and postsecondary attendance by students from low-income families. Among the most important steps are to create strong postsecondary options, create new small schools operating in districts and in the charter sector, and gather information showing whether progress is being made in areas such as graduation rates and reduction in the number of students taking remedial courses.

Taking such steps will produce many more students like the youngster who told Minnesota legislators several years ago that, despite a very troubled background, small district high schools and charter schools had "transformed my life, turning me into a productive, contributing citizen."

*Another approach to raising high school students' achievement so they are ready to succeed in college is based on incentives to individual students to raise their grades and test scores. John H. Bishop looks at the experience of an incentive program in Michigan that tied a state scholarship to a student's performance on an external curriculum-based exam, aligned with the state's expectations for what high school graduates should know. He argues that such merit-based programs, particularly when tied to state standards, can send the right signals to students, parents, and teachers, and make it easier for high schools to work toward the state's goals for students. While acknowledging and addressing criticisms, Bishop sees this as a model worth watching.*

---

## 6. Merit Scholarships for the Many: Doubling the Number of High School Students Who Work Hard in High School

### By John H. Bishop

Just about every American high school student wants to go to college, even those who are doing poorly in school. Seventy-three percent of sophomores in the bottom quartile on achievement tests say they plan to go to college. Eighty-four percent of those in the next highest quartile plan on attending college (NCES, 1993). Doubling the numbers cannot be achieved by increasing college aspirations. Aspirations are already sky high.

Why, then, did only 36 percent of 1988 eighth graders get a bachelor's or associate's degree by the year 2000? Not primarily because they failed to graduate from high school or were denied admission to a college; 75 percent spent some time in college. The problem was they did not earn enough credits to get even an associate's degree. Guess who failed to achieve their aspirations — the students with low test scores in eighth grade. Only 7 percent of eighth graders testing in the bottom quartile on a short mathematics test got a bachelor's degree, compared to 59 percent of those in the top quartile (NCES, 2003).

Doubling the numbers of successful college students will not be possible without a major improvement in the skills and knowledge of American high school graduates. We know it is possible. Students in Europe and East Asia are not only more likely to graduate from upper secondary school; they also graduate much better prepared in science and mathematics.

This paper looks at the emerging experience in Michigan, which has created a financial incentive for high school students to work hard and do well in high school. Michigan's Merit Award program is one of a growing number of state initiatives designed to aid students who meet high academic standards in high school. These initiatives vary greatly, from Georgia's HOPE scholarship and variants of it, to Indiana's Twenty-First Century Scholars program, which mixes merit with need-based aid criteria. What makes Michigan's program unique is the decision to tie financial incentives to performance on an external curriculum-based exam. In effect the state is saying; "We want to encourage performance, and we will measure students based on a clear, well-designed assessment that is aligned with the state's expectations and goals of high schools and their students." By not relying on SATs or grade point averages, the state is more tightly tying the incentive to success on the test that is the state's own way of quantifying progress toward its academic goals.

The Michigan program is not without its critics. Some would argue that all college aid should have a need-based component. Others say that the state simply cannot afford such generosity in the current economic environment. I disagree. There is certainly room for debate over the size and length of Michigan's award and for debate over the appropriateness of the assessment test. But it is my view that the potential benefits far outweigh the costs and risks. This is a program worth watching.

## Aspirations, Exams, and Performance

Why don't American high school students perform as well as their peers in other industrialized nations? One reason is that they devote less time and intellectual energy to their schooling. When homework is added to engaged time at school, the total time they devote to study, instruction, and practice is only 18 to 22 hours per week — 16 to 20 percent of a student's waking hours during the school year. By way of comparison, the typical high school senior spends nearly ten hours per week in a part-time job and 19.6 hours watching television.

American youth have high aspirations, but too many appear to believe that they do not need to apply themselves in high school to achieve their goal of going to and completing college. They know that a local college will admit them even if they don't know how to spell or write a coherent paragraph. What they do not realize is that actually completing a degree program is going to be extremely difficult if they have not developed these and other basic skills in high school.

How can our nation encourage young people to study longer and harder? The strategy followed by nations throughout East Asia and in much of Europe has been to base admission to specific universities and to specific academic programs (such as law and medicine) largely on student performance on a battery of subject-specific examinations devised by the Ministry of Education. These high-stakes exams are very different from the multiple-choice aptitude tests — the SAT I and ACT — that serve a similar function here. Each subject exam is many hours long and tied to an agreed-upon course syllabus. Students write essays and solve multistep problems showing their work. My analysis (2001) of data from the Third International Mathematics and Science Study (TIMSS) demonstrates that students in countries with such high-stakes "exit" exams outperform students in other, equally developed countries by 1.3 grade levels in science and 1.0 grade level in math.

The idea of a government-sponsored exam limiting access to postsecondary education has never been popular in America, the land of second chances. The American higher education system's open-door admissions policies are a major strength of the U.S. economy, enabling adults of any age, whatever their background or mistakes in life, to return to school and gain new skills. Nevertheless, the problem of how to motivate students remains. The strategy in 17 states, including Florida, Texas, and New Jersey, is to require students to pass a minimum-competency exam in order to graduate from high school. These are tests of basic skills, and passing scores are typically set so low that few students are induced to try harder by the threat of failing the tests. New York State and North Carolina, by contrast, give students an incentive to study through the use of rigorous, end-of-course exams that signal medium and high achievement levels, not just meeting minimum standards. The results of New York's famed Regents exams are reported on students' high school transcripts, and students earn special Regents diplomas if they pass enough of the tests. The Regents exams give students a lofty goal to aspire to, rather than a low hurdle to jump over.

## Michigan Merit Award

Michigan rejected the use of minimum-competency exams, largely because it wanted the state's high school test to reflect more challenging learning goals. Also, policymakers did not want to take the risk that a high-stakes graduation test would lower high school graduation and college-attendance rates. Instead, the state took the modest step of reporting Michigan Educational Achievement Program (MEAP) test scores on high school transcripts. However, the state university system continued to use the ACT as the admissions test, so putting MEAP scores on transcripts provided little incentive. Indeed, many high school students saw little reason to take the test: 30 percent of high school juniors did not take it in spring 1998.

In 1999, Michigan increased the reward for good academic performance by offering the Michigan Merit Award, a one-year, $2,500 scholarship to any student scoring at "Level 1" or "Level 2" on the MEAP reading, mathematics, science, and writing tests, which are first taken in spring of the junior year. Students can also earn the scholarship by meeting the standards in two subjects and scoring in the 75th percentile or higher on the SAT or ACT. Students who attend college in Michigan are eligible for the full $2,500 scholarship, while students going to college out of state can receive up to $1,000. Starting with the class of 2005, students can get up to $500 more if they meet or exceed state standards on two of the four MEAP exams in seventh and eighth grades as well. College financial aid officers are prohibited from taking the Merit Award into account when they make need-based awards, so students who earned the scholarship would not have their need-based grant aid reduced, as is common.

Merit scholarships are not new. Many states have had merit scholarship programs giving symbolic recognition to a small number of top students.

What is new is a program that awards significant financial assistance to over half of a state's high school graduates based on achievement test scores or grades in high school and college. Arkansas started the trend in 1991 when it began awarding $2,500 scholarships to graduates with GPAs above 2.5 and ACT scores of 19 and above. Georgia followed in 1993, Mississippi in 1996, Florida and New Mexico in 1997, Louisiana and South Carolina in 1998, and Kentucky in 1999. Georgia and Kentucky base their freshman awards solely on high school GPA. The other states use a combination of GPA and ACT or SAT I test scores.

*What is unique in Michigan is the decision to award merit scholarships based solely on state-developed tests that measure achievement of the state's curricular objectives.* This aligns the incentive effects of the Merit Award with the state's strategy for strengthening and upgrading high schools. Grade inflation is discouraged, and so is pushing students to drop out before they have to take state high school accountability exams.

Scholarship programs like Michigan's carry a low cost-to-benefit ratio. The total expense for the Michigan Merit Award comes to less than one percent of the state's K-12 education spending,[1] yet the program has the potential to realign incentives within the school system in a way that serves the interests of students, parents, educators, and the community. It encourages students to study harder, enhances their opportunity and willingness to go on to college, improves the educational climate in most schools, and strengthens the energy for reform among parents and teachers.

What makes Michigan's program so powerful is that the scholarships are based on students' performance on an external exam that reflects the state's recommended curriculum. If the awards were based instead on, say, high school grades, some students would respond by choosing easy courses where an "A" is guaranteed. Teachers would face little incentive to set higher standards; in fact, the pressure to inflate grades would intensify. If the awards were based primarily on SAT or ACT scores, the main result would be an increase in Kaplan's revenues from test-prep courses. The only way to win the award is to learn the curriculum well enough to pass the state's high school test. Unless the curriculum is misguided, this focuses everyone in the system on the main goal of K-12 education.

## Benefits of the Michigan Merit Award

Before the advent of the scholarship program, Michigan's young people and their parents saw few short-term, tangible benefits when school districts opted for higher standards, more qualified teachers, or heavier student workloads. The immediate consequences of such decisions were negative: higher taxes, more homework, lower GPAs, a greater risk of being denied a diploma. As a result, parents pressured teachers to be easy graders and were reluctant to pay them well enough to recruit highly qualified personnel. The Michigan Merit Award makes parents stronger advocates of higher standards and better teaching.

The fact that the scholarships go to every student who meets or exceeds the absolute standard also enhances the classroom environment. Competitive merit scholarships have the dysfunctional effect of pitting classmates against one another. The winners of traditional merit scholarships are seen as nerds, suck ups, or "Oreos" by their classmates. That is why many schools stopped awarding such honors at school assemblies. There were too many incidents of catcalls mixed with unenthusiastic applause (Suskind, 1998). The Merit Award helps to reduce anti-nerd peer pressure. Students who joke around in class will no longer be honored and rewarded by their peers because their disruptions make it harder for the rest of the class to get the $2,500 award. The fact that the cut-off score for the Merit Award was set at a level that is achievable by almost all students makes everyone believe that it is an attainable goal, one worth striving for.

The Merit Award program better enables the state to hold schools accountable for student achievement. When the MEAP high school exam was a no-stakes test, students had no reason to try their best on the primary indicator of performance in the state's high school accountability system. Many students were boycotting the test. Thus, school ratings reflected in part a school's success in getting students to put some effort into the tests. This reduced the validity of high school tests as measures of student achievement. If the state had turned the MEAP into a high-stakes exam by making high school graduation contingent on passing it, this would have affected only students at the bottom of the achievement curve. The Merit Award has given students across the board an incentive to do their best on the high school test, thus improving the fairness, validity, and effectiveness of the state's school accountability system.

Increasing the stakes attached to the MEAP assessment also improved the academic environment by focusing the efforts of teachers and students on a good test. In fact, the MEAP is a much better exam than the tests that most teachers develop for themselves and use to grade their students. It is the product of an extensive consultative process, with input from hundreds of well-regarded teachers. Trained professionals test and review all test questions for ambiguity and bias. By contrast, studies of tests developed by teachers have found that the overwhelming majority of the questions were created to tap the lowest of Bloom's taxonomic categories, knowledge of terms, facts, or principles. A 1987 study found that less than 20 percent of questions developed by secondary school history teachers required the integration of ideas. College instructors required such integration in 99 percent of their test items (Rohwer & Thomas, 1987). Most secondary school teachers test for low-level competencies because that is what they teach. The MEAP test pushes things in the other direction.

One final benefit of the Merit Award program is that it tends to redirect students away from preparing for high-stakes, multiple-choice tests like the SAT I and the ACT. This is a good thing, because the ACT and the SAT I are not comprehensive measures of a well-rounded secondary education. These admissions tests fail to assess most of the material that high school students are expected to learn: economics, civics, literature, foreign languages, and the ability to write an essay. The energy that students devote to cracking the SAT I and the ACT would be better spent reading widely and learning to write coherently, think scientifically, analyze and appreciate great literature, and converse in a foreign language. The MEAP tests have been developed with great care and are superior to the ACT, yet, despite the existence of the scholarship program, the ACT continues to carry much higher stakes because it is the primary admissions test used by Michigan colleges.

## Evidence from Canada's Moderate-Stakes System

Michigan's scholarship program is still young. Therefore, we must look elsewhere for evidence of its likely long-term effects on student performance. Analyses of high-stakes exam systems around the world have demonstrated that they lead to significant achievement gains, but these are not comparable to Michigan's moderate-stakes system. Canada presents a more relevant example. At the beginning of the 1990s, the provinces of Alberta, British Columbia, Newfoundland, Quebec, and Francophone New Brunswick administered curriculum-based exams in English during a student's junior year of high school and in French, mathematics, biology, chemistry, and physics during the senior year. Performance on the exams accounted for 40 to 50 percent of a student's final grade. This was a moderate stake because college admissions decisions were based almost entirely on high school grades and were generally made before senior-year exams were graded. After controlling for the size and structure of the school and its students' social backgrounds, schools in provinces with external exams taught their students a statistically significant one-half of a U.S. grade-level-equivalent more math and science by eighth grade than comparable schools in provinces that did not give curriculum-based external tests (Bishop, 1999a, 1999b).

Schools in provinces that used external exams were also more likely to have teachers who specialized in teaching one subject in middle school and to hire teachers who majored in the subject they would teach. Schools in these provinces devoted more hours to math and science instruction and built and equipped better science labs; their students were more likely to do experiments in science class and to agree with the statement that science is useful in everyday life. Students also talked with their parents more often about schoolwork and reported that their parents had more positive attitudes about the subject. The success of these exams led Manitoba and Anglophone New Brunswick to introduce curriculum-based external exit exams in the late 1990s.

## What Can We Expect in Michigan?

Can we expect similar effects in Michigan? Early signs are promising. Prior to the introduction of the Merit Award, only 70 percent of public school juniors were taking MEAP tests. In spring 1999, when the scholarship program became effective for high school juniors who took the state tests, participation immediately jumped ten percentage points. Participation rates continued their climb, reaching 93 percent of seniors in the class of 2002.

More important is the substantial increase in the number of students meeting or exceeding Michigan's educational standards. Test scores usually decrease as participation rates increase, yet in math the proportion of test-takers meeting the standard rose from 61 percent in spring 1998 to 67 percent for the class of 2002 (Chart 1). In reading, the proportion increased from 59 percent in 1998 to 71 percent for the class of 2002. In writing, the proportion rose from 57 percent to 68 percent. The proportion of the graduating class passing all four MEAP tests and winning a Merit Award rose 19 percent from 2000 to 2002; 46 percent of high school graduates got a Merit Award in 2002.

Michigan students have also improved their standing on other tests. Average ACT scores held constant for Michigan students, while declining by 0.2 points for the nation as a whole. They even improved slightly relative to other states in the North Central region with stable participation rates in the ACT program. Michigan scores on the combined verbal and mathematics SAT I rose five points more rapidly than for the rest of the nation.

There is also good news about Michigan's high school graduation rate. Nationally, graduation rates fell slightly during the 1990s (Chart 2). The

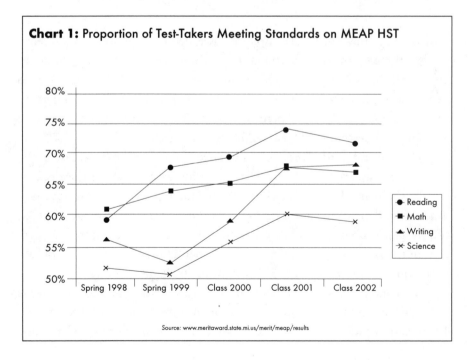

**Chart 1:** Proportion of Test-Takers Meeting Standards on MEAP HST

Source: www.meritaward.state.mi.us/merit/meap/results

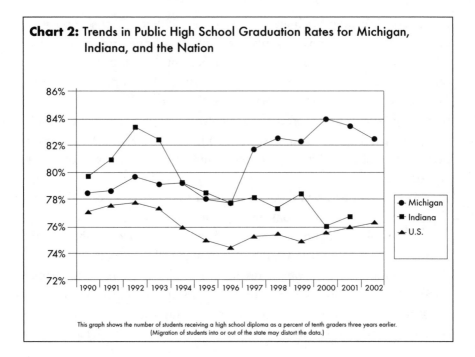

**Chart 2:** Trends in Public High School Graduation Rates for Michigan, Indiana, and the Nation

This graph shows the number of students receiving a high school diploma as a percent of tenth graders three years earlier. (Migration of students into or out of the state may distort the data.)

ratio of the number of regular diplomas awarded to the number of fall tenth graders three years earlier declined from 77 percent in 1990 to 75 percent in 1996, and rose slightly to 76 percent in 2001. By contrast, Michigan's ratio of regular diploma to tenth-grade enrollment stayed just above 78 percent through 1996, jumped to 82 percent in 1997, 1998, and 1999, and then rose again to 83.9 percent in 2000 and 83.3 percent in 2001.

The Merit Award is probably the cause of the year 2000 increase in the graduation rate. But what caused the big increase earlier in the decade? Unlike Ohio and Indiana, its southern neighbors, Michigan did not make graduation dependent on passing a test. This decision has apparently paid off. Indiana's diploma to tenth-grade enrollment ratio declined from 78 percent in the five-year period prior to implementation of their MCE graduation requirement in 2000, to 75.9 percent in 2000 and 76.7 in 2001.

A second possible explanation for Michigan's rise in graduation rates is the state's assumption of responsibility for all current educational costs of K-12 education and a funding formula based solely on the number of students attending school in the district. Liberal charter school legislation was also enacted, and in 1996 Michigan extended school choice to schools in neighboring districts, with state funds following a student to the new district. In 2001, about 5 percent of students took advantage of public school choice. School district revenue now depends directly on how many students are attracted and retained, not on the district's wealth and tax rates. This has strengthened incentives for schools to prevent students from dropping out.

Since Michigan's scholarship program enhances a student's ability to attend college, one might expect for it also to increase college-attendance rates. Indeed, Georgia's HOPE scholarship program increased the proportion of high school graduates who go to college by 8.5 percentage points in one study and by 6.9 percentage points in another (Cornwell, Mustard, & Sridhar, 2003; Dynarski, 2000). Harvard University's Susan Dynarski (2000) has studied how college enrollment rates of 18- and 19-year-olds have responded to merit scholarship programs in seven early-adopting states. She estimated that six of the seven programs had statistically significant effects, ranging from 3.0 percent in Florida to 7.3 percent in Kentucky and Georgia. In some states, the effects were larger for minority students than for white students. The program that had no significant impact — South Carolina's — restricted eligibility to those with SATs above 1100 and a 3.0 GPA, and was less generous than most of the others.

Michigan's Merit Award is considerably less generous than the HOPE scholarship and most of the merit scholarship programs in southern states. They all last for four years (if a student maintains the required GPA), while the Merit Award is good for only one year. The HOPE scholarship also pays full tuition at Georgia public universities and community colleges, and a similar amount at private colleges in Georgia. Michigan's $2,500 award covers only about half of average tuition and fees at Michigan's public four-year colleges. Consequently, one would expect a smaller response to the Merit Award than to the HOPE scholarship. In any case, the data necessary to tell conclusively whether the Merit Award influenced college attendance are not yet available.

## Should Merit Scholarships Have a Need Component?

We live in a world where the vast majority of financial assistance for attending college is need-based. In Michigan, for example, federal student aid programs provided Michigan undergraduates with over $350 million in need-based grants and interest subsidies in fiscal 2000–2001 (NCES, 2003, Table 369). The state need-based scholarship programs — the Michigan Competitive Scholarship and the Michigan Tuition Grant Program — awarded an additional $100 million to Michigan undergraduates in fiscal 2000–2001.[2] In addition, institutions of higher education in Michigan awarded over $466 million in scholarships and grants in fiscal 1996, much of which was need-based and went to undergraduates (Barbett & Korb, 1999). Federal tax credits and tuition deductions available to families with incomes under $100,000 provided another $300 million of assistance to college students. Compared to this river of need-based student aid, the Merit Award's $83 million is, indeed, a very small funding stream. For this reason, the Merit Awards need not vary with family income. There is a real incentive for universal eligibility: the simplicity of the merit-based scholarships established in seven southern states is one reason why these programs have had such salutary effects on enrollment rates.

Conditioning awards on achievement, not solely on financial need, makes it absolutely transparent what students and parents must do to seize the opportunity. Students are urged to study harder and to sign up for demanding courses. The extra learning this produces benefits the student regardless of whether she earns a Merit Award. By contrast, need-based financial aid often sends no signal, a murky signal, or the wrong signal, and stimulates undesirable behavior. The rules for determining eligibility for need-based financial aid are highly complex and vary from institution to institution. Many low- and moderate-income parents are not aware that generous, need-based financial aid will be forthcoming if their child is admitted to the University of Michigan or Michigan State University, so they do not urge their children to set their sights high and build the kind of academic record that would get them into the state's flagship institutions.

Merit-aid programs are remarkably popular. In 2002, Michigan's health-care interests put an initiative on the ballot that would have shifted tobacco settlement money originally dedicated to the Merit Award to their industry. Early polls suggested it might pass, but school administrators got the word out to parents that the Merit Award was at risk; it lost by a substantial margin. The state's fiscal crisis resulted in a second challenge. The new governor proposed in January 2003 to reduce the Merit Award to $500. The legislature demurred and the award was kept at $2,500.

As Susan Dynarski points out:

> Merit aid is a politically astute way to build support for spending on post-secondary education. . . . [When your] child receives a "scholarship" that pays for tuition, the perceived benefit is personal and immediate, inducing political support for the spending. . . . That students "earn" merit aid may also place it at a political advantage over other funding mechanisms. (2002, p. 35)

Students who blow off high school pay a very high price, much larger than they imagine when they are in school. They believe they will be able to attend college despite low grades and low achievement. But in fact their chances of completing a degree program are almost zero. They are also unaware that applying themselves in high school helps them get jobs that offer training and promotion opportunities and eventually higher wage rates. States that desire to focus the attention of students would be wise to consider merit-based scholarship programs like the ones in Georgia and Michigan. They offer little in the way of downside risks, and have the potential for wide-ranging benefits.

---

1. Michigan spent $15,385,152,000 on K-12 education in fiscal 1999–2000. The $83 million cost of the Merit Award program in 2001–2002 is less than 0.6 percent of this figure.

2. See Michigan Higher Education Assistance Authority, Annual Report 2000–2001, p. 3.

*State accountability systems can be powerful levers for changing institutional practice. What would an accountability system for "doubling the numbers" look like? It would have to induce educational providers to help underserved students persist in and complete courses of study that have value in the workplace and further education. And it would have to induce better performance across K-12 and higher education systems, which have very different accountability traditions and systems. Peter T. Ewell proposes a significant departure from current practice, emphasizing the alignment of achievement frameworks and assessments from grade 10 through grade 14, methods to credential nontraditional learning (through work or home study), and the measurement of student achievement in ways that monitor system progress and steer institutional behavior.*

# 7. An Accountability System for "Doubling the Numbers"

## By Peter T. Ewell

Essential to the goal of substantially increasing the number of underserved youth gaining postsecondary credentials is a state-level accountability system that induces educational providers to pursue three major objectives:

- Underserved students persist through the educational system to the point of earning a postsecondary credential — though they may engage in both traditional and nontraditional educational experiences and enroll in multiple institutions as they do so.
- Underserved students attain a credential of value for the workplace or further education. It does little good to increase rates of completion when those who attain a credential are deficient in what they know and can do.
- Both those objectives are accomplished for many more individuals than is currently the case, drawn from populations that have not historically succeeded in achieving either objective in postsecondary settings.

These objectives are hard to meet simultaneously, and American post-secondary institutions have tended to trade them off against one another. For example, one way to achieve the second objective, high levels of performance in the value of a credential, is to be highly selective with respect to whom an institution lets in the door. One way to achieve high completion rates is to be highly selective, but another is to reduce standards of achievement, diminishing what a credential is worth. And, as the experience of most so-called "open-admissions" institutions reveals, it is easy to achieve high levels of access so long as one does not care much about persistence or deep learning. An effective accountability system to "double the numbers," therefore, must provide incentives for education providers to avoid these historically typical short-term routes to success on individual measures of performance and to attain all the measures at the same time instead. And it must do this across the boundaries of secondary schools and postsecondary institutions — two complex and historically unarticulated educational delivery systems that have evolved quite different approaches to accountability.

## Current Accountability Tools

The range of accountability instruments available to state governments in pursuit of this goal is relatively straightforward, even if the task of deploying them is difficult. Such tools include direct regulation, performance reporting, and performance funding.

### Direct Regulation

Direct regulation is designed to confine institutions to particular courses of action and proscribe them from others. Classic examples in postsecondary education include mission definition, establishing geographic service regions, or limiting providers to only one form of instruction.

Historically, this kind of direct regulation has not worked well in higher education, and colleges and universities have often been quite entrepreneurial, "climbing the ladder" of prestige by becoming more selective (Jones & Ewell, 1993). Direct regulation has worked somewhat better in K-12 environments where more hierarchical structures and more control-oriented management structures are in place. But the more complex the system, the less leverage direct regulation will have on institutional behavior, and it is likely that improving the higher-education experience for disadvantaged groups will require an extremely complex mix of different kinds of educational providers in order to achieve the mass of participation envisioned.

## Performance Reporting

Performance reporting employs a limited set of statistical indicators about institutional conditions and outcomes that are reported publicly and prominently but are not directly consequential for institutions. Examples include the familiar institutional "report cards" that became fashionable in higher education in the 1990s (Ruppert, 1994). More recent incarnations of performance reporting are more consequential: they are linked to presumed consumer choices about which institutions to attend (e.g., the "Student Right-to-Know" Act of 1989, which requires postsecondary institutions to disclose graduation rates), harnessing market forces to improve institutional performance.

Some forms of performance reporting will probably help to increase the number of underserved youth gaining postsecondary credentials. However, like the National Center on Public Policy in Higher Education's 50-state "report card" on higher education (NCPPHE, 2000, 2002), they will need to embrace states and regions as well as institutions, and they should conceive of "benefits" in societal rather than narrowly institutional terms.

## Performance Funding

Performance funding is highly consequential for institutions because good performance yields rewards. Performance funding has always been a popular policy for public higher education, though only a few states have sustained it for long periods of time (Burke & Associates, 2002). Virtually all such mechanisms set aside a small portion of state higher education funds (5% or less) and allocate these funds to reward good performance.

This approach contrasts with recent K-12 accountability schemes that set targets and sanction institutions for poor performance. Higher education's typical approach, in which extra dollars are allocated solely on the basis of good performance, has the drawback of not investing resources to help fix poorly performing institutions. But K-12's approach, in which dollars are withheld on the basis of poor performance, can easily lead to institutional paranoia and numbers games for many institutions, while not inducing the best to do their best. An effective accountability system will probably mix both approaches.

## The Limits of Current Accountability Tools

While all these policy tools will probably be useful in helping to promote success in postsecondary education for underserved youth, the way states typically implement them has significant drawbacks. Among the most important are their focus on single institutions and the lack of either an explicit change agenda or a sense of urgency.

### Focus on Single Institutions

Current state accountability policies for higher education center almost exclusively on measures directed at one institution at a time. Needed instead are approaches that a) are directed at systemic conditions like the achievement levels of a particular underserved population or a particular region; and b) address interactions among different postsecondary providers in the state, including public, nonprofit, and for-profit institutions (Jones & Paulson, 2002). For example, instead of calculating single-institution degree-completion rates and holding institutions separately accountable for improving them, a systemic approach might begin by targeting a particular underserved population in a specific region. The next steps would be to determine overall degree-attainment rates for this population, and then induce various providers to work together to produce articulated — and perhaps multi-institutional — pathways to improve attainment.

### Lack of an Explicit Change Agenda

Most state accountability approaches are general purpose in nature, intended to assure policymakers and the public that government funds are appropriately directed and, in all too many cases, to guard against the possibility that particular "bad things" that happened in the past will ever recur (Ewell, 1998). If such systems are expensive, there is little political will to continue them when times change or funds are short.

Needed instead are accountability approaches that are tailored explicitly to achieve specific policy goals and that are implemented on a long-term basis. For example, a number of states have mandated credit transferability between two-year and four-year institutions, but this approach takes no account of whether or not students are actually prepared adequately for upper-division work. Instead, an intentional policy approach might reward both sending and receiving institutions for each member of a targeted population who ultimately earns a credential.

*Lack of Urgency*

Higher education institutions and their leaders are not infused with the culture of reform that has characterized K-12 rhetoric (if not behavior) over the past decade. Most of higher education acknowledges "no problem" with America's colleges and universities except lack of money. As a result, policy changes on issues like student assessment are pursued with far greater leisure than in standards-based reform in K-12 education. Implementing change in the higher education arena will thus require changes in attitudes within the higher education community as a prerequisite to changing behaviors.

Shifts in attitude can in part be furthered through information-based, relentlessly on-message reporting mechanisms on system condition and performance. One example is Measuring Up, the 50-state report card on higher education prepared biennially by the National Center for Public Policy in Higher Education. Another is the list of five questions about the condition of Kentucky's citizens that the Kentucky Council on Postsecondary Education formulated to stimulate policy discussion and has used consistently and persistently in public forums about the future of higher education in that state.

A second way to infuse urgency is to raise the stakes. Performance funding in higher education, for instance, has rarely ventured beyond 5 percent of an institution's base. Incentive pools of 15 to 20 percent would get more attention, especially in times of scarcity.

## A Policy Agenda for Accountability

Current accountability mechanisms deployed by state governments have had limited impact, largely because they have not been applied comprehensively so that multiple tools reinforce one another to provide a consistent set of incentives for institutions. To address this condition, several individual elements of an accountability system need to be deployed together.

*A Comprehensive Achievement Framework*

The first building block for an accountability system designed to "double the numbers" should be a comprehensive "achievement framework" consisting of attainment benchmarks in selected subject areas, such as communications, quantitative reasoning, and various content areas. Benchmarks for these areas should be set at clearly defined levels, ranging from the current equivalent of grade ten through the second year of postsecondary education ("grade 14") or the "first degree level" (the equivalent of an associate's degree). The result would resemble the "qualifications frameworks" that have been adopted by other nations to provide guidance about standards of achievement, and to which individual educational providers are held accountable. For example, Australia has established a complete national framework that sets achievement standards for each level of credentialing (e.g., secondary school completion, "first degree" level, etc.) for all subject areas; these standards serve as benchmarks for institutions when they give academic awards.

In the United States, the most promising place to begin this task would likely be at the two most important transition points for students: entry into collegiate work and "transfer" to upper-division work. Currently, state-established high school exit standards (and tests) are not aligned with college entrance requirements in any meaningful way (Venezia, Kirst, & Antonio, 2003). Similarly, college transfer arrangements are incomplete and haphazard, resting upon individually negotiated, course-based articulation agreements among institutions or broad-based legislatively imposed mandates about transferability of credit. Neither of these involve clear standards of achievement.

Constructing a comprehensive achievement framework might begin among educational providers located in well-defined geographic service regions with an established history of student flow from one institution to another. Once proven locally, the concept might gradually be expanded in scope. Existing initiatives that prove the feasibility of this approach include the Seamless Learning and Transition Consortium project (funded by the Fund for the Improvement of Postsecondary Education) and the Quality in Undergraduate Education initiative (funded by Pew Charitable Trusts). In both cases, two-year and four-year institutions work together to establish common achievement-based standards for transfer. At the transition from secondary school to college, a good example of such an initiative might be Oregon's Proficiency-Based Admission Standards System. (See "Connecting Measures for Success in High School and College," page 139, for a description of PASS.)

*An Array of Quality-Assurance Mechanisms Aligned with the Framework*
Although the establishment of a comprehensive achievement framework is critical to a successful accountability system, it should not be used to ground a single assessment approach — for example, a set of high-stakes tests. Rather, the framework would primarily provide aligned achievement benchmarks that could be referenced by a diverse family of quality-assurance approaches that can be used in combination. Among the most prominent of these approaches might be the following:

*Placement and Transition Assessments.* As noted, a major problem with current assessments used at high school exit and for college admissions and placement is that they are not aligned with one another. Using the comprehensive achievement framework, educational institutions might develop common placement/transition assessments in key abilities (e.g., communication and quantitative skills). These assessments would be designed to do "double duty"; that is, they should a) determine gaps in attainment and enable effective intervention and placement for particular individuals attempting to make a transition; and b) provide system-level information about particular points for which the skills-development "pipeline" among participating institutions is not working effectively.

These transition assessments might or might not be adopted for all transitions or for all abilities addressed by the comprehensive achievement framework. Where they are adopted, they should be public and transparent: students, faculty, and advisors at all participating institutions should be aware of the kinds of questions and problems that the assessments contain, as well as the acceptable level of performance needed to make a given transition.

*Benchmarked Assignments.* As an alternative to large-scale testing, which has a spotty record in higher education, the comprehensive achievement framework might ground a series of subject-specific tasks and problems designed to be embedded in regular courses in the last two years of high school and the first two years of college work. These would be most productive if first developed for high-volume courses — that is, courses that most students would be likely to take in any program. Examples include college-level courses in English composition, mathematics and statistics, American history, or introductory psychology. Standard grading rubrics for judging student work in response to these objectives would be keyed to appropriate levels of the comprehensive achievement framework so that student performance could be periodically checked against common standards.

Using these benchmarked assignments, educational providers within a network could assure one another that established standards were being maintained. At least as important, examples of higher-level assignments (and appropriate student responses) could be provided to "high school–level" providers by "college-level" institutions to provide guidance to students and faculty about what will be expected.

*A Teaching-Learning Audit.* Participating institutions might be obligated to engage in a periodic teaching-learning audit process conducted by a third party. This process would be designed to answer two questions: To what extent are teaching-learning processes aligned with the comprehensive achievement framework? To what extent are students demonstrating the expected attainment levels?

To address the first question, the audit might focus specifically on the extent to which curriculum and pedagogy align with the abilities articulated by the framework, and where and how students are asked to demonstrate these abilities. In this respect, the process might be modeled on the Academic Audit as practiced in the United Kingdom and other Commonwealth nations (Dill, 2000). To address the second question, samples of student work might be examined to determine whether and how student achievement at the institution meets established standards. This dimension of the audit might mirror the function of the "external examiner," which is also a prominent feature of the quality-assurance process in these nations.

An independent organization recognized by the state might run such a teaching-learning audit, much as accreditation now operates, or a state might run it directly. Institutions and providers participating in the system would agree to engage in some designated combination of these mechanisms in order to continue to be recognized by the state.

## An Alternative Credentialing System

The above mechanisms are intended to apply to formally established educational providers at the "grade-10-through-14" level. To meet the goal of doubling the numbers, an alternative method for credentialing student learning gained through work, community participation, home study, or other sources might also prove beneficial. One way to accomplish this might be to use standardized electronic portfolios (Cambridge, Kahn, Yancey, & Tompkins, 2001).

A number of institutions have established electronic portfolios as a way to archive diverse examples of student work benchmarked against commonly established standards, and there is an emerging policy discussion about how such portfolios might provide students with credible and portable credentials that they can use with multiple educational providers and with employers (Johnstone, Ewell, & Paulson, 2002). Learners would choose and develop exhibits in their portfolios to demonstrate that they have met particular components of the comprehensive achievement framework, though the exhibits themselves might come from many different venues. For a given exhibit to be appropriate for the portfolio, learners would have to not only present and document it, but also describe, through a reflective essay, why they believe it represents the ability at the level claimed. To verify achievement, portfolios might then be reviewed by a third-party organization chartered by the state to credential attainment through a rubric-based assessment process. The same electronic portfolio framework might also be used to house and integrate samples of achievement in formal education, such as completed benchmarked assignments as above. The key point is that all exhibits would be aligned with the comprehensive achievement framework.

## System-Level Measures to Monitor Collective Progress

With the above mechanisms in place, states would need a way to determine the specific subject areas in which different kinds of students are making progress and where additional investments or adjustments are needed. This need could be addressed through a set of statistical measures designed not to examine individual institutional performance, but to monitor the attainment levels of particular populations in specific areas of achievement.

Areas of achievement would be defined in terms of the comprehensive achievement framework, with data drawn from sampling the embedded assessment measures above and a sample-based statewide assessment system that might resemble the NAEP. The latter might be modeled on the state-level demonstration assessment effort being undertaken by the Pew Forum on Collegiate Learning (Ewell, 2003). Results of these measures would reveal specific performance gaps for particular populations. Such performance gaps might then be the object of state-run challenge grants to address the issue, which would be open to any educational provider, public, independent, or proprietary.

*Institution-Level Measures to Steer Behavior*
In addition to system-level measures, a set of institution-level performance indicators might be designed to monitor the performance of all publicly funded institutions — including any private or proprietary provider that wishes to participate in state-funded educational attainment initiatives. Key measures here might include acceptance of one another's benchmarked credentials; participation in periodic teaching-learning audits designed to determine curricular alignment in key abilities; and statistics on the proportion of students entering at different levels of assessed achievement who are making progress up the established ladder of attainment set by the comprehensive achievement framework.

In contrast to current state-level performance-measure systems, which are used primarily to punish institutions for substandard performance, these measures might be applied somewhat differently. For public institutions, substandard performance might be followed by action plans designed to remedy the situation, with state authorities escrowing or reallocating institutional funds to ensure that the plans are followed. For participating non-public institutions, performance levels might govern the institution's continued participation in state-funded programs.

## A New Departure

A state-level accountability system along the lines described here would admittedly be a major departure from current practice. Yet each of its elements has been proven by example (although not always in the United States). Implementing the system would therefore not require the development and testing of an entirely new set of policy tools. But it would require a state to devote substantial and sustained attention to the objective of "doubling the numbers" and to invest real resources up front — especially to establish the comprehensive achievement framework.

With respect to higher education in the states these days, both resources and political will are in short supply. In the long run, however, the potential payoff in work-force productivity and effective citizenship of substantially increasing the flow of the educational pipeline through at least the "first-degree" level should prove a compelling inducement for states to start down this difficult path.

*States have the power to use higher education funding to drive a change agenda but tend to make funding decisions that are determined by past practice, not by goals for the future. If states were serious about doubling the numbers or increasing the number of low-income degree completers, says David A. Longanecker, they would reward performance in serving low-income students. They would keep college affordable, reward institutions that serve the most educationally disadvantaged students, and reward students who complete the courses of study they begin and the institutions that enable them to complete those programs.*

---

# 8. Financing Tied to Postsecondary Outcomes: Examples from States

## BY DAVID A. LONGANECKER

If we want higher performance, why don't we use the big stick — money — to get it? This rhetorical question has led many states to develop performance funding schemes in recent years, as part of their overall set of higher education funding policies. John Bishop (see page 87) discusses how the performance-funding question is driving some states and institutions to revamp their views about student financial assistance. I focus here on how states employ performance-funding measures to reward institutional performance and, more specifically, to create an incentive for increasing student access to success.

In almost every state, the explicit public purpose for investing in higher education is to establish broad access to quality education — and to do it as economically and equitably as possible. These actions are intended to create well-educated citizens who will contribute to the state's economic, social, and civic life.

How well do most states' finance policies reinforce these policy goals? Pretty well, if you like the status quo — and not so well if you want to use finance to drive a change agenda. That's because higher education funding in virtually every state, regardless of what decisionmakers say, is determined mostly by what has been done in the past, not by what is desired for the future.

## The Four (or Maybe Five) Paths of Performance Funding

Using finance as intentional policy to achieve specific public goals is a relatively new concept in American higher education. Performance funding as we know it actually originated in 1975, when Tennessee launched a pilot program to explore the value of rewarding institutions for achieving desired performance targets via the explicit allocation of a portion of the state appropriation to higher education. In 1980–1981, Tennessee moved from a pilot to a performance-funding strategy that allocated 2 percent of the state's appropriation on the basis of institutions' achievement of specified objectives. Today, according to Joseph C. Burke and Kenrik P. Minassians (2003), at least 36 states relate funding to performance, either directly or indirectly — or so they say. However, after substantial increases in the number of states using performance funding in the 1990s, the numbers have fallen off in recent years as state budgets have become stressed. They suggest that this is in part because performance *funding*, which costs, is being replaced by performance *reporting*, which doesn't. Nonetheless, performance funding of one fashion or another still exists in most states and, as I will argue below, it actually exists even where it isn't recognized as such.

Four (or really five) generic models of performance funding have evolved.

### Skimming for Marginal Funding

The first — which I call *skimming for marginal funding* — is based on the original Tennessee model, which skimmed a modest amount of funds from the overall appropriation to reward institutions for achieving preestablished public goals. The idea that even relatively small amounts of money can cause significant change was supported by two premises:

- Institutions will work hard for new funding on the margin even if it amounts to no more than budget dust because they receive so little truly discretionary funding.
- Institutions care about their public image, which makes it important for

them to be perceived as responsive to the public goals of quality and access.

Skimming is the most prevalent performance-funding model. Generally, from 2 to 8 percent of funds are reserved for rewarding established performance outcomes. The use of this model has increased in recent years, and many more states are considering adopting it. Often, formulaic approaches to performance funding evolve from legislative mandates and reflect the angst many state legislators feel over their inability to tie their state's substantial investment in higher education to explicit results.

*The Tennessee Experience.* While Tennessee originally reserved up to 2 percent of total funding to reward institutions that performed well with respect to five specific goals, that allocation now stands at nearly 6 percent of all funding.

At first blush, the current performance goals do not appear to focus substantially on increasing access to success in higher education. For instance, only one goal — increasing graduation rates for minority students and for all other students — explicitly seeks to enhance the success of students from underrepresented populations. However, at least three other goals — achieving program accreditation, assessing learner outcomes in general education, and improving student satisfaction — focus on improvements in educational quality that almost certainly will result in greater student success. This is an important point: too often, access and quality measures are not appreciated for their interdependence in enhancing student success.

*Ohio's Substantial Effort.* Ohio commits more than 8 percent of its funding to performance objectives, and most of this funding is directed toward efforts to enhance the success of the most at-risk college students through an access challenge fund and a success challenge fund. (Ohio also provides funds for a jobs challenge fund, a technology challenge, and a research challenge fund.)

While these challenge funds help focus resources on state priorities, they do not appear to have attracted additional funds to higher education in Ohio. Rather, the various challenge funds have often simply replaced funds from other sources, leading to no net increase in total funding.

*The South Dakota Case.* One of the more recent states to enter the bona fide performance-funding arena is South Dakota, which provides about 2 percent of its funding in one of five incentive funding areas: increasing access to in-state residents, promoting work-force development in fields critical to the state, improving the academic performance of undergraduate students, improving cost effectiveness, and improving external fundraising. As in Tennessee, only one of South Dakota's measures explicitly focuses on increasing the success of at-risk students, although at least two others (increasing access to in-state residents and improving the academic performance of undergraduate students) will undoubtedly contribute to their greater success.

The original Tennessee experiment continues to define many of the parameters of performance funding. Noticeably absent from most of the states' funding efforts are rewards for improving actual student learning, probably because we lack valid and reliable measures of student learning, as so poignantly reflected in the *Measuring Up* publications from the National Center on Public Policy and Higher Education.[1] *Measuring Up* assigns every state an "Incomplete" grade on student learning. (One state, South Dakota, does provide incentive funding for demonstrated improvement in student performance.)

*Centers of Excellence*

A second model rewards excellent programs, rather than excellent outcomes. This centers-of-excellence model purports to encourage institutions to invest in their strengths rather than trying to be all things to all people. Through "focused excellence," an overall system can sustain excellence, measured in many different ways, across its institutions.

The amount of funding available for centers of excellence is generally a specified proportion of the overall budget, and it is often even more modest — generally 1 to 2 percent — than the amount reserved for performance outcomes. Colorado and Washington, for example, have "programs of excellence" that reward established centers for their renowned work and encourage other institutions to maintain focused excellence. Kentucky has perhaps the most substantial new effort based on this model. It provides over $50 million annually (about 5 percent of all state funding for higher education) in matching funds for private investments in endowed faculty chairs, and it strategically focuses student scholarships and fellowships to enhance faculty and student excellence.

Some states blend this model of incentive funding with skimming for marginal performance funding. Missouri, for example, through Funding for Results, rewards improved performance on measures of both access and quality. Through its Targeted Excellence initiative, it also rewards state institutions that clearly differentiate their missions from one another, so that no institution is trying to be all things to all purposes, but that the sum of the parts equals the desired public policy whole.

*The All or None Approach*
The third model — the all or none approach — awards all funds on the basis of achieving intentional public policy goals. The logic behind this strategy is that if performance is our ultimate objective, then performance alone should drive funding. It is hard to fault the logic of this approach. However, not all good ideas always work out as planned.

*The South Carolina Case.* In 1998 South Carolina enacted legislation that required the allocation of the entire appropriation for higher education based on each institution's ability to meet negotiated goals on 39 publicly established objectives. The process is generally considered to have been a fiasco, even by many of the individuals responsible for promoting the plan.

Two circumstances doomed this approach. First, there were too many objectives. Performance funding, in principle, works when there are strong signals. Sending 39 signals, which included virtually every public policy objective possible, meant that there were no strong signals about what was most important. Second, by negotiating targets, institutions established goals that were relatively easy to achieve. Thus, no strong forces spurred substantial change, even though the legislation had emerged because of an abiding legislative interest in seeing real change.

The notoriety of South Carolina's failed experiment has discouraged other states from pursuing the all or none approach, or at least from doing so intentionally.

*Colorado's Bold Voucher Plan.* Colorado has been toying with a new all or none approach that would take most of the state appropriation to institutions (except a modest portion dedicated to fostering the unique mission of each institution), divide this amount by the projected number of resident students, and provide the resulting amount directly to the students, who could take this voucher to any public institution. This would create the ultimate example of a funding strategy that many market-based economists and proponents have advocated for years: let the consumer choose. While this proposal has not yet been adopted by Colorado's legislature, it likely will be in the future, offering one of the most radical departures from traditional funding strategies in recent history.

Some might question whether this is really performance funding, but surely it is if your goal is broad access. Proponents ask, what better strategy is there for expanding access than to simply give the subsidy to the prospective students and let them choose the education that best meets their needs? Opponents, on the other hand, wonder whether this approach continues simply to send the old signal to institutions that enrollment is the key, not persistence and completion. Opponents are particularly concerned that, absent a strong state financial aid system (which Colorado lacks), students who are financially at risk will be even more so under a voucher plan.

### The Pretenders

The fourth model is illustrated by those states that pretend to relate budget to performance but really don't. In fact, the pretenders include most of the 36 states allegedly involved in performance funding. In most cases, these are states that have established institutional report cards of one fashion or another and that purport to take the results "into account" in the budget process. What this generally means is that the institutions that fare well on the measures argue that they should be better funded because of their exceptional performance, and the ones that show poorly either remain quiet or argue that they need more funding so that they can perform better.

And so nothing much changes. The past becomes prologue, which in most cases is comfortable but does not bode well for doubling the numbers because the circumstances that created the profound gaps in success of have and have-not students persist.

### Those Who Do It but Don't Know

What has been overlooked is a fifth model: the states that do performance funding but don't know it. Truth be told, this may be the dominant model. And it may account for why so many state policymakers are frustrated with higher education and its performance, particularly with respect to its modest performance on providing access to success for at-risk students.

Policymakers know what they want but they aren't getting it. Why? Well, the answer is really quite simple: states are getting what they are paying for; they just aren't paying for what they want. Today, most state funding formulae exist to distribute funding fairly, not to induce performance. But, in fact, they do send powerful signals to the institutions about what is important to the state. When they provide funds based on FTE enrollment, they send a strong signal that enrollment is what counts. When they provide 98 percent of funding on the basis of past practice and 2 percent on policy goals, they send a strong signal that the past is more important (49 times as important, to be precise) than explicit policy goals.

## Pay for What We Want

Most policy analysts and researchers who study performance funding argue that, after weighing the pros and cons, these performance-funding strategies work to achieve their objectives. Joe Burke, director of the Public Higher Education Program at the State University of New York, Albany, occasionally surveys the states on the status and prospects of performance funding. He has found that state officials and lay board members increasingly perceive that results should drive at least a portion of resource allocation (Burke & Serban, 1998). Brenda Albright, who helped fashion the original Tennessee performance-funding model and who remains one of the most highly respected national experts on performance funding, argues that a well-constructed model helps build public support for higher education funding by focusing the funding discussion on state rather than institutional needs, and by driving institutions toward achieving publicly established goals (Albright, 1997).

Not all who have examined these approaches, however, are so sanguine about their efficacy. Nancy Shulock and Colleen Moore (2002) of the Institute for Higher Education Leadership and Policy at California State University, Sacramento, state that the case for performance funding "is far more compelling in theory than in practice." They argue that there are "few, if any, cases of successful implementation," and that poorly designed performance-funding practices can have unintentional consequences. For example, a heavy focus on graduation rates can dissuade institutions from accepting students who are at higher risk of not graduating.

Given the goal of doubling the numbers, then, how well do state finance policies reinforce increasing participation and retention in higher education? If we truly believed in using finance to improve student success, for instance:

1. We would assure that college was affordable, particularly in tough financial times when students and families are financially strapped.
2. We would provide incentives for institutions to retain students until the completion of their programs.
3. We would assure that institutions have the additional resources necessary to provide quality educational services to the most difficult to serve students, because serving these students is obviously more costly than serving better prepared students.

Yet our finance policies, by and large, do just the opposite:

1. We talk a good line about affordability, with our mantra of low tuition in public higher education and perpetual hand-wringing about the unfortunate need to raise it, yet we ignore our own definitive research that shows that net price, not low tuition, is the key to affordability — and that, therefore, a strong state-level financial aid policy is imperative.

Despite this absolutely clear evidence, only about a dozen states have serious approaches to funding student financial assistance, and only a couple, such as Minnesota and Washington, articulate those financial aid policies intentionally with other state finance policies. Even more egregiously, our actual performance with respect to affordability runs countercyclically to our customers' ability to pay. We hold prices (tuition) down in good times when students and their parents can afford to pay, simply because we can afford to and it is politically popular to do so, but increase price (tuition) when students can least afford it, in tough economic times, because "we have no choice." In sum, most of our policies don't really optimize affordability.

2. Most states do provide an incentive to attract students through enrollment-based funding systems, yet they offer few incentives for institutions to retain these students to graduation.

Everyone knows that freshmen are cash cows who help pay for the education of upper classmen. That's the way it has always been, so it must be right. Institutions get paid even if these students don't complete the courses for which they enroll. Think about the perverse message this sends to both students and institutions. From the students' perspective, why stay and finish a tough course when you can drop it and move on? From the professor's perspective, why worry about those dropouts when it's easier to work with a smaller class? It's not surprising that about 20 percent of all courses students enroll in are never completed. (The numbers are much higher at some campuses, particularly in community colleges.) But it's tough to complete a degree if one doesn't complete the coursework leading to a degree. In other words, our finance policies don't promote successful completion.

It doesn't have to be this way — and finance policy can help drive change. The Higher Education Funding Council for England funds enrollment much as we do — but only completed enrollments. Guess what: most English students complete the courses for which they enroll, and a much larger share, therefore, go on to finish their entire educational program of study.

3. Most states pay institutions much higher public subsidies to educate the easy-to-serve students, those well-prepared students who attend our selective universities; we pay much lower subsidies to educate the most difficult-to-serve students, those poorly prepared students who attend our open-admissions community colleges.

Once again, our policies belie our purposes: we don't pay institutions what it takes to do the toughest work. And, not surprisingly, we get what we pay for: lousy performance in educating difficult-to-serve students.

That's the bottom line: we get what we pay for. In this regard, performance funding has worked remarkably well. The institutions have followed the funds. To date, however, the performance we have paid for has been driven principally by past practice rather than by future desires. That can change, but such a change won't be easily accomplished. It will be tough because change is always tough — but also because we actually may be more comfortable with the status quo than we like to believe. The status quo caters to the haves of our society, not the have nots. If we truly want to double the numbers, we simply must change this equation. If we don't change, then, truth be told, we may not mind what we have wrought quite so much as we say we do.

If we want to double the numbers, we must reward performance with regard to serving disadvantaged students. The recipe for that will require at least three ingredients:

- Reward institutions that serve the most educationally disadvantaged students (including institutions that provide remedial education), rather than those that focus on serving the most academically prepared students.
- Reward students who complete the courses they begin and also reward the institutions that enroll these students.
- Reward students who complete their course of study and also reward the institutions that serve these students.

We need not try to guess which specific strategies will work to accomplish these objectives. Rather, we need to focus on whether institutions, in whatever way they deign best, actually accomplish these objectives. The public policy objective is what is accomplished, not how it is accomplished.

---

1. For more information on Measuring Up, see *http://www.highereducation.org/reports/blg/index.shtml.*

*Federal and state policies have long placed more emphasis on access to postsecondary education than on completion. Not surprisingly, the result has been a tremendous expansion in enrollments, coupled with average or below average rates of degree completion, particularly for low-income students. Arthur M. Hauptman proposes policy incentives to narrow the performance gap. States should fund colleges at least in part based on completions, not enrollments, and they should pay public institutions more for low-income students who enroll and complete than for higher-income students. The federal government should pay a bonus to institutions for each Pell Grant recipient who completes the first year of study or earns a degree. A federal demonstration program should encourage states and institutions to develop better measures of student learning outcomes.*

# 9. Using Institutional Incentives to Improve Student Performance

## By Arthur M. Hauptman

For the past half century, federal and state policies in higher education, whether by design or unintentionally, have had the effect of promoting student enrollment over degree completion. Most states fund their public institutions based on the number of students enrolled, not the numbers who graduate. Federal student aid policies do not penalize students who take longer than expected to complete their programs of study, nor do they reward completion in any meaningful way.[1]

These policies have had predictable results. The number of students enrolled has grown to unprecedented levels. More than 15 million students now enroll in higher education every fall, meaning that in the United States one out of every 20 people is enrolled in higher education at any one time. This is one of the highest rates in the world. At the same time, the rate of degree completion in the United States is average to below average among developed countries.[2]

Despite the American success in achieving high levels of participation and the apparent difficulty in producing world-class graduation rates, the debates in Washington over the past several decades, as well as in most states, have focused almost exclusively on how to increase access to postsecondary education. Far less attention has been paid, in debate or policy, to the low levels of degree completion, particularly among low-income students for whom attrition is highest, or on whether and what students are learning while they are enrolled. This focus on access also is at odds with the broader concept of improving educational opportunity embedded in the federal legislation that created student aid programs in the 1960s and early 1970s. This concept of greater opportunity sought to provide students with a wide choice of institutions and a proper chance to graduate, and to adhere to the principle of ensuring access so that they could enroll in some form of postsecondary education.

The policy concentration on access over completion, combined with a failure to narrow differences in participation between low-income and high-income students, has led to a chronic performance gap in this country. Students from wealthier families remain far more likely to complete a degree than those from more impoverished backgrounds. Degree-completion data are sporadically collected and subjected to varied interpretations: one source suggests that low-income high school sophomores are at least six times less likely to complete a baccalaureate than students from higher-income families.[3]

To close the performance gap, the current set of federal and state policies, which emphasize increasing student demand by reducing net prices through low public tuition rates and the provision of student financial aid, require substantial reform. They need to be supplemented by policies that provide institutions with incentives to improve student performance — in the form of higher degree completion rates, particularly for low-income students — and to produce better learning outcomes.

These new policy incentives should include reforms in both state and federal policies:

• State Policies. At least a portion of state funding of public institutions should be based on the number of students who graduate or who complete their first year of study, rather than the number of students who enroll. States, through their funding formulas, also should pay their public institutions more for the low-income students they enroll and graduate than for middle- and upper-income students.

• Federal Policies. A federal program should be created that pays institutions for the number of Pell Grant recipients who successfully complete remedial programs of study, complete their first year of study, or graduate with a degree. In addition, a federal demonstration program should encourage states and institutions to develop better measures of student learning outcomes.

## Why Policy Reforms Are Needed to Narrow the Performance Gap

Much of the performance gap is a function of the realities of American society today. Students from low-income families tend to be less well prepared for college than are students from wealthier backgrounds because their families can't spend as much time or as many resources on their preschool, primary, and secondary education. Economically disadvantaged students and their families also are less able to afford not only tuition and living costs, but also the opportunity costs entailed in choosing more schooling over work. These same realities make it less likely that disadvantaged students who begin a program of postsecondary education or training will complete it. In short, low-income students find themselves shortchanged as they move throughout the education pipeline; the chronic performance gap reflects these economic and societal realities.

That gap has not narrowed over time, and it may have widened, because a variety of important public policies work against educational success for low-income students. For example, it appears that a growing number of students lack basic skills when they enroll in college. Yet the remedial courses these students require are chronically underfunded, and many of the community colleges and four-year institutions that provide remediation rely on tuition fees from these courses to fund their other activities. New policies and financing schemes are needed to improve the effectiveness of remedial programs. Similarly, closing the performance gap will require a series of serious policy reforms at both the state and federal levels to offset the underlying societal disparities that ineffectual public policies have exacerbated.

Growing concerns about performance in postsecondary education in recent decades have led to calls for greater accountability, particularly at the state level, as legislators and governors wonder what they are getting for growing investments. The reasons are many, including perceived diminution in the quality of the education provided or in the quality of the observable products of that education — the students who enroll and graduate.

To achieve greater systemic accountability, state and federal policymakers must tackle some tough questions about how to measure performance and how to instill greater accountability in the system. Thus far, the most frequently proposed and imposed means for increasing accountability at both the state and federal levels has been to set up some form of "report card" that seeks to measure how states or institutions are doing on a number of key variables, such as graduation rates.

However, these efforts are unlikely to lead to greater accountability or better outcomes any time soon for at least two reasons. First, these report cards fail to alter the fundamental incentive structure for institutions. The amount of funding that is tied to these measures of performance is too small relative to "regular" funding and is not built into the basic funding formulas. Thus, whatever funding is provided for performance is unlikely to change how institutions behave.

Second, this country has no good measures of what students learn while they are in college; therefore, we do not know whether value has been added. Measuring performance on the basis of how many students graduate will always be suspect if we are not sure whether institutions have adjusted their measures of quality downward in order to receive more funding. While we can feel confident that most institutions would not make this bargain, all it takes is for a few institutions to slip their standards to undermine the credibility of the entire system.

To address these concerns, this paper suggests that we pursue two sets of reforms to change the incentive structure for institutions. One is to modify state funding formulas to increase their emphasis on performance. The second is to create federal provisions that lead states and institutions to worry more about their performance in terms of both degree completion and learning outcomes.

## Modifying State Funding Formulas

The funds that states provide to public institutions to support their academic activities and operations are the major form of taxpayer support for higher education. Through the end of World War II, most states provided this funding largely through a political process without using any funding formula. Beginning in the 1950s, however, states began to depoliticize their funding by shifting toward formulas based on the number of students enrolled at each institution. In the 1960s and 1970s, many states began to add some measure of cost per student to the calculation. In the 1990s, in response to continuing calls for greater accountability, at least a dozen states began to fund their public institutions partially on the basis of performance measures, although this performance-based funding typically applied to a very small proportion of total funding. It was usually implemented by institutions reporting indicators of performance to their state higher education agencies, which would then review and act upon this data.

*Funding Better Performance*

To fund their public institutions, almost all states now use formulas that are based on the number of students who enroll. Few if any states fund their public institutions based on the number of students who actually complete a degree. Nor do any states base their funding on the number of students who complete a year of schooling to offset the fact that the highest level of attrition occurs in the first year of college.

As long as states continue to base their funding formulas on the number of students who enroll, it is unlikely that public institutions will change their behavior and seek to increase their students' rates of degree completion. The incentives embedded in state funding formulas need to change.

A good place to start would be for states to consider funding formulas based on how many students graduate or at least how many students complete their year of study. England is a good place to look at experience in this regard. For more than a decade it has funded its universities and other institutions based on the number of students who complete a year of study. When the Higher Education Funding Council was implementing these reforms in the late 1980s, there was consideration of basing funding on the number of graduates, but there were concerns about whether some institutions would reduce their standards for graduation as a means to increase their public funding.

The success of England's funding approach in expanding the scope of higher education without proportionately increasing the level of public resources recommends it for consideration by U.S. states that face this same dilemma. It should be noted, however, that critics of the English system argue that it has sacrificed quality as access has increased. What is difficult to assess is how much of this possible decline in the quality of the graduates that the system produces is attributable to the natural result of increasing access to the system for students who come less prepared for college than the students who would have been admitted under more elite standards.

### Promoting Equity

As noted, increasing degree completion rates overall is not enough to close the performance gap. It is also necessary to increase the graduation rates of low-income students. Even though the odds against these students' completing their degrees are steep, few state policies do much to narrow the odds. In general, states rely on student financial aid to address issues of equity, but few if any state funding formulas distinguish between students who are economically disadvantaged and those who come from better-off families. Thus, most state funding formulas provide little incentive for officials at public institutions to recruit, enroll, or graduate economically disadvantaged students.

States should consider providing more funds to public institutions for the disadvantaged students they enroll than for the more mainstream students, who are better able to draw on their parents' resources. States might also consider extending this provision to private institutions to enhance institutional incentives across the board to enroll disadvantaged students.

As in the case of funding performance, England provides a possible model for states to emulate in terms of access. The English funding council for a number of years has paid institutions a premium of 5 percent for students who come from postal codes with the lowest income profiles. Although the English continue to have their own problems with the persistent gap between low-income and high-income students, this provision certainly seems a step in the right direction. And while there is now talk of abandoning the postal code premium for some other access measure — perhaps the income profile of the secondary schools that students attend — the principle of differential funding is certainly worth consideration in the United States.

## Federal Incentives to Institutions to Improve Student Performance

The current set of federal student aid programs began with the enactment of the Higher Education Act (HEA) in 1965, one of the key components in Lyndon Johnson's Great Society. Title IV of the HEA consolidated several existing and new aid programs into an array of campus-based programs, with one for grants, loans, and work study. It also created the Guaranteed Student Loan program as a bank-based alternative to the then-existing federally financed National Defense Education Loans, a campus-based aid program.

The HEA also moved beyond student aid to authorize the so-called TRIO programs that sought to improve the preparation and capabilities of low-income students by linking high schools with colleges and universities.[4] The Education Amendments of 1972 further expanded the reach and scope of federal student aid by expanding eligibility for all federal student aid to students in proprietary schools as well as creating the Basic Grant (now Pell Grant) program.

A major debate preceded the enactment of the 1972 amendments. The argument was over whether student aid should continue to be provided via the educational institutions through a set of campus-based aid programs of grants, loans, and work study, as had been laid out in the initial HEA, or be shifted to a more student-oriented approach in which aid would be provided directly to students, who could then "vote with their feet," with the federal funds to follow the student. After much heated debate, the student-based philosophy won out, principally through the enactment of the Basic Grant program.

To accommodate those legislators and lobbyists who argued for a continuing role for institutions in the student aid structure, the 1972 legislation provided that a wide range of institutions would receive annual federal payments based on the number of Basic Grant recipients they enroll. These "cost-of-education" payments recognized that enrolling economically disadvantaged students entails more effort by institutions.

The cost-of-education payments were never funded, however, and eventually their legislative authorization was dropped. Yet the rationale remains strong to get institutions to engage more in helping to solve the problems of increasing access for low-income students. Several recent studies also make it clear that elite institutions still enroll disproportionately low numbers of Pell Grant recipients, confirming that postsecondary access remains very uneven.[5]

### Improving Student Progression

It has become apparent since the shift to a more student-based philosophy three decades ago that just providing student aid is not enough to address the underlying problems entailed in improving student access and performance. One critical reform is that institutions must have more incentive to become and remain involved in the process of identifying, enrolling, and graduating economically disadvantaged students.

In this view, there is much reason to believe that the design of the student aid programs contributes to the performance gap. As a rule, federal and state student aid programs do little to encourage greater degree completion. Federal legislation as a matter of policy typically allows students to remain eligible for aid far past their expected date of graduation. There is no reward within the federal aid programs for recipients to complete their degree promptly, nor is there much, if any, penalty for noncompletion.

When this issue has been raised in debate, one typical response is to consider ways to "punish" students who do not complete their degrees in a timely fashion by, for example, reducing or eliminating their eligibility for aid after a certain number of years beyond when they should have received a degree. The problem with this punitive approach is that, if anything, it will exacerbate the performance gap and its consequences.

Difficulties with focusing on punishing students by withholding aid suggest that it may make more sense to consider how to encourage institutions to improve student performance. One possibility is for the federal government to reward institutions on the basis of their ability to improve the performance of low-income students.

Along these lines, the federal government could establish a provision in which they would pay institutions for each low-income student — as measured by the number of Pell Grant recipients — who meets certain performance standards. These standards might include aid recipients who successfully complete remedial courses of study (as determined by independent measures), complete their first year of study (when the most attrition occurs), and receive a degree.

This provision would represent a twist on the cost-of-education payments contained in the 1972 Education Amendments that were supposed to complement the shift to student aid. But rather than paying institutions for the low-income students they enroll, this proposed payment approach would compensate institutions on the basis of the performance of their Pell Grant recipients.

*Encouraging Better Student Learning Outcomes*
Another obvious measure of performance is whether and what students learn while enrolled. But for various reasons, including the long tradition in this country of protecting academic freedom, federal and state policymakers have shied away from intruding upon institutional processes to try to measure what students learn. Institutional officials over time have reinforced this nonintervention policy by citing the difficulties entailed in trying to measure precisely what it is that students learn. Thus, very little is known about what students know when they graduate or how much value was added relative to what they knew when they started.

This tradition of insulation helps to explain the absence of any national or even state tests being applied at the time that U.S. students receive their degrees. It also helps to explain why whatever progress may have been achieved by the school reform movement in this country over the past two decades in raising standards for K-12 education is likely to be eroded in higher education.

Given the tradition of nonintervention in institutional practices and the absence of any real measure of student learning, it would be unrealistic at this time to urge federal or state policymakers to pursue the introduction of funding systems that are based on what students actually learn. Nevertheless, the imperative to develop measures of value added by the postsecondary education process remain strong. To meet this imperative, other policy avenues should be explored.

At least several states, including Nevada and Washington, have had serious discussions in recent years about developing better measures of student learning outcomes as part of broader accountability initiatives. Similarly, faculty and officials at a handful of institutions have had such discussions. These efforts should be encouraged.

One reasonable role for the federal government is to create incentives for states and institutions to act in this regard. For example, a federal demonstration program could be created to encourage states and institutions to develop measures of student learning outcomes. Once such measures are developed and effectively implemented — a process that would take a number of years — it would be possible to begin funding institutions and students on that basis. Moreover, this new federal emphasis on student learning would help ensure that the K-12 standards movement of the past two decades would finally be carried forward into the hallowed halls of higher education.

In sum, real progress on closing the performance gap is unlikely to occur without fundamental changes in policy and philosophy at both the state and federal levels. Policymakers can no longer depend on changing student behavior principally through providing more and more student financial aid to try to keep up with rapidly growing tuition and other costs of attendance. We must also look for ways to motivate institutions to do a better job of seeing that their students complete their program of study with appropriate protections for maintaining levels of quality. That is what the reforms suggested here are intended to stimulate.

---

1. This paper draws on other recent work by the author, including a draft paper prepared for the Brookings Institution and the Progressive Policy Institute, entitled "Returning to First Principles: A Strategy for Improving the Effectiveness of Federal Student Aid," and a chapter prepared with P. Michael Timpane entitled "Improving the Preparation and Performance of Low Income Students in Postsecondary Education" for a volume on low-income students and higher education, published by the Century Foundation in 2003.

2. It should be noted that educational attainment — the proportion of the population of a certain age with a degree — is still high in the United States by international standards. This high level of attainment is the result of so many people enrolling in the first place. Even if relatively few complete a degree, the size of the entering class ensures a high rate of attainment.

3. At least several recent estimates from disparate data sources look at changes over time in the probability of students from different socioeconomic groups graduating from a postsecondary education program. The problem with all these estimates is that no data

sources regularly collect data on the degree-completion rates of students based on their socioeconomic status when they entered college. Several of these estimates are substantially larger than the six times probability stated here, which is based on the 1992 status of a survey of 1980 high school sophomores as reported in the *Digest of Education Statistics*, 2000, Table 307.

4. The TRIO programs initially consisted of Upward Bound, Talent Search, and Special Services. They were subsequently supplemented by Education Opportunity Centers.

5. Robert Shireman, while a program officer at the Irvine Foundation, conducted an informal analysis of the enrollment share of Pell Grant recipients at different institutions, and Donald Heller has more recently prepared a more formal analysis of enrollment patterns of Pell Grant recipients for the volume published by the Century Foundation cited in note 1.

# SECTION TWO

## Lessons from the Field:
## Innovations in Systems, States, and Schools

---

## *Introduction*

The success of the call to "double the numbers" and to reduce achievement and attainment gaps in secondary and postsecondary education will require significant policy changes like those proposed in Section One. It will also require significant changes and improvements in practice in schools and colleges serving low-income students. Fortunately, a growing body of experimentation and innovation in both policy and practice, in states, localities, and at the national level, points toward better ways to organize educational opportunity and progress for low-income students. In this section, we turn from broad policy frameworks and strategies to innovations "in the field" — programs and policies being tested in the crucible of actual schools, districts, communities, and states. The vignettes and snapshots that follow complement Section One with "visions of the possible" that have emerged in both policy and practice in response to weaknesses in the ability of too many high schools and postsecondary institutions to provide sufficient motivation, rigor, and support to low-income and minority students.

This section is structured around two clusters. The first set of chapters explores policy tools and strategies that states are using to change some of the most basic assumptions about how high schools and colleges should be organized, and how the two sets of institutions should interact. These tools include accountability systems, financing mechanisms that promote individual and institutional success, and incentive systems that can alter institutional behavior. The second cluster reports on innovative school and program models that appear to hold promise for helping low-achieving high school and college students perform better, persist in school, and succeed in moving through the "pipeline."

*Accountability, financing, and incentives:* Various experiments are underway to revamp state systems of standards, assessments, and accountability so that they send clearer signals to high schools, faculty, and students about what it takes to succeed in college.

David Conley of the University of Oregon reports on the Oregon Proficiency-based Admission Standards System and the Association of American Universities' Standards for Success effort, both of which connect measures of success used in high school with the skills and knowledge it takes to be ready for college.

Sheila Byrd, director of the American Diploma Project, describes and assesses the progress of this five-state initiative to help states align high school standards and assessments with the expectations of colleges and employers. The project recently published a set of new math and English standards that colleges and employers feel are rigorous enough to guarantee success in college or career.

Michael Kirst profiles the California State University system's decision to use the state's high school exit assessment as its placement exam for incoming freshmen.

Other authors describe how states are using various policy levers in an effort to plug some of the worst leaks in the education pipeline.

Hans L'Orange of SHEEO, the organization of state higher education executives, reports on the progress of Texas, Florida, and Maryland as they try to build integrated K-16 data systems for tracking student progress, not just through high school but through college as well.

Scott Evenbeck and his colleagues in Indiana describe that state's program of scholarship incentives for low-income students to raise their aspirations for college and their enrollment in state colleges and universities.

Some states and state university systems are integrating results of the National Survey of Student Engagement into higher education performance indicator systems. As NSSE's creator George Kuh and his colleague Brian Bridges report, states can use this survey to recognize and reward colleges whose students are more fully engaged in learning, which correlates well with persistence and success in college.

Finally, Lara Couturier of Brown University's Futures Project assesses the potential impact of a new trend in state higher education policy that involves granting more autonomy to state-chartered colleges in exchange for more accountability for student results. She looks at how low-income students can benefit or suffer, depending upon the terms of the agreement between state and school.

*School and program models:* Moving from policy to practice, these chapters highlight some of the most exciting innovations in schools and programs designed explicitly to increase the likelihood that students will succeed both in high school and after. The authors describe schools that have been successful or demonstrate promise in helping low-income and low-achieving adolescents get ready for and succeed in learning after high school by improving the quality of high school learning, smoothing the transition between high school and college, and minimizing the dislocation that students feel when they enroll in a community or four-year college program.

There is a crying need for more, and more varied, quality learning options and environments for older adolescents, particularly models that can help minimize the inefficient transition from high school to college learning. As No Child Left Behind demonstrates, supply is a serious problem: not enough good schools that can help low-achieving students catch up so they leave high school prepared to succeed in postsecondary institutions.

Several emerging models hold promise for different ways of organizing high school and its relationship to college credits and credentials. Monica Martinez and Christine Donis-Keller report on the growing movement of small theme high schools, such as the career academies that are emerging as alternatives to large comprehensive high schools. Donna Rodrigues describes the remarkably successful high school for low-achieving students in Worcester, Massachusetts, that she launched in 1997 as a partnership between the public schools and Clark University. Joel Vargas profiles statewide dual enrollment programs in Texas and Washington and assesses the potential of these programs to help low-income students gain college experience and earn college credits while still in high school. Nancy Hoffman makes the case for the growing number of "early college high schools" that combine high school and postsecondary courses and credits in a single small school, frequently located on a college or university campus. Lili Allen, Sue Goldberger, and Adria Steinberg examine schools that combine quality academic instruction with technical training in accelerated programs; these can be particularly appealing to older adolescents who need to work while earning a diploma and a degree.

A final chapter, by Barbara Leigh Smith of Evergreen State College, looks at Washington State's experience with using learning communities in the first year of community college or university as a way to help students stay in and complete degree programs.

*One way for states to promote better secondary school outcomes for all students is to connect high school instruction and state testing more directly with measures of college success. This approach is feasible but not easy. David Conley describes the progress and challenges facing two efforts to better align high school curricula with entry-level college courses: Oregon's groundbreaking Proficiency-based Admission Standards System (PASS), and the Standards for Success initiative co-sponsored by the Association of American Universities and the Pew Charitable Trusts.*

---

# 10. Connecting Measures for Success in High School and College

## By David Conley

States are clearly seeking to increase the academic rigor of a high school education. They have combined academic content standards and assessments with increasingly stringent course requirements to engage more students in academically challenging programs of study. Unfortunately, these efforts are rarely connected to or coordinated with what students will do with their academic skills and knowledge after high school, which for most students is some form of postsecondary education. The challenge is to connect high school instruction and state testing more directly with measures of college success.

Two important projects demonstrate both the feasibility and the difficulty of creating a consistent set of expectations that span high school classes and entry-level college courses. One is Oregon's groundbreaking Proficiency-based Admission Standards System (PASS); the other is Standards for Success, a national project co-sponsored by the Association of American Universities and the Pew Charitable Trusts. They serve as examples of how high school and college programs of study can be connected more directly.

The ultimate goal of connecting high school and college more directly is to increase the number of students eligible to be admitted to and prepared to succeed in postsecondary education. The two projects examined here make more explicit the requirements for college success. This can be particularly valuable to students from groups historically underrepresented in postsecondary education, since these students are often the least aware of what is required to succeed and, subsequently, the least prepared to succeed.

## Proficiency-based Admission Standards System

In Oregon, school reforms instituted in the early 1990s led to a state assessment system focused on the tenth-grade Certificate of Initial Mastery (CIM). This in turn led high schools to focus on enabling more students to pass these assessments; however the CIM as initially designed had no relationship to the admissions criteria of the Oregon University System's seven campuses. The state was pressuring high schools to increase the number of students earning CIMs, but students had little incentive to do so.

The university system responded by developing a set of proficiency standards keyed to university admission, and then created an entirely new and unique admission system that would allow students to demonstrate proficiency in place of high school grades and required courses. In 1994, the State Board of Higher Education adopted this system — PASS — as official admission policy for all seven campuses. The board even set the goal that PASS become the "preferred" form of admission, to be fully implemented in concert with the Certificate of Advanced Mastery (CAM), a companion to the CIM that was designed to be awarded at the twelfth grade.

PASS utilizes data from two hitherto untapped sources: state test scores and teacher judgments of student classwork. The assessment system includes multiple-choice test scores, performance tasks, and classroom-based "work samples." Work samples are assignments, devised and scored by teachers, that measure student performance in relation to state standards.

Students demonstrate college readiness through performance on seven "proficiencies" in math, six in English, and four in science. Each of these proficiencies has criteria and sub-criteria, thereby creating a means to score student work and rate student test scores. Students receive a rating of 1 to 5 for each proficiency: 1 = does not meet the standard, 2 = working toward the standard, 3 = meets the standard, 4 = high-level mastery of the standard, 5 = exemplary achievement of the standard. Each rating is based on one or more of the following data sources: state multiple-choice test scores; state performance task scores; classroom-based collections of student work; and national college-entry test scores, including the SAT II, AP, and International Baccalaureate.

A college admissions officer receives a proficiency profile that demonstrates student knowledge and skill on PASS proficiencies, which are directly linked to college success. This facilitates and improves admissions decisions, as student strengths and weaknesses can be better noted. Because proficiency scores derive from common criteria statewide, their reliability and stability can be more accurate than grades. Because scores are centered on a 5-point scale, they distribute students better than the current 4-point scale, where most students are clustered above 3.25. Scoring of student work can be conducted at the high school on a departmental level to help ensure reliability. "Moderation panels" external to the school validate scores of 4 and 5.

Perhaps most significant is the fact that PASS allows students to demonstrate college readiness, regardless of the high school courses they take. This can be particularly important for high schools seeking to increase the number of students who are college eligible, because students can demonstrate college readiness in any course. Clearly, courses geared toward developing the skills that underlie the PASS proficiencies will be better at helping students prepare for college, but any class can be designed to enable students to develop and demonstrate one or more PASS proficiencies.

Based on this description, one might conclude that teachers enthusiastically embrace a system that was based on assessment of actual high school work, that allowed teachers to make important instructional and curricular decisions, that engaged teachers in a key role as scorers of student work, and that provided an alternative to the state test. The reality has been somewhat different. Although teachers from 64 Oregon high schools participated in developing and piloting PASS, and many continue to utilize it to varying degrees, many others have not embraced this method. PASS will remain optional through 2006, since it is implemented in concert with state high school reforms that have not yet been fully implemented.

Some view PASS as extra work; some question why they should be asked to make decisions for admissions officers; still others are content with their current grading system and see little need to standardize their judgments with colleagues or external criteria; and some question whether out-of-state colleges and universities will accept or value PASS proficiency scores. This last concern does not seem justified, in light of conversations with admissions officers who, once PASS is explained to them, indicate that they will be able to process PASS profiles with relative ease, given its numeric system. The state education department, for its part, has yet to implement the CAM fully, due to design difficulties and a generalized sense that high schools are overloaded implementing the CIM, leaving PASS in an ongoing state of policy limbo.

## Standards for Success

Teacher reactions to PASS demonstrate the difficulties involved in creating a new means of assessing college readiness. Teacher acceptance is likely to be limited as long as proficiency-based policies are essentially voluntary and limited to a single state. Establishing a broader connection between high school standards and assessments and university admission will likely require a national model.

A first step in this direction has been taken by Standards for Success, a recently concluded three-year project. Over 400 faculty members from 20 schools in the Association of American Universities across the nation participated in nine meetings and contributed course syllabi and student work from the freshman-level classes they taught. The resulting set of standards identifies the knowledge and skills in six academic content areas that students should master to succeed in entry-level university courses.

These standards are a resource to which high school teachers and curriculum planners can refer when developing classes or programs of study. The university course syllabi and student work samples provide additional insight into the level of challenge that students face upon entry to the university. The high school curriculum can be calibrated better to be on a trajectory to prepare students for postsecondary studies. The four years of high school study can be designed to develop the intellectual skills and habits of mind that allow students to gain the most from a university education.

An equally important goal of Standards for Success is to provide state education departments with information on how their standards and assessments match up with university success standards. Because no state standards or assessments are fully coordinated with university admission and success, the alignment that does exist is more a function of chance than intent.

Standards for Success analyzed 60 state assessments to determine their alignment with the knowledge and skills for university success. Findings indicate widely varying degrees of alignment among state tests, with only moderate connection to university standards for even the best-aligned assessments. In other words, students preparing for these tests are not necessarily engaged in learning activities that will equip them best for university success.

The College Board has adopted these college-readiness standards for inclusion in 2005 as a foundational element of the SAT, PSAT, and AP tests. The College Board's goal is to provide better diagnostic feedback to test-takers, letting them know what they should be doing in high school to prepare better for college success.

The challenge these college-readiness standards face is how well they fit with existing state standards. Many high schools are already overwhelmed trying to meet state and federal accountability requirements. Adding a new set of standards, one that benefits students but for which students are not held directly accountable, will not be looked upon as an opportunity by many high schools. An additional question is the degree to which universities will actually embrace the notion of consistent standards tied to entry-level courses. If universities base admission on standards tied to entry-level courses, this implies that those standards will consistently serve as the prerequisite for success in those courses. Many colleges and universities are just now awakening to the need to incorporate standards into their general education curriculum.

## Primary Goals

Currently, the information generated by high school tests and, in particular, classroom-level student work is left at the high school door and not passed along to postsecondary education. Grades, course titles, and Carnegie units are all that survive from four years of instruction and assessment. Standards for Success and PASS offer models for states that wish to enhance alignment and improve the focus and challenge level of their standards and tests.

With a system of standards and assessments in place, high schools would be more free to organize the curriculum as they see fit. Distinctions among "college prep," "general ed," and "vocational ed" courses would have little meaning when the goal is for students to master challenging standards that ensure their preparation to succeed in postsecondary learning. This freedom could lead to a greater integration of conceptual and applied learning, to the benefit of all students. It would also greatly reduce the impetus for tracking if students in the same class could choose different assignments to demonstrate proficiency related to common standards.

If systems are well aligned, more students will have the opportunity to keep open the widest range of post–high school options possible. This, after all, should be one of the primary goals of the reform of the American secondary school.

*It is difficult to assess the value of most high school diplomas granted in the United States. What does a diploma guarantee to colleges or employers in terms of student knowledge, skills, and capabilities? The American Diploma Project (ADP) is a five-state effort designed to determine what colleges and employers want to see from high school graduates — and to work with states to encourage the use of information on student achievement of ADP standards in decisions about admissions, placement, and hiring. Sheila Byrd discusses the power of this approach — and its challenges.*

---

# 11. Do American High School Diplomas Guarantee Postsecondary Success?

## By Sheila Byrd

Imagine that we could magically double the number of students receiving a high school diploma in America, and that all of those newly graduated students were dispatched by their respective K-12 systems to pursue the postsecondary credential of their choice, as nearly 80 percent of current high school diploma holders do. How would we describe what they had learned in their 12 years of school?

Would the diploma be a guarantee to those students that they could now begin credit-bearing coursework at a two- or four-year college?

How would they survive a four-year baccalaureate business administration program at DeVry University?

What sort of professional placement in the armed services could they expect?

Could they get a job that ensures a family wage, benefits, and the promise of further education and training?

Current answers to these questions are "not necessarily," "they might not," "who knows?" and "probably not."

However hard we work to increase the number of students who receive a high school diploma and advance to the postsecondary program of their choice after graduation, we must be equally diligent in our efforts to ensure that a high school diploma actually signifies that students have learned something of value, that the diploma conveys a "real-world" currency beyond the walls of our local high schools. We must insist that an American high school diploma reflect the achievement of credible and commonly valued academic expectations, and that students, parents, college admissions counselors, and employers all trade in that same currency. Doing so can play a big role in making sure that all students, especially underrepresented populations, will get the access to a rich curriculum that is required for postsecondary success.

Sixty percent of employers recently surveyed by Public Agenda said that a high school diploma is no guarantee that the typical student has even learned "the basics." Between 60 and 75 percent of employers said that recent job applicants/freshmen lack the basic skills in grammar, reading, basic math, and work habits to succeed either at work or in college. Interestingly, however, 74 percent of teachers said that a high school diploma is a guarantee that a student has mastered "the basics."[1] Clearly there is a critical disconnect between what we think we are teaching students and what they are in fact learning.

Unless a high school diploma actually means something to both the students themselves and the people at the institutions who receive them after high school, the diploma will continue to be no guarantee at all of "postsecondary success," broadly defined.

## Redefining the Value of an American High School Diploma

In response to this problem, the American Diploma Project (ADP) was established in 2001 by Achieve, Inc., The Education Trust, the Thomas B. Fordham Foundation, and the National Alliance of Business.[2] The goal of the ADP is to help states guarantee that a high school diploma does in fact convey the accomplishment of core knowledge and skills in English language arts and mathematics — knowledge and skills that have a clear and convincing applicability in whatever field a student chooses after graduation, whether it's the workplace, a postsecondary academic institution, or the armed services.

There are two essential components to our work.

First, building on research conducted in its first year, ADP has developed a new set of benchmarks in English language arts and mathematics that every state can use to analyze the quality and rigor of its current high school graduation standards and assessments.[3] We chose these two content areas because they are fundamental: they are the languages used to access all other content areas.

Second, we asked five states that we selected as partners to change their policies so that standards-based assessment data would begin to matter beyond high school.[4] We knew it wouldn't be enough to establish new benchmarks, however compelling and innovative they are. We also knew that we had to increase the demand for good information about student achievement. ADP has therefore been encouraging postsecondary institutions, employers, and the armed services to ask for and value information about student achievement of standards in the admissions, placement, and hiring processes.

In the first instance, as we developed the new benchmarks, we learned that there really is a "greatest common factor" among the many sets of state standards that have been developed over the last decade, and that some sets of state standards actually do compare favorably to what employers and postsecondary institutions alike say they need students to have learned before they arrive at their doors. Our research revealed that these historically divergent sets of expectations have actually converged in a way that we might never have imagined.

Regrettably, not many sets of state standards compare favorably to this converging set of expectations, as exemplified by the new ADP benchmarks. ADP expects that the new benchmarks can help states in the near future to refine their expectations so that they will comport not only with expectations for success in the workplace, but will also — simultaneously — align to the needs of postsecondary institutions and the military. Quite a few states in recent years have demonstrated that it is possible to make mid-course corrections to standards and assessments without starting over from scratch.

To generate demand for student achievement data from employers and postsecondary institutions, ADP determined that performance on standards-based high school graduation assessments must, as a matter of policy, matter (to the extent possible) both to the students who take them and to the postsecondary institutions and employers who receive high school graduates into their systems. In other words, standards-based assessment data must be used as one criterion in college admissions and employer hiring practices.[5] Although we recognize that large-scale state assessments do not represent the full picture of a student's achievement, we also believe that requiring students to demonstrate proficiency on fair but rigorous standards-based assessments is a necessary (if not sufficient) first step toward making diplomas meaningful again to all stakeholders.

## Implementing ADP Goals: Indiana and Texas

Indiana and Texas offer examples of what ADP states are doing to move state policies in the direction of "making standards matter" and making the diploma meaningful again.

### Indiana

Demonstrating the power of policymakers working together across sectors, Indiana's Education Roundtable began meeting in the late 1990s on an informal basis to discuss critical issues in improving education in Indiana. Formalized through legislation in 1999, the Roundtable is now charged with making recommendations concerning education to the governor, the superintendent of public instruction, the General Assembly, and the Indiana State Board of Education. The Roundtable also assumed the duties formerly held by the State Standards Task Force. Most recently, the Roundtable drafted a "P-16 Plan to Prepare Students for Success in College," which exhibits a comprehensive vision for streamlining P-16 policies in the state and in many ways represents an ideal vision of how ADP goals could be implemented.

The plan's high school component focuses on the implementation of the "Core 40," a college and workplace readiness curriculum, as the default curriculum for Indiana students. The plan includes the use of the Core 40 tests in admissions, placement, and financial aid decisions at the postsecondary level (beyond the graduation requirement that students pass the tenth-grade "graduation qualifying exam"). Indiana has refined the content of all of its state tests so that they align to its new state standards, which compare favorably with the new ADP benchmarks.

Indiana's P-16 plan also addresses the addition of student test scores to electronic transcripts, as well as the initiation of predictive validity studies of the tests, as ADP has recommended. Other ADP states are conducting similar studies so that they will be assured of the efficacy of their standards-based tests in indicating later success.

## Texas

Texas currently requires high school students to pass the English language arts and mathematics portions of the Texas Assessments of Knowledge and Skills (TAKS) in order to graduate. These new, more rigorous assessments are well aligned with the Texas standards, which compare favorably to the ADP benchmarks.

Furthermore, predictive validity studies are underway to track student performance in college relative to TAKS scores, and in 2004, the Texas Board of Higher Education will set a "college readiness" score on the TAKS that will presumably be higher than that set in 2002 by the State Board of Education for high school exit. New legislation suggests that TAKS may replace the Texas Academic Skills Program as the state's college placement test.

On the employer front, the Texas Business and Education Coalition, an unwavering supporter of the state's standards-based reform efforts, recently established a "Meeting the High School Challenge" initiative designed to assist rising 11th graders with passing the new TAKS.[6] A joint effort of the coalition, the Texas Education Agency, the University of Texas, and Texas A&M, the initiative will help develop extra resources and provide teacher and principal training and other support for a successful 11th-grade TAKS program.

The Texas Business and Education Coalition also developed the Texas Scholars program, which provides incentives for students to follow the state's now mandatory Rigorous High School Program, a college and workplace readiness curriculum that, as Indiana's Core 40 requirement would do, provides all students with the opportunity to be exposed to the rich curriculum that will prepare them to have choices upon graduation. The newly established Center for State Scholars will implement similar programs in many more states over the next few years.[7]

## ADP State Efforts: Different Paths/Same Goals

Texas and Indiana illustrate that there is more than one way to make standards-based achievement matter to students and other stakeholders. Other ADP states are proceeding in similar ways, accounting for special circumstances.

In Kentucky, for example, policymakers plan to revisit the form and substance of the current state standards and assessments so that individual student scores may be generated, and therefore be useful for conveying information about individual student achievement. The refined college and workplace readiness standards will be benchmarked against ADP benchmarks. Pilot college admissions projects that would include consideration of 12th-grade writing assessments and/or a student's writing portfolio are also in the planning stages.

Nevada policymakers will use ADP research to inform potential refinements to Nevada's High School Proficiency Exam (HSPE) in English language arts and mathematics. The HSPE is already a requirement for graduation, but it should increasingly reflect more of the content of Nevada's recently revised state standards, which compare favorably with ADP benchmarks. The Nevada Board of Regents is also working to revise the requirements for high school graduates to receive Millennium Scholarships, currently offered to students based on grade point average. In the future, scholarship students will be required to have followed a rigorous college and workplace readiness curriculum, detailed by the Board of Regents and informed by the new ADP benchmarks.

In Massachusetts, studies are underway to identify the relationship between student performance on the Massachusetts Comprehensive Assessment System (MCAS) graduation tests with postsecondary success, so that decisions may be made about how MCAS data might be useful to postsecondary admissions and employer hiring processes. ADP research found that the Massachusetts standards align favorably with ADP benchmarks, and that the MCAS does a good job of covering much of the content that is useful to postsecondary institutions and employers for admissions and hiring purposes.

## Looking Ahead: Challenges for States

ADP states are not unique in their struggle to make better connections between high school exit expectations and the exigencies of the postsecondary world, broadly defined. Revising standards and assessments so that they reflect the rigorous, convergent expectations of the various postsecondary worlds will take states a long way toward providing useful information to their employers and postsecondary institutions about student achievement.

Beyond this important alignment — and even if their standards and assessments are well aligned to college and workplace readiness benchmarks — states may still need to revisit the relationship between state standards and assessment systems to state graduation requirements and locally monitored measures of student progress. Much important content in rigorous state standards cannot be measured by large-scale, on-demand assessments. For example, ADP benchmarks require students to complete an "extended essay" or research project. Both employers and postsecondary institutions insist on the usefulness of this vital skill. State standards-based assessments, while absolutely necessary, may not necessarily be sufficient indicators that our students have learned everything they need to have learned before leaving high school.

To ensure that all students, especially underrepresented populations, are assured of the opportunity to become college- and workplace-ready, states will also need to look beyond the content of state standards and assessments. Making sure all students have access to the rigorous content of ADP college and workplace expectations will require an insistence on a rigorous core curriculum for all students. Texas has taken the lead in this regard by requiring a college and workplace curriculum of all students. States will have to wrestle with human and material resource issues to address this crucial aspect of ADP goals, but equality of opportunity will depend heavily on equality of expectations in the first place.

The need for all students to follow a rigorous college and workplace curriculum also precipitates the need for more and better career and college counseling in our high schools. Currently, the ratio of students to counselors is several hundred to one.

Finally, asking private employers and postsecondary admissions officers to demand good information from K-12 systems about their potential employees and students is an extremely difficult proposition. It requires a constant grassroots effort to change entrenched cultures that are not used to getting good information about actual student achievement of rigorous standards from K-12 systems. In the case of postsecondary institutions, they have relied heavily on the "devils they know" — sporadically useful mechanisms, such as national standardized tests and grades. When shown good tests aligned to rigorous standards, however, postsecondary faculty confirm that those tests tell them what they need to know for making admissions and placement decisions. Employers, too, who have had waning faith in high school diplomas, confirm that if students were to leave high school having mastered the content and skills delineated in the ADP benchmarks, they would be more confident about hiring high school graduates.

Using standards-based data for college admissions/placement and hiring purposes, as described here, also requires a systematic way of gathering and sharing information in the first place. Some ADP states are developing common student identification numbers so that high schools, postsecondary institutions, and employers may track student progress and provide useful information to one another. New federal requirements for the disaggregation of student achievement data are making it easier for policymakers to develop these information-sharing systems. ADP states are discovering that developing electronic transcripts is one way to make data sharing easier.

## Conclusion

It is an encouraging sign that so many states were willing to be part of the American Diploma Project and to revisit and refine their standards-based systems so that they really are giving all students the best chance to master the content and skills they will need when they leave school. Throughout the last decade, states surely believed that by setting standards they would raise expectations and therefore enhance the eventual opportunities for all students. The American Diploma Project has helped our states and other "companion states" to hone their standards-based reform efforts on evaluating the efficacy of their current expectations and increasing the ability of the system to provide everyone involved with a commonly shared understanding of a student's achievement after 12 years.

ADP looks forward to working with other states to ensure that their hard work on standards-based reforms during the last decade really will produce the results they originally intended: to provide a rich and rigorous academic experience to all students, so that choices about their postsecondary future are not made *for* them but *by* them.

---

1. See *www.publicagenda.org/issues/pcc_detail.cfm? issue_type=education&list=14*.

2. The NAB dissolved in 2002, after completing its research for ADP.

3. See *www.americandiplomaproject.org* for reports.

4. ADP partner states are Indiana, Kentucky, Massachusetts, Nevada, and Texas.

5. See *www.americandiplomaproject.org/legal_research.html* for ADP research that describes the legal issues surrounding the use of assessment data.

6. See *www.tbec.org/meetingthehschallenge.shtml*.

7. See *www.centerforstatescholars.org/index.php*.

*How can college expectations and high school graduation standards be better aligned, so that remediation rates at broad-access colleges can be reduced? Michael Kirst describes a rare K-12/higher education collaboration that has tackled this dilemma. California has modified the assessment given all 11th graders to better reflect the expectations for college readiness of the California State University (CSU) system and its 23 campuses. CSU is the first statewide system to adopt a K-12 assessment as its own placement test for first-year students. This approach lessens the need for multiple, often conflicting tests, while raising high school standards and the consequences of the state's high school assessment test.*

# 12. Using a K-12 Assessment for College Placement[1]

## By Michael W. Kirst

Across the nation, high percentages of high school graduates are entering college, but they increasingly need remediation to succeed there. As a result, colleges are expending a great amount of resources on remediation instead of on college-level education, while large numbers of students never get past the first year of college.

In the California State University (CSU) system, which has 408,000 students on 23 campuses, remediation rates have risen over the past decades, along with concerns among public and state policymakers about the high number of poorly prepared students entering CSU from California public high schools. High remediation rates raise questions concerning the quality of public schools, and about the K-12 content standards and accompanying state tests developed by the California State Board of Education. Furthermore, the high level of CSU remediation is expensive. About 25,000 out of 40,000 first-time CSU students need some form of remediation. The university must absorb the cost of providing classes not offered for college credit. Parents and students bear additional expenses because remedial courses do not count toward graduation; consequently, students take longer to finish degrees.

In the mid 1990s, this problem prompted the CSU Board of Trustees to establish the Trustees' Subcommittee on Remedial Education to explore solutions. As a result, the state has modified the exam administered to all 11th graders to better align it with what students require to enter CSU prepared to succeed. CSU is the first statewide system to adopt a K-12 state assessment as its own placement test for first-year students. This is an important breakthrough in K-16 assessment policy, and it promises to provide clearer signals to high school students who have been uninformed about the discrepancy in standards between their high school grades, tests, and CSU placement.

This policy can also help reorient high school seniors to an intensive academic experience that will help them attain placement at the expected credit level (i.e., nonremedial). It is a rare collaboration between secondary and postsecondary education to help solve a mutual problem that neither education level can attain on its own.

## Evolution of the Problem

By state policy, CSU accepts the top third of California high school graduates, most of whom have a 3.0 average in the same number of academic courses required for entering the system.[2] However, except for students with high SAT scores, all incoming CSU students must take placement tests in English and entry-level mathematics before they can enroll in any first-term classes. Students who don't meet the cutoff scores on either test must take and pass remedial courses before enrolling in the typical course sequence for the general education degree. If test scores are particularly low, a student might first need to pass a low-level remedial course, then advance to a higher-level remediation course.

The CSU central office determines the cutoff scores, but each institution determines the specific process of remediation and development (e.g., the specific courses, the number of levels of remediation/development). At Sacramento State, for example, placement tests serve as gatekeepers to Math

1 and English 1A, which begin the typical course sequence in those subjects. Students take the math test only once: it is not readministered after completing remedial coursework as a check for mathematics understanding.

Currently, more than half of entering freshmen taking the CSU placement test require remediation in English or math before beginning college-level coursework (47% fail English, 37% math). It was numbers like these that led the CSU Board of Trustees to establish the Subcommittee on Remedial Education. In January 1995, a study committee presented the trustees with background information on remediation in the CSU system, along with several preliminary recommendations.

The initial recommendation, which the trustees approved, was to eliminate remedial courses by 2001. In the absence of swift progress, however, the CSU trustees soon established benchmarks for a 12-year period. The first of these targets was that by 2001 the need for remediation for regularly admitted freshmen would decline by 10 percent from 1996 levels. This target was not met. The new interim benchmark was a 50 percent reduction of 1996 remediation rates by 2004. The trustees' current goal is that only 10 percent of first-time students will need remediation by the final target date of 2007, a reduction of 90 percent.

Two other proposals surfaced to mitigate remediation. The first was to delay admission of students needing remediation until they could demonstrate they were prepared for college-level work. The other was that CSU bill high schools for the cost of remedial coursework to bring students' performance up to college-level expectations. Neither proposal has been enacted, but CSU did accept their underlying premise: that CSU could best reach its remediation targets for 2007 with a solution that spanned the state's K-12 and postsecondary education systems.

As CSU realizes, meeting the 10 percent remediation goal by 2007 will require three key steps:

- High school teachers and students must understand CSU placement standards;
- K-12 schools and students must know as early as possible about their progress in meeting CSU standards;
- K-12 students who are not ready for college-level math and English classes must be helped before they enter CSU.

## Actions to Solve the Problem

In the late 1990s, CSU began to discuss the remediation problem with a K-16 voluntary body called the Intersegmental Coordinating Committee (ICC) of the California Education Roundtable. The roundtable brings together representatives of all education levels in the state; it consists of the heads of the three California public higher education systems (the University of California, California State University, and California Community Colleges), plus a representative from the private colleges, and the state's K-12 chief state school officer, who is elected. The ICC is composed of high-level administrators serving under each of the roundtable leaders.

After consulting with ICC, CSU decided to try several new strategies to reduce remediation. Reflecting the key steps needed to reach the 2007 goal, these initially focused on improving communication with K-12 schools about placement standards and assessments; encouraging high school juniors to take the CSU placement; and providing high school preparation for students with low scores.

This approach, however, proved insufficient. The state already required so many K-12 assessments that schools and students resisted taking CSU's placement test. California already has a high school exit exam, based mostly on grade 7-9 standards, as well as the California Standards Tests, which reflect the state's 11th grade standards. Moreover, the cost and staff CSU needed to assist the huge California K-12 education system effectively was daunting. Finally, several studies demonstrated significant discrepancies between required K-12 state tests and CSU's placement exams (Le, 2002; Venezia, Kirst, & Antonio, 2003).

Rather than administer another exam to high school students, in the late 1990s CSU decided to negotiate directly with K-12 policymakers to merge CSU placement standards into the existing California Standards Tests, which are given to all students in 11th grade. A new policy and test design group was formed, representing CSU and the California State Education Department (an advisory group to the California State Board of Education and the CSU Trustees). This group examined test items from several K-12 tests for their relationship to CSU standards, and to find similarities between K-12 and CSU standards.

The State Board of Education negotiated with CSU to enhance the existing K-12 standards-based test to meet CSU placement standards. For example, as CSU requested, a writing sample was added to the existing K-12 multiple-choice language arts test, as was an increased focus on Algebra II in the math test.

To develop this K-12 early assessment program, CSU gained support from the legislature, the California State Board of Education, the CSU Department of Education, the University of California, California Community Colleges, CSU faculty, and organizations of K-12 teachers and administrators. The development of an augmented 11th grade state assessment proceeded with these multiple stakeholders in mind.

In 2003, CSU set the scores that high school juniors would need to achieve to be exempt from its placement exams, and the state sent test results to rising seniors by August 1. Low-scoring students can now use the senior year for intensive preparation to meet CSU placement standards.

## Common K-16 Standards

CSU's merged K-12 assessments strategy has many advantages, making this new K-16 collaboration deserving of close scrutiny by other states with high remediation rates. First, it gives a timely, targeted signal to students and schools of the need for added K-12 preparation. Moreover, by coordinating K-16 standards, it reduces the total testing time for students in high school and at CSU. In fact, it raises the stakes for statewide high school tests; previously, students saw no purpose for the 11th grade test because the SAT was used for admission and CSU had a separate placement test. This increases the academic focus during the senior year of high school for students who are not meeting CSU's placement standards.

Just as important, the strategy reforms and consolidates multiple K-16 school assessments, while providing better data for K-16 accountability concerning students' K-12 preparation for CSU. Instead of the previous lack of alignment between the standards for exiting high school and those for entering CSU, there are now common standards and performance levels across secondary and postsecondary education.

The CSU placement initiative is likely to be more successful than prior policies for a number of reasons. First, both secondary and postsecondary education will be working together. Previously, secondary educators had been unaware of CSU's placement standards, and high school students did not receive clear signals about what they needed to know for placement at the credit level.

Moreover, CSU found that a top-down strategy from the university was insufficient, and collaboration with K-12 had more promise. And, finally, in this era of tight and even shrinking state budgets, the combination of assessments saves the state money and testing time.

---

1. This paper benefited greatly from a speech given by Dr. David S. Spence, executive vice chancellor of California State University, at a conference sponsored by the National Center for Higher Education and Public Policy, Los Gatos, California, June 2003.

2. The University of California accepts the top 12 percent of state high school graduates, but the two systems require the same number and types of high school courses.

*If states are to significantly reduce the leaks in their educational pipelines, they need data systems that track student progress and outcomes — not just to the end of high school, but across the divide into and through postsecondary degree programs. States are in different stages of developing coordinated data systems. Hans P. L'Orange highlights the progress of Texas, Florida, and Maryland in addressing technical, political, and financial challenges. States are encouraged to learn from and build on the early work of other states so that data systems tracking student progress and success over time can be more efficient, and can be powerful tools for improving decisionmaking within institutions, at each educational level, and, ultimately, across the K-16 spectrum.*

# 13. Data and Accountability Systems: From Kindergarten through College

## By Hans P. L'Orange

The tremendous interest in increasing the depth and breadth of educational achievement in the United States has drawn new attention to standards, accountability, and data systems. It has also become clear that the data systems in many states, originally constructed to provide routine reports or to audit expenditures, do not always meet the assessment and accountability challenges of the 21st century. What is needed are data systems designed to document the achievement of students, schools, and colleges across the K-16 continuum, as well as improve the ability to respond to questions about a state's investment in education. These systems will be required to monitor student progress across the continuum and to identify barriers within systems, enabling early assessment and leading to possible intervention strategies.

The good news is that data systems for accountability and improvement are for the most part plentiful. However, their largest shortcoming is their isolation from one another: rarely are the data systems for K-12 students and postsecondary students linked together. The value of a K-16 data system in raising the levels of educational achievement for young people, including those groups underrepresented in gaining secondary and postsecondary credentials, can only be analyzed when data are available across all components of that system.

States are in different stages of developing coordinated data systems, but some data are already being shared across systems. Many postsecondary systems contain admissions information, including a student's final high school grade point average. Work attempted prior to entering a postsecondary institution — in the form of transfer credits or prior college-level work — is also available in certain systems. Extracting this information has permitted many states to develop feedback systems that allow high schools to receive information about their graduates' postsecondary performance. A comparison of what students have learned in high school to what they attempt to learn in college is a promising development in the evolution of K-16 data systems. And several states have programs that go a step further, explicitly linking data and demonstrating the power of partnerships in creating comprehensive systems.

## Effective K-16 Data and Accountability Systems

Effective systems share several common characteristics. First, they inform stakeholders of the condition of education at various levels: states can identify effective educational practices and diagnose problems. Effective systems also have the ability to identify programs, schools, and students that are successful, in addition to those needing assistance to become more successful. Specifically at the K-12 level, such systems help students and teachers focus on the course content that must be mastered in postsecondary education. And good systems can be used to assess and improve achievement that, in turn, can result in more students meeting the standards required for both admission and success at the next level.

Unfortunately, in many cases the systems that contain data on student learning rely on data captured at predefined grade levels and most often by a survey test. This point-in-time assessment, often used to compare performance across schools, does little to support judgments about the academic growth of individual students over time.

Effective systems that truly follow individual students across levels and over time are often more complex. Such longitudinal systems, typically called "unit record" systems, collect a wide range of demographic and performance data at regular intervals. They require the use of consistent definitions for individual variables, making valid comparisons possible. This consistency requirement also provides a mechanism to ensure that providers submit accurate data, especially when the data are used to compare institutions. Unit record systems offer an additional benefit: they can be used to answer "what if" questions, which can take accountability questions to higher levels (e.g., What combination of high school courses best prepares a student for postsecondary education?). Several states have developed promising systems that provide a mechanism to address these questions.

## Texas PK-16 Public Education Information Resource

The Texas PK-16 Public Education Information Resource (TPEIR) is a cross-agency effort building on the data and expertise of the Texas Higher Education Coordinating Board, the Texas Education Agency, and the State Board for Educator Certification. Their goal is to provide "ready access to public primary, secondary, and higher education information for purposes of research, planning, policy, and decision-making," from prekindergarten through the bachelor's degree.

TPEIR objectives include:

• Enhancing the analysis and reporting capabilities of both agency staff and external stakeholders;
• Supporting trend analysis, with some data from as early as 1989;
• Providing access to consistent results (everyone gets the same answers); and
• Reducing the agency time needed to fulfill requests for data.

Data for the repository come from the three partners. The data that are held in common and can most logically be linked are on students, staff, and teacher certification. The Higher Education Coordinating Board furnishes data on degree programs, courses, classes, testing results, and facilities. The Texas Education Agency and the Board for Educator Certification supplement the common data with district data and certification data.

The challenges for Texas include sheer size: managing the mass of data could become cumbersome. Texas has almost 1,200 school districts, and those districts, along with the state's postsecondary institutions, generate massive amounts of data. Currently, 680 million records are loaded in a very large warehouse, with the expectation of adding another 300 million records annually. Specific reports provide information about graduates at all levels, along with higher education admissions and enrollments. Cross-agency reports detail PK-16 linkages, including high school to postsecondary progression and the sources of certified teachers.[1]

## Florida K-20 Education Data Warehouse

Florida's new education data warehouse addresses many of these same issues. The structure provides "stakeholders in public education — including, but not limited to, administrators, educators, parents, students, state leadership, and professional organizations" with information on public school students from kindergarten through their graduate-level studies, including work force information available to the Florida Department of Education. This is accomplished by extracting and integrated data from existing source systems including a robust K-12 data system that has been in place for more than ten years, along with data from community colleges, the state university system, the Florida work-force development information system, and student assessment files.

The warehouse is a single repository of data concerning all students served by the public K-20 education system, as well as information on facilities, curriculum, and staff. The system provides:

- K-20 public education data integration;
- Analysis over time;
- A student-centered perspective;
- Both historical and current data, beginning as early as 1995;
- Confidentiality, with personally identifiable information removed; and
- State-of-the-art analytical capabilities.

The warehouse is a joint project among all the divisions of the Florida Department of Education. The various agencies work as partners to provide the data for the warehouse. This obviously makes data-sharing much more feasible, and the warehouse provides the capability of analyzing information from several sectors.

The lofty objectives and goals of the Florida effort include:

- Providing complete, timely, and accurate data with easy access and manipulation;
- Supporting an integrated technical environment, bringing in data from multiple sources and organizations;
- Merging historical data with current data in a structured repository; and
- Creating comprehensive data definitions.

A challenge for Florida will be to ensure that the benefits from a partnership among multiple agencies don't disappear when issues arise across bureaucracies.[2]

## Maryland Partnership for Teaching and Learning K-16

While Maryland has not built a comprehensive data warehouse, its efforts highlight the importance of partnerships in K-16 efforts. The Maryland Partnership for Teaching and Learning K-16 is beginning with an alliance of the Maryland State Department of Education, the Maryland Higher Education Commission, and the University System of Maryland.

The partnership is considering some very specific questions, as it notes on its website: "What should college graduates know and be able to do? What should our high school students know and how will we know that they have learned it? What should our teachers know and be able to do, and how will we know they have reached the standards we expect? What can we learn from the most successful programs and practices in our state and around the country that will help us raise the achievement of all our students in reading, writing, mathematics, and citizenship skills for success?"

The Maryland partners have recognized that, even though large quantities of data are collected, the information often is not accessible in a manner needed to do appropriate analysis and address the questions being asked. An emerging concept is the establishment of a Maryland Education Data Network. In this case, "network" implies linking, integrating, and making more usable the vast quantities of existing data that are stored by numerous parties in the state. Maryland currently has no plans to create a single database or warehouse managed by one agency. Instead, its early conceptual model includes a single electronic comprehensive record or portfolio that would accompany each student throughout his or her education.

The state still has to resolve many issues, but it is considering a very different approach from other states to following students and measuring their achievement.[3]

## Issues and Challenges in Creating a Successful K-16 System

Even though Texas, Florida, and Maryland are addressing some common issues and share some common characteristics, each approaches the challenges that arise in its own way. And while lessons certainly can be learned from each state, it is a mistake to think a single model or "magic fix" will work in every situation. A supportive state environment is critical to a successful effort, and each state environment presents its own unique set of challenges.

Regardless, a unified approach with support across all levels is critical to developing a shared system. There is often a tendency to look for a quick technical solution when considering the development of a K-16 data system, but addressing the policy environment and political issues must come first. Determining the goals for the entire state, regardless of sector, should be addressed early in the process of developing a data system. Sectors often act independently, potentially at cross-purposes with one another. Identifying common goals and providing a means for the elementary, secondary, and postsecondary sectors to work together addresses some of the "turf" issues that inevitably arise. Many states have found that voluntary and cooperative relationships between state boards of education and higher education systems are key to any success behind their efforts.

Related issues revolve around the costs of creating systems where the sectors involved are funded separately. A shared system requires shared responsibility: successful systems have either created a separate funding mechanism or explicitly mandated how cost-sharing will occur. There can also be a tendency to provide "one-time" funds, but effective data and accountability systems require sustained support. That can be a challenge in difficult economic times, and it is just one of the reasons why it is so important to address long-term state goals at the outset.

Technical issues can become barriers as well. Many postsecondary systems identify students through their social security number or another system-generated unique identification number. Most elementary/secondary systems use a different but still unique number. Reconciling these numbers as a student transitions between levels can be difficult without systematic planning.

Ownership of the data must also be addressed. This will be the case whether the data lives in a single warehouse, in shared multiple databases, or in an electronic student portfolio.

Privacy is a related and critical issue. All students, regardless of level, have a legal and ethical right to privacy. Safeguards must be built into any K-16 system to ensure that privacy is maintained while still allowing the benefits of tracking a student's achievements to be realized.

The steps taken in Texas, Florida, and Maryland illustrate that states can create coordinated or linked systems that allow them to truly assess the benefits of K-16 data systems, but challenges are also prevalent. As the purposes of information continue to evolve and challenging issues are addressed, states can build on one another's efforts. Exemplary data and accountability systems will become more efficient. They will be designed and implemented in ways that truly increase the ability of policymakers and practitioners to focus on data that improve decisionmaking — within an institution, within a particular educational level, and ultimately across the entire spectrum of K-16 education to help ensure that more of our young people gain the quality education they need and deserve.

---

1. For more information on TPEIR, see *http://texaseducationinfo.org.*

2. For more information on Florida's data system, see *http://edwapp.doe.state.fl.us/doe.*

3. For more information on the Maryland Partnership for Teaching and Learning K-16, see *http://mdk16.usmd.edu.*

*Many states have turned to merit scholarships as a way to spur middle and high school students to work harder so they can qualify for college scholarships. Scott Evenbeck and his colleagues discuss Indiana's Twenty-First Century Scholars, which targets merit scholarships at low-income students. In addition, the state of Indiana links a statewide college information and counseling service to the scholarship. Receipt of a Scholars grant appears to improve the odds that a student will prepare for, enroll in, and persist in college in Indiana.*

## 14. Twenty-First Century Scholars: Indiana's Program of Incentives for College-Going

By Scott Evenbeck, Philip A. Seabrook,
Edward P. St. John, and Seana Murphy

The Twenty-First Century Scholars Program was created in 1990 as Indiana's way of raising the educational aspirations of low- and moderate-income families. The program's mission is to increase high school and college graduation rates by ensuring that all Indiana families can afford a college education for their children. Inspired by the I Have a Dream tuition-promise program, then-Indiana Governor Evan Bayh proposed the program, and State Representative Stan Jones, now Commissioner for Higher Education, stewarded the legislation.

Income-eligible eighth and ninth graders who enroll as Scholars are promised free tuition at a state college or university, or a like portion of tuition if attending an independent institution in Indiana. The program is limited to students who qualify for free or reduced price lunch.[1]

Between 1986 and 1998, Indiana rose from 40th in the country to 17th in the percentage of high school graduates enrolling in college.[2] This remarkable improvement can be attributed in no small part to a number of state policy initiatives: the Twenty-First Century Scholars Program, state efforts to improve access to college preparatory curricula in high schools, and increased state-funded support services for middle and high school students.

## Program Components

The Twenty-First Century Scholars Program differs from other "merit-based" scholarships in a significant way: it provides clear and early signals to students as to why they should prepare for a college education, accompanied with supports and information about college opportunities that help make that possibility a reality. In return for the promise of free tuition, students who enter the program in the seventh or eighth grade take this pledge of good citizenship:

- I agree to graduate from an Indiana high school with a high school diploma.
- I will achieve a cumulative high school GPA of at least 2.0 on a 4.0 scale.
- I will not use illegal drugs or alcohol or commit any crime.
- I will apply for admission to an Indiana college, university, or technical school as a high school senior.
- I will apply for student financial aid by March 1 of my senior year of high school.

The "pledge ceremony," which involves students and their family members, creates a significant ritual for the young people beginning the program and for their parents, who are encouraged to support their child's fulfillment of the pledge.

The pledge is just a first step. A statewide program has been established — coupling financial aid with academic support and parental involvement — to translate words into change in young people's lives. Overall, 65,599 students have enrolled in the program since 1995, when the first Scholars headed to college. Just under 25,000 Indiana youth have fulfilled the pledge and graduated through the 2002–2003 academic year.

The Twenty-First Century Scholarship supplements a student's need-based financial aid from the state up to the level of tuition at Indiana's public colleges. Unlike so many other state merit-aid programs, this is targeted to those in the state least likely to be able to afford a college education.

In 1999–2000, the average Twenty-First Century Scholarship for participants attending public colleges was $1,457, supplementing an average need-based state grant of $1,645.[3] Indiana's estimated total costs for Twenty-First Century Scholarships in 2001–2002 were $8,074,640 for 5,773 students. This is below one original projection of $15 million in annual costs. The variance is primarily due to the fact that not all eligible students participate, despite extensive recruitment efforts.

Support for Scholars goes beyond the financial assistance. Across the state, 16 regional offices recruit students to take the "pledge," working with school counselors, advisors, and family members. The regional offices solicit parental involvement and coordinate the programs that equip students — and parents — with the academic, social, and cultural skills that young people need to succeed in secondary and postsecondary education. The offices also engage all sectors of the community in efforts to encourage students to pursue postsecondary education.

Programming for high school students includes campus visits, workshops, tutoring, and other activities designed to foster student success. The Twenty-First Century Scholars GEAR UP program, for example, includes partnerships with colleges and universities. Upper-division Twenty-First Century Scholars are mentors to lower-division Scholars. Mentors and protégés both benefit, with the results showing up in their persistence in higher education.

Indiana's administrative and program costs for the nonscholarship component of the Twenty-First Century Scholars program were estimated at $2.3 million in 2001–2002 (St. John, Musoba, Simmons, & Chung, 2002).

## Documenting the Results

In the program's early years, educational researchers, working with the Indiana Department for Higher Education and the nonprofit Indiana Career and Postsecondary Advancement Center, studied the Scholars Program, produced early estimates of its impact, and helped inform its development. This initial analysis of state data from 1998–1999 examined the effect of receiving a Twenty-First Century Scholars award on whether freshmen and sophomores enrolled in Indiana's public colleges and universities stayed in school for the full year (St. John, Musoba, & Simmons, 2003). The findings indicated that both Scholars grants and other state grants were associated with successfully completing the academic year.

Based upon this initial research, the National Governors Association highlighted the potential of the program, and the Lumina Foundation for Education funded a more complete evaluation. An evaluation team at the Indiana Education Policy Center developed a procedure for merging three datasets: a statewide survey of eighth graders in the high school class of 2000, financial aid application information and student records from public colleges and universities for freshman in 2000–2002, and information on applications for federal student aid by high school seniors in 2000.[4] The new database followed a cohort of Indiana students from eighth grade through the second year of college, making it possible to compare Scholarship recipients to other students, and to assess the impact of the Scholars program on college enrollment (or destination) and persistence.

Evaluators found that receipt of a Twenty-First Century Scholars grant substantially improved the odds that a young person would enroll in both public and private colleges. For example, Scholars were more than four times as likely to enroll in a public four-year college than non-Scholars with similar backgrounds. Scholars were also more likely to apply for student aid than their comparable peers (St. John, Musoba, Simmons, & Chung, 2002).

The effects of being a Twenty-First Century Scholar on persisting through the first year of college were also positive, although the positive effects were similar to those of receiving any state financial aid.[5] Given that Scholars were more likely to attend college in the first place, the authors concluded that the program had positive net effects on the number of low-income students in Indiana who attained at least one year of college (St. John, Musoba, Simmons, & Chung, 2002). Scholars also incurred on average less educational loan debt than other financial aid recipients — debt that has been shown to be negatively associated with college enrollment and persistence (Kaltenbaugh, St. John, & Starkey, 1999).

The Twenty-First Century Scholars Program provides a model for states seeking an alternative to a merit-based scholarship program. The components and results of the program are being used to inform the redesign of the Michigan Merit Scholarship Program as part of a legal challenge by the American Civil Liberties Union and the National Association for the Advancement of Colored People (Heller, 2003; St. John & Chung, forthcoming). Unlike the Michigan Merit Scholarships, which usually go to high-income students with high odds of enrolling without grants, the Scholars program has proven to increase enrollment of low-income students (St. John, Musoba, Simmons, & Chung, 2002).

A recent, more comprehensive evaluation of the Twenty-First Century Scholars Program, based on a follow-up analysis of the database for the 2000 cohort, examined impacts on eighth graders' aspirations to attend college, college applications, and college enrollment (St. John, 2002, 2003).[6] Taking the Scholars pledge in eighth grade was positively associated with aspiring to attend college and applying for student aid (i.e., earning the Scholars award). In addition, receiving a Scholars award substantially improved the odds of enrolling in college (St. John et al., 2002).

This body of research confirms that the balanced approach used in the Twenty-First Century Scholars Program — combining information on college and encouragement for low-income students to prepare for college with financial support for enrollment — enables more students to prepare for college while in middle and high school, to enroll in college, and to persist in their program of study. Not only are there strong indications that this approach works, but the program also provides a viable model that other states can replicate.

---

1. The program conducts random validation of income eligibility as quality assurance.
2. See St. John, Musoba, Simmons, and Chung (2002), based on compilation of data from *Postsecondary Education Opportunity*, August 2000 (*www.postsecondary.org*).
3. Information about program costs is from St. John, Musoba, Simmons, and Chung (2002).
4. Students in the Twenty-First Century Scholars Program apply for federal student aid, so the aid application by students who take the pledge is an indicator of having completed the requirements for a scholarship.
5. It was not possible to examine persistence in private colleges because student records on continuous enrollment in private colleges were unavailable. However, researchers had information on the award of state grants to students enrolled in private colleges, so they could estimate the impact of the scholarship on enrollment in private colleges.
6. The Balanced Access Model provides an alternative to the logic of the college pipeline

model used by the National Center for Education Statistics (1997). The NCES pipeline model examines the impact of background on preparation and enrollment, but ignores the impact of finances on aspirations and enrollment. The Balanced Access Model combines the pipeline logic with explicit consideration of the role of finances in aspirations formation and college enrollment.

*One important predictor of student persistence in college is the quality of students' high school preparation. Several chapters in this book address that issue. Another predictor of success is "student engagement," the amount of time students invest in educationally purposeful activities and how institutions organize their resources to induce students to engage in those activities. The National Survey of Student Engagement (and the companion Community College Survey of Student Engagement) asks students about classroom participation, study time, faculty contact, and interactions with other students. Brian K. Bridges and George D. Kuh demonstrate how this data is being used for institutional improvement and argue that NSSE can also be used by states as a performance indicator in higher education oversight, performance reporting, and accountability systems.*

---

# 15. The National Survey of Student Engagement: A New Tool for Postsecondary Accountability

By Brian K. Bridges and George D. Kuh

The public is enamored with rankings of all kinds, and that includes rankings of colleges and universities. Popular magazines use everything from student entrance exam scores and faculty-student ratios to library holdings and alumni giving to create their lists. Although some of this information is useful, the rankings focus primarily on inputs and resources, which is misleading when evaluating collegiate quality. Such measures say nothing about institutional performance, and they tell us very little about the quality of the undergraduate experience — what students actually do during college and what they gain from their educational pursuits.

At effective colleges and universities, students are satisfied, devote substantial effort to their studies, and learn at high levels. Most important, given the goal of "doubling the numbers" of underserved young people who gain a postsecondary credential, they persist to complete their educational objectives. A key predictor of student success is a concept called student engagement: the amount of time and energy students invest in educationally purposeful activities and how institutions organize their resources to induce students to engage in those activities. More engaged students tend to be more satisfied and graduate at higher rates than their less engaged counterparts. Knowing the degree to which students take part in educationally purposeful activities can serve as a proxy for institutional quality, especially in the absence of other measures, and hence for a school's capacity to serve all students.

## A Tool for Strengthening Institutional Accountability for Student Success

Research has shown that a number of educational practices correlate with high levels of student engagement. These include student-faculty contact, cooperation among students, time on task, high expectations, and respect for diverse talents and ways of learning. Also important are institutional environments that students perceive as inclusive and affirming and where expectations for performance are clearly communicated and set at reasonably high levels. These institutional factors improve student satisfaction and achievement on a variety of dimensions (Astin, 1984, 1991; Chickering & Gamson, 1987; Kuh, 2001; Kuh, Schoh, Whitt, & Associates, 1991; Pascarella, 2001; Pascarella & Terenzini, 1991).

Until recently, there was no reliable way to assess student engagement across the universe of postsecondary institutions. Since 1999, though, the National Survey of Student Engagement, launched at Indiana University with support from the Pew Charitable Trusts, has annually collected information directly from tens of thousands of randomly sampled undergraduate students about the quality of their educational experience. Co-sponsored by the Carnegie Foundation for the Advancement of Teaching and designed by a group of national assessment experts, NSSE (pronounced "nessie") asks about classroom participation, faculty contact, interactions with other students, study time, and the school's support of their efforts, all of which are linked to desired outcomes in college.

Equally important, NSSE results point to aspects of student and institutional performance where improvement is highly desirable and possible, such as persistence and success in major field courses. Studies conducted by the National Center for Higher Education Management Systems (Ewell, 2002) and NSSE, in cooperation with RAND (Kuh, Carini, & Klein, 2003), suggest that lower-ability students tend to benefit disproportionately from the effective educational practices measured by NSSE — a particularly important finding, given the challenges low-income and low-achieving students face in staying in college through degree completion.

Schools are using their student engagement results in a variety of productive ways. The past several NSSE national reports highlight some examples, including institutional efforts to reform general education curricula, guide accreditation self-studies, reallocate resources, justify funding requests, and communicate with prospective students, parents, and alumni. NSSE encourages participating institutions to report their results to constituents as appropriate in order to prompt discussions about how this information can guide institutional improvement efforts.[1]

## Student Engagement as a Performance Indicator

Higher education governing boards and state oversight agencies are beginning to incorporate student engagement and NSEE reports into performance indicator systems. For example, the University of Massachusetts system prepares a "Report on Annual Indicators" each spring as part of a legislatively mandated performance measurement system. The report includes a variety of measures of academic quality, student satisfaction, access and affordability, service to the Commonwealth, and financial health. The system compares each campus' NSSE student-satisfaction results to the aggregated system average, as well as to that of peer institutions (defined by Carnegie institutional type), in order to identify areas for improvement. NSSE results are also examined in the system's report on access and affordability, including the experiences of undergraduates who are from the first generation of their family to attend college.

The University of Wisconsin Board of Regents' annual accountability report has begun to include NSSE data to explain to Wisconsin citizens how the university's resources are being used to promote student learning and other goals. NSSE data are used to estimate progress toward improving learning competencies, enhancing campus learning environments, and improving academic support programs, all of which relate positively to student persistence. Wisconsin has also adapted selected NSSE questions to survey recent graduates about how well their educational experience prepared them in such areas as critical thinking and problem-solving. The system expects to use this information to demonstrate the university's contribution to an educated citizenry that is well prepared to contribute to the increasingly complex state and global economies.

South Dakota's six public universities, which participate in NSSE, are using the results for multiple purposes. The Board of Regents receives annual reports for institution and system-wide performance. The results are also compared against NSSE's five national benchmarks of effective educational practices: academic challenge, active and collaborative learning, student-faculty interaction, enriching educational experiences, and supportive campus environment. The student engagement sections of the reports provide lay members of the board with additional information on the principles of good practice in undergraduate education upon which NSSE is based. Individual South Dakota universities are using the results to gauge student perceptions of the quality of their academic experiences and to inform student retention efforts.

Student retention has become an even higher priority as the system is considering adding a new performance funding indicator based on persistence from the first to second year. The system is also participating in a study conducted by the National Center for Higher Education Management Systems to examine the relationship between student engagement as measured by NSSE and performance on the system's general education proficiency examination (Ewell, 2002).

In 1999, the Texas legislature required that all state agencies and public universities begin to address customer satisfaction. The University of Texas (UT) system uses NSSE survey questions to meet its state legislative mandate on customer satisfaction and to help assess institutional performance in the system's newly created Performance and Accountability System. The UT system is also developing a test of academic skills that will be correlated with student engagement indicators.

Other states and university systems using NSSE in some way in their performance reporting approaches include the New Hampshire state universities, Texas A&M, and the University of North Carolina.

## Additional Student Engagement Survey Initiatives

With more than 700 four-year colleges and universities participating in NSSE, it appears that student engagement is a performance indicator whose time has come. The Community College Survey of Student Engagement, which is based on NSSE, completed its first national administration in spring 2003, with about 120 two-year colleges participating. A faculty version of NSSE was recently field tested with 16,000 faculty members at about 150 colleges and universities. The results are intended to help interpret how students respond to engagement questions at the participating campuses.

Building Engagement and Attainment of Minority Students (BEAMS) is a major multiyear national initiative designed to reduce the national higher education attainment gap for African American, Hispanic, and Native American students by increasing graduation rates at minority-serving institutions — historically black colleges and universities, Hispanic-serving institutions, and tribal colleges and universities. The American Association for Higher Education, NSSE, and the Alliance for Equity in Higher Education are working together with participating colleges and universities to analyze the scope and character of student engagement on their campuses and to implement action plans to improve engagement, learning, persistence, and success. Funded by Lumina Foundation for Education, BEAMS is intended to showcase the strengths of these campuses while identifying areas for improvement that strengthen the capacity of minority-serving institutions to engage their students in effective educational practices.

Most students come to college with habits of engagement already well established, for better or for worse. Academic disengagement of high school seniors is at an all-time high, which shapes how they perform when they get to college (Kirst, 2001; Sax, Lindholm, Astin, Korn, & Mahoney, 2001). Drawing on NSSE's experience, visibility, and utility, the High School Survey of Student Engagement (HSSSE) is being developed to help teachers and administrators identify areas where improvement is needed in K-12 schools, to signal to high school students where they need to devote more time and energy to succeed in college, and to pave the way for a smoother, more productive transition to postsecondary education. HSSSE is working with the Community College Survey of Student Engagement on a College and Careers Transition Initiative, which will administer the survey in about 40 participating high schools.

As the various NSSE initiatives indicate, student engagement data represent an essential but underused source of information for both accountability and institutional improvement efforts. NSSE and its expanding cadre of partners are helping change the way in which the nation conceives and assesses quality in higher education. Used well, these surveys and the information they generate can inform and drive efforts to enhance the learning and personal development of *all* students, especially those who have historically been underrepresented in postsecondary education.

---

1. See *www.iub.edu/~nsse*.

*As state governments place greater emphasis on accountability for results in higher education, some colleges have asked the state for a changed "deal": greater autonomy (e.g., in tuition-setting, budgeting, employment, procurement) in exchange for greater accountability. By looking at the experience of two public colleges, the Colorado School of Mines and St. Mary's College of Maryland, Lara K. Couturier assesses the implications of this trend for access and attainment for underserved students.*

# 16. Balancing Autonomy and Accountability in Higher Education

## By Lara K. Couturier

When St. Mary's College of Maryland became the nation's first "charter college" in 1992 — securing new procedural freedoms in exchange for meeting specific performance standards — its leaders never imagined that more than a decade later the institution would be the poster child for a debate over autonomy and accountability.

In 2001, nine years after St. Mary's founding, the Colorado School of Mines effectively became the nation's second charter college, when the state legislature granted it "exemplary" status.

Today, as higher education budgets are being slashed in the current economic downturn and policymakers look to the market to restructure the public sector, these alternative models are being watched closely. Lawmakers in most states have discussed or enacted measures to move traditional public colleges and universities in a direction similar to that of St. Mary's and "Mines."[1]

The levels of autonomy and accountability in the models under consideration vary dramatically, from "compacts" in Washington, to "privatization" in Wisconsin, and "contracts" in Florida. A "New Partnership" for the

Massachusetts College of Art, modeled after St. Mary's, was signed into law in 2003 (personal communication, F. Newman, July 1, 2003). Similar new relationships also can be found in Sweden, Denmark, and Austria, plus instances of increased autonomy in countries such as Indonesia and the Slovak Republic.

As political and academic leaders analyze these new models, the debate revolves around how to remain competitive for research funding, maintain contracts and donations, attract the "best and brightest" students, and boost prestige. The examples of St. Mary's and the Colorado School of Mines reveal some of the dangers and some of the promise inherent in these new relationships with a question that is rarely asked: What is the impact of increased autonomy on higher education's ability to meet the public's needs, especially in terms of access and attainment for underserved students?

## St. Mary's College of Maryland

In 1992, the leadership at St. Mary's envisioned a new funding and governance structure for the state's only public honors college (St. Mary's College of Maryland, 2002). Administrators negotiated with the state to gain a lump-sum budget and new autonomy from state regulations, including more control over such areas as employment and procurement. The legislation imposed a ceiling on state support, dramatically elevating the role of private revenue, and a plan was set in motion to double tuition over five years. In return, the small liberal arts institution agreed to maintain its distinctive role and mission. To assuage fears about rising tuition closing off access for low-income students, the college agreed to double its financial aid budget by putting a portion of new tuition revenues into need-based aid (Berdahl, 1998; Schmidt, 1998). It also agreed to demonstrate that it had met its goals through presentations to the legislature and through Managing for Results, an accountability program for Maryland state agencies (personal communication, T. Meringolo, November 25, 2002; personal communication, M. O'Brien, July 7, 2003).

The college's performance has been highly scrutinized. Evaluations conducted by Robert O. Berdahl in 1996 and 1999 revealed high performance and strong political backing for continuing the experiment. St. Mary's has enjoyed improvements in curriculum, SAT scores, governance, graduation and retention, faculty quality, fundraising, and physical facilities. A Middle States accreditation team gave the school a glowing report in 1995 (Berdahl & MacTaggart, 2000; Berdahl, 1998; personal communication, M. O'Brien, July 7, 2003). *The Washington Post Magazine* depicted St. Mary's as a bastion of both quality and diversity. Nearly one-third of the college's students are first-generation, and its five-year graduation rate for the past two years has met or exceeded 75 percent (Naughton, 2001).[2]

But in the late 1990s, St. Mary's ran into difficulty maintaining enrollments for students of color. Critics argue that institutions with more autonomy naturally focus on ways to boost the statistical measures that ensure high marks in popular rankings such as those in *U.S. News & World Report*. Consciously or not, St. Mary's did just that. As St. Mary's grew more elite and more expensive, access fell. The percentage of first-time, full-time freshmen who were African American dropped from a peak of 14.1 percent in 1994 to 6 percent in 2000, and the percentage of all freshmen of color bottomed out at 12.5 percent.[3]

The leadership at St. Mary's quickly acknowledged this issue and stepped up recruiting efforts to reverse the trend, establishing innovative relationships with area high schools and community colleges (personal communication, M. Apter, July 2, 2003; personal communication, T. Meringolo, November 25, 2002; St Mary's College of Maryland, 2003). By fall of 2002, the percentage of entering students who were African American had risen to 8.3 percent. The percentage of entering students of color was up to 17.1 percent, and is estimated at 18 percent for fall 2003 (personal communication, F. Lanzer, July 8, 2003).

In other words, St. Mary's used its new freedom to improve. When performance fell in an area for which it was held accountable — in this case, maintaining access for a diverse population — the leadership acted to rectify the situation. And despite the dip in diverse enrollments experienced in the late 1990s, students of color are a higher percentage of the total student body now than before the legislation passed.

Moreover, St. Mary's has high rates of retention and graduation for students of color, and President Maggie O'Brien's dedication is obvious: "We have not hit [our] goal [of matching the state's demographics]. . . . But we never stop striving to get there and actively work on new programs . . . to increase our enrollments of students of color" (personal communication, M. O'Brien, July 7, 2003). As a result, says O'Brien, St. Mary's maintains political support, even among Maryland's Black Caucus.

But St. Mary's still has a long way to go — in Maryland, students of color comprise 39 percent of all enrollments at four-year public institutions (Almanac, 2002–2003). The question remains: How can charter status push St. Mary's to improve access and attainment for underserved students?

## Colorado School of Mines

When the legislature granted the Colorado School of Mines exemplary status, it gave the college a lump-sum budget and more control over tuition and academic programs. The legislation also exempted Mines from the higher education commission's system for assessing and reporting performance. In return, the leadership signed an agreement that clearly defines performance criteria for the school as a highly selective engineering college. Performance criteria include the strength of transfer agreements with community colleges, increases in graduation rates, responses to employer surveys, and pass rates for the Fundamentals of Engineering examination (personal communication, R. Kieft, July 17, 2002).[4]

It is too early to report definitive results of the Mines performance agreement, which was completed in early 2002. However, there are indications of improved performance already. Enrollments of students of color climbed to 14.3 percent in 2002, after a three-year drop in the years leading up to the change in legislation. The freshman-to-sophomore retention rate of students of color for fall 2001 to fall 2002 exceeded the 84 percent rate for the freshmen class as a whole (Colorado School of Mines, 2003a, 2003b). Applications are up by 60 percent over the last two years, and the number of minority applicants increased 92 percent from 2001 to 2002. Despite the weak economy, fundraising is going well, and Mines has responded to the needs of local industry by creating several new master's programs quickly — a process that could have taken as long as two years under the old system (Colorado School of Mines, 2003a; personal communication, J. Trefny, June 30, 2003).

Some changes give cause for concern, however. The performance agreement requires Mines to narrow its exception window for accepting applicants who fall below the minimum admissions criteria, effectively tightening admissions standards (personal communication, J. Trefny, June 30, 2003). Mines' president John Trefny has explained that the purpose of this change is to ensure that all admitted students are prepared to succeed in the college's rigorous academic setting, but a side-effect will be to make it more elite. Starting in 2003, the Board of Trustees also gained the authority to recommend tuition increases (personal communication, J. Trefny, June 30, 2003). The combination of tighter admissions standards and higher tuition could make Mines less accessible to underserved students.

Moreover, despite the careful crafting that went into the performance agreement, it does not include accountability for maintaining a diverse learning environment, and it does not specify financial aid goals except for a minimum standard. The result is a flexible, entrepreneurial relationship that includes clear accountability in a number of important areas but lacks a mandate to improve opportunity for underserved students.

President Trefny has made his commitment to providing opportunity clear. An impressive array of outreach, bridge, and retention programs is in place, and Trefny has pledged that 15 percent of tuition increases will be funneled directly into financial aid (personal communication, J. Trefny, June 30, 2003). Sixty-five percent of Mines students receive need-based aid.[5] But what happens when the leadership changes? Who will be watching, and how will the institution be held accountable?

These questions troubled State Senator Penfield Tate, who cast the sole vote against the exemplary institution legislation. "No one I talk to says they want this charter college system so they can come up with a more diverse, more reflective student body that provides opportunities for a broader cross-section of society," Tate said. "They're saying we want money, and if we have a whole bunch of money we'll figure out a way to educate everybody. But how to educate everybody is sort of the afterthought" (personal communication, P. Tate, August 16, 2002).

## The Optimal Balance between Autonomy and Accountability

In most areas, St. Mary's and Mines are performing well under their new status, but the charter model in its current forms has proven a mixed blessing to underserved students. Will all public institutions with increased autonomy follow a competitive pattern of growing more elite and expensive? Can the charter college model be leveraged to improve access and attainment for low-income students and students of color?

The implications extend far beyond the small number of institutions that are identified as charters. The dizzying array of new initiatives cropping up around the country — from charters to vouchers to public corporations — will, in the end, look much like the arrangements found at St. Mary's and Mines: more autonomy over operations, increased external fundraising, and new forms of accountability to the state. Increased autonomy in certain areas — such as budgeting, procurement, and employment — will help institutions to operate in today's competitive environment, but institutional leaders must also be held accountable for recruiting, retaining, and graduating low-income students and students of color.

If they are not, it is likely that these new relationships will encourage institutions to focus more on institutional self-interest (i.e., prestige and revenues) and less on serving an ever-expanding share of the population. A quick review of discussions around the country — Arizona, Colorado, Texas, Ohio — reveals that academic leaders deflect most questions about access being harmed by pledging increases in financial aid. Financial aid is critical, but access and attainment experts have concluded that it is not enough. A complex array of preparation, outreach, orientation, remediation, and retention programs is needed. The charter must hold institutions to a higher standard.

Accountability for educating underserved students should not be ambiguous, nor should it be left to the changing priorities of institutional leaders. The Colorado Commission on Higher Education and Mines' leadership painstakingly negotiated the performance agreement, whereas the method of accountability at St. Mary's is much more loosely defined within the legislation. On the critical issue of access, however, the legislation holds St. Mary's to a performance standard of "increased access for economically disadvantaged and minority students," while the performance agreement for Mines does not. And Colorado governor Bill Owens has publicly stated his opposition to the use of race as a factor in college admissions, making this a tricky political issue for Mines (Martinez, 2003).

Wherever possible, the ideal would be a combination of the two arrangements: an explicit agreement such as that found at Mines, with a clear commitment to underserved students such as that found at St. Mary's.

The new charter model holds great promise for institutions, but that promise will be better met through a performance agreement that holds institutions accountable for taking proven, definitive steps to improve access and attainment. The results could be good for everyone: the institutions operate with more flexibility, the state knows that the institutions are working toward the public good, and more underserved students will have the opportunity to attend college.

---

1. Examples include: Arizona, Colorado, Florida, Hawaii, Illinois, Maryland, Massachusetts, New Jersey, North Dakota, Ohio, Oklahoma, Oregon, South Carolina, Texas, Virginia, Washington, West Virginia, and Wisconsin.

2. Data from "Retention of First-time Full-time First-year Students by Race," a table supplied by Fran Lanzer, Research Assistant, St. Mary's Office of Institutional Research.

3. Data from "Race of First-time Full-time First-year Students," a table supplied by Fran Lanzer, Research Assistant, St. Mary's Office of Institutional Research.

4. See also "Performance Agreement: Colorado School of Mines and CCHE for FY 2002–2007," February 11, 2002.

5. See *www.finaid.mines.edu/PR_TOC.html*.

*Theme or "focus" high schools create a strong identity, coherent curriculum, and sense of community among students and faculty. The best of these schools, unified around a particular theme such as a career area or a pedagogical approach, demonstrate increased graduation rates, increased college attendance, stronger faculty-student relationships, and reduced disciplinary problems, among other preconditions for achievement gains. As Christine Donis-Keller and Monica Martinez note, the schools often achieve these outcomes with a more vulnerable student population.*

---

# 17. Theme Schools: A Model for Restructuring High Schools

By Monica R. Martinez and Christine Donis-Keller

At the High School for Environmental Studies in New York City, students study the environment through a variety of required and elective classes, work on hands-on projects throughout the city, and run a rooftop garden. At the New Gate School in Sarasota, Florida, students prepare for college through a research-oriented curriculum and projects both at the school and in the community. And at the Cristo Rey Jesuit High School in Chicago, Illinois, students combine a Catholic college preparatory curriculum with corporate internships designed to defray the costs of tuition.

All three of these innovative institutions are theme schools: public or private high schools purposely organized around a particular curricular, instructional, or philosophical concept.

Theme schools, which are often implemented as charter or alternative schools, or as part of the restructuring of large high schools into smaller units with individuated identities, offer an antidote to the alienating and diffusely organized comprehensive high school. Developing, restructuring, or redesigning a school around a theme, whether that theme is curricular, pedagogical, or philosophical, provides a vision for student learning and a substantive purpose for structural reforms and new teaching practices. By coalescing around a theme, a school can help ensure that its central focus is intellectual quality, and it can foster coherence and a sense of community among students and faculty.

Also referred to as focus schools, theme schools often employ a combination of approaches across three domains. The High School for Environmental Studies has a curricular theme: it integrates the theme of environment into the students' entire educational experience, including core courses, daily activities, and extracurricular activities. Alternatively, a theme school may provide elective courses in a particular theme area or discipline (e.g., arts, science, history) or an interdisciplinary topic (e.g., social justice).

The New Gate School is organized around an instructional approach: a pedagogy focused on Montessori principles constitutes the theme. Schools that employ the Socratic method are another example of this model.

As a Jesuit and Catholic school, Cristo Rey strives to prepare all students for college, and to promote the religious and cultural heritage of the families it serves, thereby emphasizing a *philosophical orientation* (or worldview) centered on both intellectual and character development. Other examples include schools that focus on democracy or that employ the Ten Common Principles of the Coalition of Essential Schools.[1]

The Institute for Educational Leadership's (IEL) Theme High Schools Network (THiSNET.org) database currently contains hundreds of examples of theme schools in operation nationally. Supported by the Bill & Melinda Gates Foundation, THiSNET connects these high schools, providing practitioners with support and ideas for successfully developing and implementing theme schools.

## Linking Theme Schools to Student Success

Two types of research relate to theme schools and their benefits for reaching and engaging students who face special barriers to success in high school and postsecondary education.[2]

Most of the research focuses on particular features of these schools, rather than on thematically based schools per se. Specifically, while theme schools are not always small schools, a great number of them work with significantly smaller enrollments than the standard high school. Three critical features contribute to the success of students in both small schools and theme schools: curricular equity, instructional coherence, and engendering a committed community.

## Essential Features of Theme Schools

*Curricular equity* plays an important role in distinguishing theme schools from their comprehensive counterparts. In traditional schools, racial and ethnic minority students are disproportionately distributed in lower academic tracks and ability groups (Berkner & Chavez, 1997; Gamoran, 1987; Lucas, 1999; Thomas, 2000), limiting their access to knowledge and subjecting these students to lower expectations. Theme schools, by design, expose all students to the same curriculum, instructional practices, or philosophy and orientation to learning. Research suggests that a commonality of academic experiences, in particular providing minority students with a rigorous and constrained curriculum, promotes academic achievement as well as more equitable educational outcomes, including increased college participation (Adelman, 1999; Lee, Ready, & Johnson, 2001).

Theme schools also structure the school's culture, curriculum, and pedagogy to foster *coherence*. Schools that are coherent offer a "set of interrelated programs . . . that are guided by a common framework for curriculum, instruction, assessment, and learning climate pursued over a sustained period" (Newman & Wehlage, 1995). Coherence provides an integrated way for students to understand their academic work by providing a frame in which to build on previous knowledge. By centering the curriculum, instruction, and pedagogy on a theme, schools help students incorporate new understanding into prior knowledge. This can increase student engagement, and it is a feature often missing in comprehensive high school settings (Bransford, Brown, & Cockling, 1999; Pittman, 1998).

Third, theme schools provide a clear focus that acts like a magnet, *drawing together parents, teachers, administrators, school staff, and students around a few important ideas* (Hill, Foster, & Gendler, 1990). The active engagement of these groups develops communities of commitment. Unity of purpose, a clear focus, and shared value for student learning are key to improving student achievement, particularly for minority students (Hill & Celio, 1998).

Researchers also have documented the need for students, particularly those who have dropped out or are at risk of doing so, to experience affiliation and membership and to have support for college aspirations. Students who feel disconnected from teachers are more likely to disengage and drop out of school (Croninger & Lee, 2001). Through shared values, a common agenda of activities, and an ethos of caring in social relations, theme schools can create a sense of collective responsibility for students' learning among teachers (Goddard, Hoy, & Hoy, 2000).

In schools with high levels of collective responsibility, students learn more in all subjects, and students from lower socioeconomic backgrounds appear to achieve at the same level as their more wealthy counterparts (Lee, Smith, & Croninger, 1996; Lee et al., 2001). Teachers in this context can play an important role as sources of support and influence. They can help and encourage students, as well as provide information about course selection and the college planning process (Gandara, Gutierrez, & O'Hara, 2001; Noeth & Wimberly, 2001).

## The Benefits of Theme Schools

Research on the effectiveness of theme schools has not kept pace with their growth, nor has it been comprehensive in making explicit the links between practices and outcomes. What has emerged from the literature are a number of positive student outcomes, including increased graduation rates, increased college attendance, overall increased achievement, stronger relationships between faculty and students, stronger student communities, fewer disciplinary problems, and increased student engagement (Ancess, Darling-Hammond, & Ort, 2002; Hill et al., 1990). Theme schools often achieve these ends with a student population facing greater odds than their more traditional counterparts.

Research on career academies, which are among the most prevalent forms of theme schools, shows that they work well to raise academic achievement, significantly reduce dropout rates, and increase both attendance rates and the number of students completing a basic core curriculum of English, social studies, and math and science courses (Kemple & Snipes, 2000). Designed to promote challenging, relevant, and academically demanding instruction through a career focus such as health sciences or environmental technology, career academies also increase student graduation rates and grade point averages over those of their comprehensive school counterparts (Elliott, 2002; Elliott, Hanser, & Gilroy, 2001). These findings are particularly salient, given what we know about the link between student preparation and access to postsecondary opportunities, and to success once enrolled (Adelman, 1999).

## Public Policy to Expand Theme High School Success

To promote the growth of theme schools, state policymakers need to pay special attention to issues of resources, standards, flexibility, and autonomy. Just as important, alternative and charter schools need intensive support and the ability to leverage federal, state, and foundation grants.

*Envision and stimulate the expansion of theme schools to prepare high school students for the work force and postsecondary education.* California offers an example. Under a state law passed in 1984, the California Department of Education developed the Specialized Secondary Program. Using a statewide competitive grant process, school districts are awarded four-year grants to plan and implement specialized theme programs in any area. The state invests $20 million annually in 290 funded academy programs (McNeil, 2003). More recently, New Jersey, citing a mission to promote multiple pathways to success, has embarked on a partnership initiative with local industry to develop and create a number of career academies, including a partnership with Pfizer, Inc., to establish a medical science academy (New Jersey Department of Education, 2003).

*Provide incentives and structures establishing alternative schools.* The number of alternative schools, fueled by philanthropic support and warmly welcomed by students and parents seeking more diverse educational choices, has grown extensively in recent years. Once considered special schools for dropouts or students with behavioral problems, alternative schools also have become a mechanism for diversity and choice. It is these alternative schools that most often organize their teaching and learning around a curricular, instructional, or philosophical theme. Some states permit districts to establish alternative schools, others require that alternatives be offered, and some states provide special funding and exemptions for these schools from certain state regulations.

Some states are even offering a form of vouchers to private providers of alternative education. For instance, the Minnesota legislature enacted Education Options (originally named the High School Graduation Incentives Program) to "encourage all Minnesota students who have experienced difficulty with the traditional education system to enroll in public and private alternative programs in order to complete high school." Using per-pupil basic revenue, districts may establish their own alternative programs or contract with a nonprofit, nonpublic school to provide education for eligible students (Beales & Bertonneau, 1997). Charter school policies are also a significant engine for creating new types of alternative schools.

*Remove barriers to the establishment and operation of theme schools.* Perhaps the biggest impediment to the promulgation of theme schools is the fact that innovation can be struck down by state mandates, specifically standards and assessment. For example, during the 1990s, at the same time that New York City was encouraging the expansion of small theme schools that used alternative pedagogy and assessments, New York State was beginning to increase high school graduation requirements, culminating in the requirement that all high school seniors pass a series of standardized exams to graduate. Recognizing the unique character of the city's new schools, the state issued a handful of waivers, allowing the innovators to employ their own assessments. However, the waiver was revoked in 2001, which forced these schools to accommodate what they felt was a test-driven curriculum at odds with their existing curricular frameworks.

Policymakers must address how the implicit promises of theme schools can have autonomy and flexibility to help students choose a unique path to success. Alternative measures of outcomes, including monitoring high school completion and postsecondary enrollment, should be included in state assessment.

Theme schools are intentionally unique. Designed to offer an alternative to standard educational offerings, the policy barriers they encounter may rarely be the same from one school to the next. Policymakers must provide the autonomy and flexibility that is necessary for the successful implementation of theme schools that promote a professional culture and provide students with a curriculum that emphasizes the development of depth of knowledge.

---

1. This definition of theme schools rests on a framework developed by Raywid (1994).

2. In addition to the research cited here, Stanton-Salazar (1997) identifies a theoretical context for personalization and access to adults, looking at the role of social support networks (i.e., access to teachers, guidance counselors, and other adults within the school) as a way to facilitate minority student learning and educational attainment, especially for Hispanic students.

*Several distinct models are emerging that emphasize bringing college experiences into the secondary school years, including dual enrollment programs and early college high schools. This kind of early exposure to college can be a powerful spur to further education, particularly for students from communities or families where college-going is not the norm. Donna Rodrigues describes another variant of this strategy: University Park Campus School, a partnership between Clark University and the Worcester Public Schools that serves about 210 students in one grade 7-12 school. This small school has had remarkable success preparing at-risk students who are behind academically to engage in demanding, college-level work. The school ranks near the top among Massachusetts schools on the state's tenth-grade assessment, and three-fourths of juniors and seniors earn college credits before graduating from high school.*

---

# 18. Making the Most of a University/ High School Partnership: University Park Campus School

## By Donna Rodrigues

When Damian Ramsay enrolled at the University Park Campus School six years ago as a seventh grader, he could barely read a fourth-grade textbook or tackle a basic multiplication problem. Today, Damian, a tall, bespectacled 18-year-old, devours the works of Dickens and Fitzgerald.

Damian is one of 31 students who graduated from the University Park Campus School on Sunday. His story is not unlike those of his classmates. They live in Main South, a neighborhood notorious for its high crime rate and low academic standards in this blue collar city of 173,000. High school graduation was questionable for these students; college did not seem to be an option. But that is where each is heading this fall.[1]

Stories of urban schools often tell of dismally low levels of academic achievement, decrepit facilities, insufficient resources, and pervasive violence.

Rarely do these schools receive public attention for academic excellence. University Park Campus School (UPCS) defies this picture. Founded through a joint effort of the Worcester Public School Department and Clark University, the school has become the highest-performing open-admissions urban high school in Massachusetts.

University Park started with an ambitious premise: that all students, regardless of their starting place, would master a demanding, honors-level curriculum and be fully prepared for college success. To achieve that goal, the school would provide a small, personalized learning environment with a strong core academic curriculum and ample time and support for learning. Exemplary teaching practice and a professional culture deeply committed to the school's mission of college success for all would ensure that no student would be left behind. The partnership with Clark University would play a vital role in establishing a highly effective professional community and a college-going culture.

## The University Park Achievement

University Park opened in September 1997 with 35 seventh-grade students. Adding a class each year since then, UPCS now enrolls close to its design maximum of 210 students. In 2001, four years after they entered, 100 percent of the initial class passed the state's rigorous exit exam, the Massachusetts Comprehensive Assessment System (MCAS), which students first take in the tenth grade. And these students did not just pass: they outperformed many of their grade-level peers from affluent areas of the state. When University Park tenth graders took the test in 2001, they ranked 13th in Massachusetts in math and 53rd in English, putting UPCS 34th overall among the state's 332 high schools. More recent classes have done even better: in the latest round of testing, UPCS sophomores ranked third in the state in math and sixth overall. Here are some other achievements of this open-admission urban high school:

- All 31 members of the first graduating class were admitted to college, even though many had begun seventh grade reading at third- or fourth-grade levels.
- Not a single student has dropped out of UPCS.
- UPCS is the only Massachusetts high school at which no student failed

any MCAS tenth-grade grade test in the past three years.
- Three out of four students take courses at Clark University while they are juniors or seniors at UPCS.
- The cost of educating each student is essentially the same as at other Worcester public high schools.

These are the same kinds of students who "are not supposed to graduate from high school." All are drawn by lottery from Main South, the poorest neighborhood in Worcester, and reflect its demographics. The vast majority of UPCS students enter at least two grade levels behind in reading, and 70 percent qualify for free lunch. A third of the students are Hispanic, 19 percent are Asian American, 7 percent are black. About 60 percent come from homes where English is not spoken. In the class of 2003, 30 percent were students with special needs.

## The University Park Model

What has enabled University Park to succeed where so many others fail?

First and foremost, the school is committed to success for all its students. The goal is not that students graduate from high school, not that they pass the MCAS test, but that all students, no matter where they start, leave UPCS prepared to do college-level work.

The achievements of University Park can be attributed to this unyielding commitment to student achievement and success, to the concept that "there are no sparrows and blue jays: all will soar."

This commitment is embodied in several design principles:

*Offer an honors curriculum for all:* All students take a common core curriculum benchmarked to the requirements for entering Clark University. Beginning in ninth grade, all classes are honors classes and expectations are high for all, with a strong emphasis on mutual respect and support rather than competitiveness. Few academic choices are provided; instead, the school focuses its limited staff dollars on the core subjects of English, math, history, science, and foreign languages. Students can take AP classes starting in tenth grade and courses at Clark beginning in 11th grade.

*Provide catch-up strategy in grades seven and eight:* The seventh and eighth grades have been designed to address core literacy, numeracy, and English language skills, so that students are ready for college-prep work by grade nine, no matter what their literacy levels were upon entering the school. Summer classes and extra time before and after school are part of the model in the early grades.

*Recruit and build staff with deep commitment and expertise:* University Park's ambitious academic program depends on a powerful professional learning community, with teachers who can quickly learn from one another, solve problems together, and develop expert strategies to meet the needs of diverse learners. The three veterans who were the entire first-year faculty helped build an expert teaching staff, modeling effective practices for younger, less-experienced teachers. Today, most of the faculty are young, yet they continue the school's unyielding belief that all students can succeed and do demanding, honors-level work. UPCS teachers have the same academic expectations of their students that prep school teachers have for theirs: all students will enroll in college, and it is their job to prepare students for this trajectory.

A critical factor has been common planning time every Wednesday, with that time structured constructively. During these sessions, teachers work together to plan interdisciplinary units, ask and give advice, set and revise common goals, examine data and evaluate progress, study student work, develop plans to address areas of concern, and discuss important school matters like budget and staffing.

*Offer accelerated instruction with adequate support:* To maximize instructional time, the school turned to an instructional model that demanded longer days (8 hours a day) and longer blocks of instructional time (90 minutes) with fewer teachers. Teachers stay with their class for two consecutive years to minimize disruptive changes. (The longer day requires about $100,000 in additional costs to the district. Because of budget cuts, the school day was shortened to 6.5 hours in 2003–2004.)

*Make no decisions without data:* Standardized test data are analyzed carefully for each student. Student work and data are reviewed during every Wednesday's common staff planning time. Teachers are well-versed in state and district curriculum frameworks and use that knowledge in their lesson planning.

*Create a school community that allows no one to fail:* "We are all in this together" is more than a motto. It describes a school culture in which each person measures his or her own success by how well the school community achieves its mission. Collaboration is the norm, as faculty, students, families, and community partners work together to solve problems and improve results. Teachers and students are encouraged to take risks and are not afraid to share mistakes or ask for help. Everyone must understand and agree to meet certain conditions, and UPCS makes these expectations clear to prospective students and their families:

- Students must be willing to put in the extra hours for school and homework.
- Coursework and homework are difficult.
- Absences are not tolerated.
- Failure is not an option.

*Build college partnerships to enhance students' confidence and commitment to learning:* The university–high school partnership is both deep and broad, as detailed in the next section. The University Park steering committee, with representation from the school district and Clark University, has been deeply involved in all major decisions about creating and operating UPCS.

## The Partnership between Clark University and UPCS

The close relationship between UPCS and Clark makes concrete the goal of college and the standard to perform at the college level. UPCS students come to see a future for themselves that includes college — not only as a dream but as an expectation. This sense of being part of a college community helps give students the motivation and confidence they need to persevere in demanding academic courses. At UPCS, the students say, "It is cool to be smart."

UPCS students and teachers are on the Clark campus nearly every day, not only using the labs or the gym but also observing and interacting with Clark students. UPCS students in grades seven to ten take miniseminars taught by college faculty. They can take courses at Clark in 11th and 12th grades, although these do not substitute for the core high school classes. Three-quarters of the school's students take at least one Clark course by the time they graduate from high school. The university gives University Park students free tuition for courses they take at the college. If students are admitted to Clark after they finish UPCS, they pay no tuition and receive credit for the college classes they took in high school.

The students' physical encounter with the campus is an important part of their becoming "little Clarkies." They are on campus regularly and have free use of the gym and library. Many serve as counselors in an on-campus summer recreation camp for neighborhood children sponsored by the university. They get a Clark ID early in their University Park experience. As early as seventh grade, students walk through the campus pointing out their future dorm rooms.

For Clark faculty and students, the high school is a teaching lab. Cohorts of education graduate students share responsibility with their mentors at the school throughout the year. University mentors, teacher mentors, and graduate students observe in classrooms regularly in a structured collaborative learning process called "rounds." At any given moment, up to one-third of the teaching at University Park is conducted by Clark education students, and an additional one-third by former education students who are now full-time UPCS teachers.

## The Power of Bringing College Experiences to Low-Achieving Students

University Park has had remarkable success preparing low-income, low-achieving students for college. It draws on the strengths of the public system and the private university, integrates a small school reform model with teacher development, and gets at-risk kids through high school and into college. It is an oasis of hope and opportunity for a rough inner-city neighborhood, and home to a diverse group of children who are motivated by a dual promise: success in a college-prep program and free tuition at Clark University.

The partnership with a college — with exposure to the place, the faculty, the students, and the level of learning that the college demands and expects — informs, motivates, and challenges students to succeed. The power of college experiences transforms young people into students who believe college is for them.

University Park Campus School is, as Tom Del Prete of Clark University's Hiatt Center for Urban Education says, "a partnership in education reform, teacher quality, student achievement, and community renewal." It sends a powerful message of possibility to urban schools across the nation: academic achievement for all students is within reach.

---

1. "Hard Work Opens College Door for Whole Class," *New York Times*, June 4, 2003. Copyright © 2003 by New York Times Co. Reprinted with permission.

*Thirty-two states have enacted statutes supporting dual enrollment programs, which enable high school students to enroll in college courses and earn college credits before they graduate from high school. These programs are popular with students and parents and have been growing rapidly. Most dual enrollment programs are open only to students who demonstrate high academic achievement in ninth and tenth grade, but some think that dual enrollment can be an important component of strategies to increase access to, and success in, college for underrepresented groups. Joel Vargas looks at variations in dual enrollment programs in Texas and Washington State and identifies a need for further research on issues related to financing, quality, students served, and college access and persistence.*

# 19. Dual Enrollment: Lessons from Washington and Texas

## By Joel Vargas

It is increasingly common to find students taking college courses even before they graduate from high school. Indeed, this is a trend endorsed and encouraged through state dual enrollment policies.

Through dual enrollment, sometimes known as postsecondary option enrollment programs, high school students can enroll in college courses and often earn secondary and college credit simultaneously. Dual enrollment is typically associated with "gifted" students or students in technical preparation programs coordinated with community colleges (e.g., Tech Prep). However, some have considered whether dual enrollment can improve the transition from high school to college by exposing students earlier to postsecondary expectations and by making college more accessible to students otherwise discouraged by such barriers as cost or distance (Bailey, Hughes, & Karp, 2002; Kirst, 2000). For example, Virginia has considered dual enrollment as a way to alleviate impending pressures on institutional enrollments and to "save money for students, state governments, local governments, or some combination of all three" by moving students faster through the education pipeline (Bailey & Karp, 2003).

By 2001, 32 states had enacted statutes supporting dual enrollment (Michelau, 2001), and these programs enroll a significant number of young people. In Washington State, for example, in the 2001–2002 school year, 14,313 high school juniors and seniors — about 9 percent of the state's 11th and 12th graders — took one or more courses on college campuses (Washington State Board for Community and Technical Colleges, 2002).[1] Nationally, over the next five years, thousands of youth who are underrepresented in higher education will attend early college high schools, a new model drawing on dual enrollment and designed so that all students can graduate with two years of college credit or an associate's degree in four to five years (see "Challenge, Not Remediation," page 213).

At a 2003 forum co-sponsored by the American Association of State Colleges and Universities and Jobs for the Future, education practitioners and policymakers analyzed dual enrollment policies in Texas and Washington, two states that are prominent in advancing this option. Differences and similarities in regulations and ground-level issues between these states surfaced during the forum. The lessons are instructive for dual enrollment policy — and for better determining the potential of this approach to increase access to, and success in, college.[2]

## Washington

Washington's "Running Start" began as a component of Learning by Choice, 1990 state legislation broadening access to educational options. The law entitles qualified high school juniors and seniors to take up to 18 hours of courses on community college campuses at no cost. Students qualify for admission usually by passing a standard college placement test. Their high school districts pay for tuition, but students are responsible for other costs, such as books and transportation. Districts reimburse colleges based on a standard statewide per-credit rate for academic and vocational courses.[3]

Running Start has grown steadily, beginning with just over 5,000 participants enrolled in community college courses in 1993–1994. In 1994, it expanded to include four-year state universities in areas lacking community

colleges. In 2001–2002, 14,313 dual enrollment students took college courses throughout the state.

Running Start has spurred incredible growth in dual enrollment, but it
has also caused concern. Since money follows the students, the same incentives for students and colleges to participate are disincentives for high
schools, which surrender per-pupil state funding to pay tuition. At the 2003
forum, Linda Whitehead, superintendent of the Marysville, Washington,
school district, reported that in many communities little per-pupil-generat-
ed funding remains after paying a Running Start student's tuition. Thus,
high schools are legally mandated to inform students about dual enrollment
options but in practice are conflicted about doing so.

Conversely, the funding formula may encourage efficiency and productive competition. For example, Running Start appears to have saved
millions of dollars in public expenditures because students earn high
school and college credit simultaneously.[4] Also, attempting to prevent
their highest-performing students from taking dual enrollment courses,
some high schools have created more Advanced Placement and
International Baccalaureate programs.

That is good news — as long as curricular and instructional upgrades
extend to all parts of the school and do not lead to tracking.

Beyond funding, there are other concerns about dual enrollment. For
example, some faculty at four-year colleges have expressed doubts about the
readiness of Running Start students for their courses. In addition, teachers
unions suspect a threat to jobs when college faculty teach at high schools
under another dual enrollment program, College in the High School (CHS).
Taking a different approach from Running Start, CHS enrolls high school
students in college courses on their high school campuses, with adjunct college faculty teaching the courses. Unlike Running Start, CHS is not a legislatively directed or singularly defined program. Rather, it is based on a variety
of local contracts between high schools and colleges outlining arrangements
for tuition — often covered by students themselves.

## Texas

In 1995, the Texas legislature essentially affirmed existing dual enrollment
agreements between community colleges and local school districts. South

Texas Community College, for example, had long made courses available at neighboring high schools, increasing access for rural students who might have otherwise been discouraged by distance.

Few statistics are available about the statewide composition of dual enrollment courses in Texas. However, Teri Flack, deputy commissioner of the Higher Education Coordinating Board, estimates that about 28,000 Texas students participate, with two to three thousand dual enrollees at the four-year universities.

Texas students can earn transferable dual enrollment credits if they are high school juniors or seniors, meet college eligibility requirements, pass the state's high school exit exam, and pass the relevant subject areas of the state's college placement exam.[5]

To help ensure the quality of dual enrollment courses, the Higher Education Coordinating Board adopted a set of rules in 1999. It specified that courses be "composed solely of concurrent, Advanced Placement (AP), and/or college credit students." It also said that instructors must meet institutional standards comparable to those applying to regular college faculty.

Community colleges and — beginning in the fall of 2004 — universities may waive tuition.[6] Thus, students may or may not have to pay tuition, depending upon local agreements. Whether or not colleges waive tuition, they receive state funding based on their contact hours with dual enrollment students. The year after South Texas Community College started waiving tuition for these students, participation more than doubled, according to Nick Gonzalez, the college's head of public school relations. Yet according to a 1998 Texas Higher Education Coordinating Board survey, only nine of 61 community colleges reporting dual enrollments waived tuition and fees (Rylander, 2000).

Until recently, Texas legislation instructed the commissioners of education and higher education to develop rules for avoiding "double dipping" — having state funds pay twice for the same student's education. Accordingly, high schools lost per-pupil state funding for students not enrolled in at least four hours of *high school credit–only* courses.

These restrictions were a notable point of contention in Texas. The focus on minimum high school credit–only seat time reportedly inhibited access for students in high schools with block schedules. These schools were leery of letting students dually enroll because their schedule did not translate easily into the minimum number of high school–only contact hours. Gonzalez contends that these restrictions were shortsighted, not accounting for savings in financial aid that the state could realize from encouraging more students to finish college faster.

In 2003, the state eliminated the requirement to reconcile duplicate funding. As a result, Texas may see big increases in dual enrollments, if the experience in Illinois is any indication. When the Illinois Community College Board gave credit-hour grants to community colleges for dual enrollment students, even while high schools kept per-pupil funding, the number of secondary schools participating the following year increased by 240 percent (Andrews, 2001).

Other questions surrounding dual enrollment in Texas relate to course integrity. The Texas Higher Education Coordinating Board has ongoing concerns about maintaining the quality of college-level courses taught at high schools. While the state has rules regarding the qualification of teachers and the composition of courses, it has no required benchmarks for dual enrollment courses. Gonzalez reports that there is evidence of the success of dual enrollment efforts at South Texas Community College. He believes that students who normally would not consider college generally thrive in these courses and intend to continue their education beyond high school. However, Deputy Commissioner Flack notes that the school is probably "ahead of the curve" in documenting the quality of its dual enrollment program.

## Key Lessons, Unanswered Questions
Texas' and Washington's dual enrollment policies suggest that different funding formulae for dual enrollment courses provide varying incentives for participation. Key issues affecting access include how college tuition is paid and how "double dipping" is managed. When students do not have to pay tuition, access is greater. When state funding follows the student, high schools may be inclined to limit access, but they perhaps also feel pressured to improve learning options if dual enrollment is an entitlement.

Whether expressed as questions about the maturity of students or the qualifications of instructors, concerns about the quality of dual enrollment courses are also prevalent and persistent. Although most states, like Texas and Washington, regulate who can enter and teach courses, forum participants agreed that outcome data about dual enrollment are sorely needed but still lacking.

Policymakers and practitioners also should be alert to potential tensions on the ground. Dual enrollment may spark turf battles, as intimated by teachers unions' concerns about on-campus college faculty, college faculty's circumspection about teaching unprepared students, and high schools' concerns about losing their "best" students.

The most significant policy choices revolve around questions of whom the courses should be for and who should pay. Yet there is a question that precedes those issues: Beyond improving access to college, why should states encourage dual enrollment and what is the evidence that it can achieve the state's educational objectives?

For example, can dual enrollment help to eliminate the "senior-year slump" for students who intend to go to college but who, without guidance or mandate, do not prepare themselves with rigorous courses in 12th grade and subsequently need remediation? (Bailey et al., 2002; Kirst, 2000). Some studies suggest that dually enrolled students subsequently perform better in college than those with no history of dual enrollment (Spurling & Gabriner, 2002; University of Arizona, 1999; Windham & Perkins, 2001), but more research is needed that controls for participants' backgrounds and accounts for different policies.

Is dual enrollment appropriate for students who typically have difficulty completing high school and entering college? The experience of middle colleges suggests the answer is yes, given proper support. These small high schools located on community college campuses have long served such students well, seeing them through high school, often with college credits to their name. More research is needed on whether the effects of dual enrollment are similar for students from different social and academic backgrounds and, if so, under what conditions.

Finally, can states realize savings through increased efficiency in the secondary to postsecondary transition or through increases in the human capital of dual enrollees? While the experience of Running Start suggests an affirmative answer, more evidence is needed from other states, which frequently lack any data about the composition of statewide dual enrollment participation.

Overall, a recent comprehensive synthesis of dual enrollment research is informative. According to Bailey and Karp (2003), policymakers need more information about student characteristics, the content of courses, variations in program size and design, and participant outcomes vis-à-vis comparable nonparticipants. Research, the authors note, should also clearly explain if and how dual enrollment — and differences in the comprehensiveness of programming — affect the college access and success of traditionally lower-achieving students.

Answering these questions rigorously and systematically is a necessary prerequisite for making the best policy choices about dual enrollment — and for justifying those choices to the public and to decisionmakers.

---

1. Figures about statewide high school enrollment come from the website of Washington State's Office of Superintendent of Public Instruction, *www.k12.wa.us/dataadmin/ GRACES01.pdf*. Running Start figures come from the Washington State Board for Community and Technical Colleges (2002).

2. Forum panelists: Pam Praegar, Spokane Falls Community College; Brian Levin-Stankevich, Eastern Washington University; Linda Whitehead, Marysville School District; Joyce McGlaston, Marysville School District; Teri Flack, Texas Higher Education Coordinating Board; and Nick Gonzalez, South Texas Community College. Other forum participants: Thomas Bailey, Institute on Education and the Economy; Linda Campbell, Antioch University Seattle; Cecilia Cunningham, Middle College National Consortium; Keith Egawa, Antioch University Seattle; Edward Elmendorf, American Association of State Colleges and Universities; Christine Enyeart, Jobs for the Future; Peter Ewell, National Center for Higher Education Management Systems; Yvonne Freeman, SECME, Inc.; Eduardo Garcia, National Council of La Raza; Luis Genao, National Council of La Raza; Barbara Gombach, Carnegie Corporation of New York; Leslie Haynes, Jobs for the Future; Nancy Hoffman, Jobs for the Future; Richard Kazis, Jobs for the Future; Jan Kettlewell, Board of Regents of the University System of Georgia; Joann Lighty, College of Engineering, University of Utah; George Mehaffy, American Association of State Colleges and Universities; Hilary Pennington, Jobs for the Future; Travis Reindl, American Association of State Colleges and Universities; Stefanie Sanford, Bill & Melinda Gates Foundation; Jan Somerville, The Education Trust; Brett Visger, KnowledgeWorks Foundation; Michael Webb, Jobs for the Future.

3. Sources about Washington's dual enrollment are the forum and its participants, unpublished research conducted by Michael Webb of Jobs for the Future for the Early College High School Initiative, Robin Rettew of the Washington Higher Education Coordinating Board (Washington Higher Education Coordinating Board, 2001a,

2001b, 2002, 2003; Rosenthal, 2003).

4. $34.7 million in 2001–2002, according to the Washington State Board for Community and Technical Colleges (2002).

5. Sources for Texas' dual enrollment experience are the forum and its participants, unpublished research conducted by Michael Webb of Jobs for the Future for the Early College High School Initiative, Rylander (2000), the Texas Education Agency (personal communication [memo], August 30, 2002), and the Texas Higher Education Coordinating Board (2002).

6. Recent legislation allows universities and state colleges to waive tuition, as community colleges have long been allowed to do.

*Early college high schools are one exciting version of small schools that are designed to minimize the difficulty of the transition to postsecondary learning and credentials for students from underserved groups. These schools, which number about two dozen in 2003–2004, combine grades 9-14 (sometimes 7-14) in a single institution that gives students an integrated secondary/postsecondary course of study with strong supports and other benefits of small-school environments. According to Nancy Hoffman, the challenges of getting these schools up and running, because they bring the two worlds of K-12 and higher education under a single roof, demonstrate ways that state policy must change if blending secondary and postsecondary learning opportunities is to become routine and more equitably available, and not just a reward for traditional high achievers.*

---

# 20. Challenge, Not Remediation: The Early College High School Initiative

## By Nancy Hoffman

Between the ages of 14 and 22, a period that might be called emerging adulthood, young people develop a plan for the future and the beginnings of a vocational identity, albeit at different rates and with different goals.[1] Since the advent of the comprehensive high school, Americans have behaved as if the "natural" break in that period comes at age 18, marking a rite of passage from youth to adulthood, from the regulated world of public schooling to greater freedom, independence, and responsibility. For some, age 18 marks the effective end of further education. For most, it is the beginning of a period of some experience with postsecondary education.

For young people and their educational futures, there appear to be advantages to blurring the existing divide between high school and what comes after. What if high school graduation were not a turning point, but merely a pause on the educational continuum? What if the turning point came later, when students were already launched into college? An early experience of college-level learning is particularly important for adolescents who come from low-income, immigrant, and minority families — young people for whom preparing and planning for college do not come automatically, as they do to those from wealthier families in this country. One clear indication of the growing interest in bringing college experiences directly into the lives of high school students is the increasing popularity of dual enrollment, advanced placement, and other types of early exposure to college learning.

Other authors in this volume argue that the nation needs a system of multiple pathways or options to better serve the needs of older adolescents, particularly those from underrepresented populations.[2] As most of these arguments emphasize, there is a need to help more young people make a smooth and successful transition to and through college. One new pathway receiving significant attention is the early college high school, a small school that bridges what is now the ninth grade through the second year of college. The most important contribution of the early college high school is that *it goes beyond aligning the standards for high school exit and postsecondary entrance to create new schools that combine high school and college learning and result in both secondary and postsecondary credits.*

If, as a nation, we want to double the number of underserved students successfully completing postsecondary credentials, we can learn a great deal from this radical experiment. Further, efforts to implement this new kind of school highlight changes that would have to be made in the design of current secondary and postsecondary systems if blending high school- and college-level academic work is to become a more common, even routine, element of the educational experience of high school youth.

## What Are Early College High Schools?

Early college high schools blend high school and college learning into a coherent educational program. These autonomous small schools are demonstrating ways to meet the intellectual and developmental needs of young people who now fail to complete high school or drop out in the first years of college.

Early college high schools are committed to the following design elements:

- The curriculum is designed so that all students can achieve two years of college credit or the associate's degree in four to five years while still in high school.
- Students start college work as soon as they are able, based on their performance, possibly as early as ninth grade.
- The eventual completion of a baccalaureate degree is assumed for all students.
- Schools reach out to or include seventh and eighth graders in order to prepare all their students to take college-level courses in high school.

Since March 2002, the Bill & Melinda Gates Foundation, with Carnegie Corporation of New York, the Ford Foundation, and the W. K. Kellogg Foundation, has provided over $60 million in funding to the Early College High School Initiative to establish about 140 schools over five to seven years. The foundation dollars cover planning and start-up costs and are intended to leverage long-term funding from a variety of public and private sources.[3]

As of the 2003–2004 school year, 24 schools that meet the criteria of the early college high school model are up and running. These include charter schools, "regular" public schools, and schools in which a college has contracted with a district to serve a certain number of youth. Most of the schools are starting with a single class of seventh, ninth, or tenth graders, adding subsequent grade levels one year at a time. All the schools are built on formal partnership agreements joining secondary with two- or four-year postsecondary institutions.

With those common elements, these early college high schools are taking diverse approaches. A number of them focus on science, engineering, and technology. Many serve students whose first language is not English. And while all the schools have committed to creating a college-like culture and environment, some familiarize students with the demands of college-level work and campus life as early as ninth grade, while others begin with college courses in the 11th or 12th grade.

Ideally, early college high schools are located on or near a college campus, easing the process of formally integrating the secondary and postsecondary curricula and experiences, with secondary and postsecondary faculty assuming teaching responsibilities together. College courses do not merely supplement some high school courses; rather, they replace those courses, eliminating time wasted during the junior and senior years and making it possible for students to advance where they are strongest while gaining confidence and skills in areas of challenge. Problem-based, experiential, and collaborative methods of instruction are expected pedagogies, and adults provide guidance and support through the first two years of college.

For students and their parents, a particularly attractive aspect of the early college high school design is the assumption that students will earn college credits and credentials without having to pay tuition and without the daunting trial of completing financial-aid forms and multiple college applications. From the moment they are issued college ID cards, meet college students and professors, begin to learn about the demands and rewards of postsecondary education, and spend time on campus, early college high school students become "college people," adolescents who see themselves, and are seen by others, as college-bound (Murphy, 2004).

Growing numbers of students are taking advantage of dual and concurrent enrollment programs that provide access to one or several college courses, and a few institutions similar to early college high schools have long existed, mainly attended by gifted (and often alienated) students with economic means. The current crop of early college high schools extends the reach of such models to a more vulnerable group of students, using the challenge of college not to reward prior achievement but to motivate. While early college high schools may some day be the choice of many young people, these new early college high schools are intended for low-income students and students of color who have not had access to strong precollegiate preparation.

In creating 140 new schools, the Early College High School Initiative draws on lessons learned from a broad base of experiences, including dual and concurrent enrollment programs, middle colleges, small schools, advanced placement and other accelerated curricula, and studies of time wasted in the senior year. It also further tests the conclusion of Clifford Adelman (1999), a researcher at the U.S. Department of Education, that "the best predictor of college completion was not how good [students'] high school grades or SAT scores were, but how difficult their high school courses were. The harder the courses, the better they did in college. This was particularly true for minority students."

Data from middle colleges serving at-risk students, from schools with open enrollment in Advanced Placement courses, and from one-of-a-kind schools — for example, University Park Campus School, which collaborates with Clark University in Worcester, Massachusetts (see "Making the Most of a University/High School Partnership," page 197) — support the counterintuitive proposition that challenge, not remediation, is a powerful motivator for students who lag behind, regardless of their prior high school preparation (Hoffman, 2003). But early college high schools put academic challenge forward under special conditions: in a setting no bigger than 400 students, where peer and adult-student relationships are strong and respectful, and where young people get intense and relentless academic and social support.

## Who Is Creating Early College High Schools?

The schools in the Early College High School Initiative are sponsored by a wide variety of intermediary organizations charged with creating and supporting new schools. Several of these organizations operate across regions or the entire country. For example, SECME works throughout the South with historically black colleges and universities, and the National Council of La Raza has helped to launch a network of community-based schools in Arizona, California, and Washington, DC. The Middle College National Consortium, now in its tenth year of establishing high schools on community college campuses (where students get some college credit but not the associate's degree), is assisting in the transformation of some of the schools in its network into early college high schools. The Woodrow Wilson National Fellowship Foundation is creating schools at private and public liberal arts institutions, some quite selective. Portland Community College in Oregon is in the process of replicating Gateway to College, its successful contract school for 16- to 20-year-old dropouts at ten sites nationwide.

Other intermediaries in the initiative are state- or district-based. These include Antioch University Seattle, which is creating a network of schools for Native American students in Washington; KnowledgeWorks Foundation in Ohio; the Utah Partnership Foundation; and the Foundation for California Community Colleges. The Office of Academic Affairs of the City University of New York (CUNY) is collaborating with the New York City Board of Education to add ten early college high schools to the three that already exist in the CUNY/New York public schools system. Parallel to that initiative, North Carolina and Texas also will seed early college high schools with the help of funding from the Bill & Melinda Gates Foundation and support from their state governments.

Interest from other states is also surprisingly robust, even before the data is available to confirm that such schools can indeed meet their promise: to save money by accelerating students' education and to ensure that many more underserved students gain access to postsecondary learning and the middle-class wages that follow. The initiative has received many inquiries from states that want to do something innovative and high profile to increase postsecondary attainment rates.

## Implications for Education Policy

At the level of implementation, the partners in the Early College High School Initiative are addressing a number of immediate challenges related to the "mis-" or non-alignment of secondary and postsecondary education:

- *How to reconcile the high school and college systems for awarding course credit:* Carnegie units and college credits do not match. Calendars and schedules are inconsistent between the sectors, and neither system is truly based on student performance.
- *How to facilitate secondary-postsecondary teaching partnerships:* College professors are not credentialed to teach high school students on a high school campus, and some postsecondary institutions do not accept college credits earned in high school.
- *How to blend funding streams from systems financed with different assumptions:* In many states, per-pupil allocations cannot follow students into college classes. Even in states with dual enrollment legislation, students often must choose high school or college credit for a course, or may take college courses only in addition to a full high school program.
- *How to construct co-governance across sectors:* Secondary and postsecondary sectors are governed differently, and they have different cultures. Even where there is a history of K-16 collaboration, the two systems often play a "blame game" rather than assuming mutual responsibility for student outcomes.

Even as the intermediaries gain experience in starting and operating early college high schools, the initiative has begun to raise two even more fundamental questions about the policies and structures that characterize the nation's education system. What would have to change if all young people today required — and should be entitled to — education at least through two years beyond the high school diploma? And is our current mainstream pathway — from high school into a community college or four-year institution — properly organized and sequenced?

## The Consumer Voice

These and other critical questions of policy and data remain to be addressed, yet students (and their families) are already voting "with their feet." Here are the sorts of comments these "consumers" of public education make when they hear about early college high schools and ask to attend them: "I want to save money on college. I want the chance to prove I can do college work. I'm not afraid of working hard even if I've messed up in the past. On a college campus, I know I can be safe and that my teachers in a small school will care about me."

Schools and school districts, states, and postsecondary systems are also recognizing the advantages of helping underrepresented students earn college credits while in high school. Although we do not yet have the cost analysis that would confirm that taxpayer dollars are being saved on schooling, we do know that students who attain a college degree out-earn their high school graduate peers by 70 percent and thus contribute substantial tax dollars to their states' economies.

The enthusiasm with which a wide array of sectors has greeted the Early College High School Initiative suggests that there is deep interest in the potential of innovative small schools that make postsecondary education accessible and the attainment of a college degree much more likely. If this is the case, and if early college high schools are, in the end, to fulfill their promise, we will need to know a great deal more about how they can best achieve that goal — and we must use that knowledge to help "double the numbers."

---

1. Arnett (cited in Waidtlow, 2002) uses the term *emerging adulthood* to describe a developmental stage distinct from adolescence and young adulthood, occurring between the

late teens and through the twenties. During this period, identity issues are prominent, with few normative expectations imposed on young people by society.

2. See, for example, "Multiple Pathways — and How to Get There" (page 21) and "High School and Beyond: The System Is the Problem — and the Solution" (page 47).

3. Jobs for the Future, the Boston nonprofit where I work, guides the initiative on behalf of the funders and provides conceptual coherence, policy, and technical assistance. For more information on the initiative, see *www.earlycolleges.org*.

*For many young people, poor academic preparation and the need to earn an income conspire against their persistence and success in secondary school, particularly in college. Lili Allen, Sue Goldberger, and Adria Steinberg highlight a number of innovative schools and program models that integrate secondary and postsecondary learning, while also incorporating technical skill development opportunities that can expand the options for low-income students who are pursuing and earning postsecondary credentials.*

---

# 21. Pathways to Postsecondary Credentials: Schools and Programs That Blend Education and Employment

## By Lili Allen, Sue Goldberger, and Adria Steinberg

A significant percentage of the nation's youth will not be able to attain a postsecondary credential without receiving some attention to their need to develop the marketable skills and job market connections that will help them move up from the lowest paying and most volatile sectors of the economy. This is particularly true for college students from lower-income families or households.

This chapter describes a number of schools and programs that integrate not only secondary and postsecondary learning, but also academic and technical education. These models begin with a commitment to high academic achievement, and also recognize the importance of work and marketable skills to the ability of many young people to afford college and be better equipped to stay in college and earn a credential.

Young people have a variety of needs that make this type of pathway to postsecondary credentials appealing — and necessary. In addition to the need to earn money during their high school and college years, some young people can derive significant benefit from obtaining specific marketable skills as a "leg up" in their pursuit of quality postsecondary technical education. Another advantage is pedagogical: some young people respond well to the integration of a rigorous academic program with a hands-on, technical approach to learning.

## The Need to Work While in School

National research indicates that two of the most important risk factors for noncompletion of postsecondary degree programs are part-time enrollment and academic underpreparation, followed by single parenthood and financial independence from parents (Berkner, He, & Cataldi, 2003). One of the key reasons that low-income students have such low completion rates in postsecondary education is that many work long hours in order to be able to afford college. They struggle to balance work with part-time enrollment in college, which frequently begins with multiple remedial programs to bolster their academic skills. This combination contributes to the high rate of attrition of lower-income and lower-achieving students, particularly in their first year of college. An analysis of the college-age population indicates the following:

- The percentage of students who must work while in college is significant. In 1999–2000, more than a quarter (27%) of undergraduates had dependents, and 13 percent were single parents. While 80 percent worked part-time, a full 39 percent of college students were employed full-time (U.S. Department of Education, 2003).
- Employment options for working students have narrowed over the last decades. High school no longer delivers the marketable skills and/or credential necessary for young people to compete in today's labor market. Without these skills, working college students struggle in low-paying "youth jobs."
- Young people who drop out of high school and make their way to a high school completion program face the highest barriers: they often must fully support themselves while they are progressing toward a diploma and then toward a college degree. This population is quite large: in 2000, 3.8 million 16- to 24-year-olds lacked a high school diploma and were not attending high school or college (Toft, 2002). One in three Hispanics and one in five blacks fell into this category.[1] Yet most programs for this

population help participants achieve a GED or other type of high school diploma, and do not serve as feeders into postsecondary institutions or careers with advancement potential.

For many young people who want to earn a high school credential and prepare for further learning, programs that develop both academic and technical skills and that are linked to clear paths to a good job can be an attractive option. Such programs can provide accelerated entry into technical employment, which can then be a springboard to further formal education and can help make that education financially feasible. They also provide low-income youth with the kind of adult connections and information about career options that can help them gain access to employment outside of "youth ghetto" jobs. And because they are built on a college-prep curriculum, they are not a second-class track to lesser opportunities. They provide an alternative route to postsecondary credentials.

There is a misconception in some circles that access to technical programs in college is easy for anyone who completes high school. In reality, entry into postsecondary technical programs that lead to well-paying jobs and careers is highly competitive. Low-income youth coming from low-performing high schools often find such programs beyond their reach. Close connections to employers in high school or in alternative diploma programs can give students a leg up in the competition for access to health, technology, and other postsecondary programs. This is particularly true if these programs offer some form of work-related credential along the way.

For young people who must work while they learn, schools and programs that combine technical and academic skill development and credentialing can make it easier to juggle school and nonschool responsibilities. At the secondary and postsecondary levels, better ways to integrate accelerated academic and technical skill development can help more low-income students persist in and complete their programs.

Programs that combine education and employment have long been part of a U.S. high school education, and a range of efforts to "modernize" such blends of education and employment have been implemented in the past decade. Tech Prep and other vocational education strategies to link high school and postsecondary technical training programs in 2+2 models are one example. The innovation and experimentation spurred by federal school-to-work investments also grappled with this challenge. Career academies and other small school models demonstrate the power for some high school students, particularly low-income and low-achieving students, in linking rigorous academic instruction with work experience and a career focus.

This chapter identifies a number of innovative programs that blend education and employment for older adolescents. We focus in particular on programs that appear able to accelerate academic progress while imparting specific, marketable technical skills with value in the labor market. Most of the models highlighted below combine secondary and postsecondary learning in programs that emphasize accelerated progress, marketable technical skills, and, typically, high-quality work experiences. When implemented well, these approaches can help districts and states create additional alternative pathways to high school completion and postsecondary credentials that can be of particular value to older adolescents struggling to find their way forward in our complex economy.

## New Routes to Academic and Technical Skills

For years, high school vocational education was the programmatic answer to young people who either sought a marketable skill or had a passion for hands-on learning. Today, vocational education must do more than prepare students for immediate employment after graduation: an academic core must complement vocational coursework so that all students are prepared for college or other learning programs that open routes to good jobs.

The pressures on high school vocational education programs are significant. Academic expectations and requirements are crowding out vocational offerings, contributing to the dramatic decline in the number of high school vocational concentrators (Jacobs & Grubb, 2002). Academic rigor in vocational programs remains a challenge; while academic course-taking has increased among vocational students, they continue to lag behind their peers in the percentage of students completing a college preparatory curriculum. At the same time, the complexity and cost of technical programs and their equipment is rising, making it more and more difficult for high schools to provide quality technical instruction on site.

For these and other reasons, community colleges have become the preferred institution for the delivery of technical skills programs. The nature of this education has changed, with a greater focus on academic competencies and the provision of access to professional and semi-professional occupations. These programs also tend to be in fields that align with those at the four-year college and graduate level, which facilitates transfer from community college to further education. In other words, entry into these programs opens more doors toward completion of four-year college (Jacobs & Grubb, 2002).

However, community college technical programs are generally designed for older students with college experience. Recent high school graduates are more likely to enter developmental courses (i.e., remedial education) than technical courses of study that offer the payoff of marketable skills. Forty percent of community college students take at least one remedial course, as do 29 percent of undergraduate students overall (Bailey, Jacobs, Jenkins, & Leinbach, 2003). As a result, huge gaps exist in how young people — particularly low-income, low-performing students — gain access to the technical training that promises a payoff in terms of both marketable skills and access to further education. Lower-performing students have too often been locked out of college-level technical courses, and high-end technical high school programs usually have very selective entry requirements.

Jobs for the Future has begun to identify and document the potential to address this gap of new school and program models that combine college preparatory curricula with instruction in marketable technical skills, with an ultimate target of a postsecondary technical credential. We are particularly interested in models that experiment with new institutional arrangements across secondary and postsecondary sectors. In these programs, technical education opens doors because it is combined with academics and college opportunities.

These ambitious efforts take a variety of forms around the country:

- *Early college models that feature a technical course of study leading to a two- or four-year institution.* For example, at Washtenaw Technical Middle College in Ann Arbor, Michigan, a charter high school on a community college campus, students take a combination of high school and college academic and technical courses to graduate. After completing core courses, students move into Washtenaw Community College courses on one of six career pathways. Graduates are prepared to find employment in a technical field or expand their opportunities at a four-year university. The middle college students outperform community college students in their college-level courses, with a pass rate of about 80 percent. The school has increased the percentage of students graduating with both a high school diploma and a community college certificate or associate's degree from 26 percent in 1999 to 92 percent in 2002.

- *Early college models that feature a humanities-based course of study leading to postsecondary technical opportunities.* The California Academy for Liberal Studies (CALS) Early College High School, opened in fall 2003 in Los Angeles by the National Council of La Raza, features a humanities curriculum that uses project-based and arts-based learning. One of its partners is Los Angeles Trade Technical College, which offers students the opportunity to pursue graphic arts training at the college level while they are in high school. The CALS Early College High School is an outgrowth of the CALS middle school, which has outperformed all neighborhood schools and most statewide schools on California's high-stakes test.

- *Programs that offer technical certification, a high school diploma, and up to one year of credit toward an associate's degree:* ISUS Trade and Technology Prep, a charter high school in Dayton, Ohio, offers a program for high school dropouts that combines high school academics, college-level technical courses at a local community college, and hands-on skills practice.[2] Students can earn a high school diploma and college credits and advance toward national construction certification or computer-related certifications. Despite entering the school facing numerous challenges to success, 60 percent of ISUS students are meeting the graduation requirements — including passing statewide assessments and college courses — in two years.

- *Programs that intensively prepare students for the academic demands of college and smooth pathways to technical fields.* In Oregon, Portland Community College's PCC Prep uses a similar approach. It has created a continuum of services to help high school dropouts make it to and through college and onto pathways to high-skill careers. Through PCC Prep's Gateway to College program, students enter intensive skill-building and study-skills programs customized to their needs and skill levels, then take a set of college courses matched to individual career goals and aligned with career pathways that lead to a certificate or associate's degree. Eighty-three percent of students entering in 2001–2002 achieved the reading level required to enroll in college-level courses, and 60 percent of students completed all college preparatory requirements and went on to enroll in a full college-credit course of study.

- *"Thirteenth-year" post–high school programs that prepare students for college and for well-paying entry-level jobs, delivering both technical training and college credits.* Boston's Year Up, a one-year, intensive educational and work-force training program, provides urban young adults, 18 to 23 years old, with a combination of technical and professional skills and a paid corporate internship. Students also get a leg up on college education through a dual-credit arrangement with a local college; Year Up courses count for credit toward an undergraduate degree. The goal is to prepare urban young people for successful transitions to higher education, professional employment, and leadership positions in their community. During the first six months, students focus on skill mastery in a technical field through a curriculum that is constantly market-tested and updated to reflect the latest employer demand. During the second six months, participants use their skills as interns in local partner companies. Year Up has a 92 percent graduation rate; 90 percent of graduates are placed in technical positions within four months of graduation, with an average salary of $16 per hour. In addition, 60 percent of first-year graduates applied to college; 100 percent were accepted.

These programs serve a wide range of populations, from dropouts (ISUS), to high school graduates lacking a clear pathway to adulthood (Year Up), to high school students wanting a more technical course of study linked to postsecondary credentials (Washtenaw). Many, if not most, programs such as these have historically served a motivated population; like traditional dual enrollment programs, technical training programs that integrate high school and college tend to be set aside for those high school students who have proven that they can manage college coursework. Similarly, most dual enrollment legislation defines college readiness fairly narrowly, in terms of Carnegie units attained and grade point averages. But both the changing economy and changing demographics make these programs a critical component of a state or local portfolio of learning options. This type of integrated educational model can be especially beneficial for students who are behind in their coursework, who are older, or who have dropped out of school.

These programs also provide an intriguing answer to an underlying question about career and technical education: how early should young people choose a career pathway? The programs described here do not foreclose options; rather, they open doors to higher-paying careers while keeping open the possibility of higher education. They respond to older adolescents' immediate and long-term needs: academic and technical skill development, portable technical credentials, and postsecondary opportunities.

## The Challenge

We have much to learn from early experiments of technically focused, blended programs. For example, how do such programs balance acceleration and remediation to ensure that students who are behind can move quickly to college readiness while also beginning technical coursework? What curriculum, instructional strategies, and support services make this possible? Which technical programs of study are amenable to taking college courses early? Finally, which institutions are most likely to deliver technical training that pays off?

In this chapter, we have focused primarily on arrangements between high schools and community colleges and have included a description of the in-house training program provided by Year Up. This small, entrepreneurial organization was able to redesign its training program quickly when the economy shifted and businesses were demanding a new skill set of entering information technology employees.

Like the early college high school model (see "Challenge, Not Remediation," page 213), school designs that integrate academic, technical, and postsecondary education into a coherent pathway presume that students will rise to the challenge if given more demanding learning requirements, along with clear paths to postsecondary learning and attainment. The challenge is for educators is to work through the operational issues to make such hybrid institutions possible for those young people who most need to accelerate their progress to postsecondary credentials.

1. See *http://nces.ed.gov/programs/coe/2000.*
2. ISUS is redesigning its postsecondary partnership to ensure that both the funding and the instructional practices support ISUS students' success in postsecondary education.

*The greatest attrition in community colleges and higher education broadly is in the first year. Over 500 colleges and universities nationwide have redesigned their first-year program to emphasize learning communities, small groups of students who take a common set of courses. Learning communities can make a big institution seem small, build a sense of community and engagement among students and faculty, and help students meet higher expectations. Barbara Leigh Smith describes the experience of Washington State community colleges in implementing learning communities, demonstrating how state policy can interact with institutional action to support retention and improved outcomes for lower-achieving students.*

## 22. Beyond the Revolving Door: Learning Communities and the First Two Years of College[1]

### By Barbara Leigh Smith

Many contend that higher education needs to rebuild its core competency in undergraduate education, using what we now know about student learning to serve an increasingly diverse, mobile, and less selective student body (see, e.g., Guskin & Marcy, 2003; Massy, 2003). This will be no mean task, particularly in an environment of financial uncertainty.

The first two years of college, which do little to engage new students and build a sense of community, pose a special challenge. First-year students report a mismatch between their preferences for experiential learning and the widespread use of passive lectures and large, impersonal classes (Sax, Keup, Gilmartin, Stolzenberg, & Harper, 2002). As a result, the first year is often a revolving door; many students enter but subsequently leave our colleges and universities in the freshman year.

Learning communities, now offered at more than 500 colleges and universities, are a campus-level response to this challenge. They intentionally restructure the curriculum by enrolling students in a common cluster of two, three, or more courses. This creates opportunities for active learning, more time on task, and closer relationships among students and faculty, all proven ingredients in promoting student persistence and achievement.

A growing body of research indicates that learning communities are effective, even on large campuses (Grubb et al., 1999; Taylor, Moore, MacGregor, & Lindblod, 2003; Zhao & Kuh, 2003). Building on a rationale similar to that of the small schools movement in K-12 education, learning communities can make a big institution seem small, build a sense of community and engagement, and help students rise to high expectations.

The experience of Washington State, where the learning community movement began in the mid-1980s, suggests ways that states can support similar innovations to enhance student success. It demonstrates ways to promote innovation through a convergence of state policy initiatives with grassroots efforts at the campus and inter-campus levels.

## The Evolution of Learning Communities in Washington

The learning community effort began in Washington with a simple but unusual boundary-crossing request. On 1983, looking for ways to revitalize his institution, Ron Hamberg, a dean at Seattle Central Community College, arranged for a team of ten teachers and administrators to visit Evergreen State College, a four-year institution organized around a form of learning community: team-taught, year-long interdisciplinary coordinated studies programs.

Dean Hamberg later recounted the story:

> We spent the morning observing classes, visiting seminars, and talking with students and faculty. In the afternoon, we stayed to discuss the philosophy behind the educational program. The intellectual engagement of the community was contagious. One visit was enough to convince us that we should try to import the model to our college. We've been doing learning communities ever since.

As Seattle Central expanded its initiative to create learning communities, word spread quickly among the state's higher education institutions. It became apparent that learning communities had a powerful effect on students, faculty, and institutions, and that they offered a low-cost, community-building approach to improving our colleges and universities. In 1985, with seed money from the Exxon and Ford foundations, Evergreen established the Washington Center for Improving the Quality of Undergraduate Education to support the budding reform effort. By 1987, when the Washington Center became state-funded, 17 institutions were affiliated with it, and ten were offering learning communities. The center had a small staff and an annual budget of $200,000.

In the ensuing years, learning communities have proliferated across Washington. With modest assistance from the Washington Center, the common interest in improving undergraduate education has been nurtured through conferences, curriculum planning retreats, and collaborative writing projects. The inter-institutional relationships have led to new solutions for old problems. Tacoma Community College, for example, developed a lower-division bridge program leading into Evergreen's multicultural upper-division program. Co-location has provided opportunities for lower- and upper-division students to mingle, inspiring an informal mentoring process and a community of aspiration. A similar inter-institutional program developed between Evergreen and Northwest Indian College for students on six Indian reservations.

Community colleges led the way in developing learning communities, with strong communication networks among the two-year colleges promoting the rapid dissemination of models and practices. The most integrated form of learning community — team teaching — was common in the beginning years. Through team teaching, faculty members developed models for teaching and learning while at the same time reinventing collegial relationships. Large teaching teams spread the innovation through peer networks. At many colleges, senior faculty led the way, giving the movement credibility, leadership, and well-honed skills in collaborative teaching and learning. The critical issue of who joins a movement often defines the effort and can become a real factor in its expansion. On some campuses, the initiators worked hard to recruit others. On others, the teams became inbred, prompting jealousy from outsiders.

A largely stable cadre of community college administrators supported the endeavor and one another in the beginning stages, which was especially important when key organizational changes were needed. The initial composition of the Washington Center planning committee promoted collaboration. Institutions sent members in pairs: a key academic administrator and a faculty member. Much time was spent sharing experiences and discussing the literature, resulting in considerable alignment about the purposes of learning communities among faculty and administrative leaders.

The adaptability of the learning community idea was an asset. Institutions began offering a variety of models, but also continued with team-taught learning communities. The simple model of linking two courses became especially common, proving to be a practical model in many institutional settings. As the effort matured, institutions began thinking more strategically about learning community goals. They began to build programs around classes that large numbers of students fail and gateway courses to the major. Some institutions developed learning communities for students in developmental education, while others focused on students pursuing the associate of arts degree. Many emphasized the first quarter of college, thinking it set the culture and expectations for new students. In a number of institutions, vocational and professional programs were a natural site for learning communities. Transfer interest groups — yet another type of learning community — formed at the University of Washington and became a means of helping transfer students.

An early relationship between the Washington Center and the State Board for Community and Technical Colleges (SBCTC) was a key factor in the expansion of learning communities. Washington's 33 technical and community colleges are organized under this state board, while the four-year institutions are more loosely connected through a higher education coordinating board. The Washington Center and the SBCTC began collaborating soon after the learning community effort began, when the board decided to try to improve quality through an educational rather than a regulatory approach. This collaboration joined grassroots action with state goals.

At the four-year colleges and universities, learning communities emerged more slowly. The University of Washington was one of the first to start learning communities. Its program, along with that of Seattle Central Community College, was found to be highly effective by the first major study of learning communities (Tinto et al., 1994). The university now has more than 100 freshmen interest groups (FIGs) each fall, a model that has become widespread in U.S. research universities. The FIG program is also a highly competitive student leadership opportunity for seniors who act as peer advisors, and the program has become a platform for reforms in such areas as service learning, technology, and diversity.

Other Washington four-year institutions came into the learning community effort later, mostly through first-year initiatives. State efforts to improve institutional performance through accountability measures made learning communities look attractive, especially when research suggested that students in learning communities had higher retention rates and completed their degrees more rapidly. At North Seattle Community College, for example, a five-year study found that 55 percent of the learning community students completed the AA degree, compared with 13 percent of the non–learning community students (North Seattle Community College, 2003). Such results have been replicated in two- and four-year colleges across the nation, with especially dramatic increases in areas of the curriculum that typically have high failure rates (Taylor et al., 2003; Zhao & Kuh, 2003).

By 1998, almost every two- and four-year public college in Washington offered learning communities, and the movement had also expanded nationally to hundreds of colleges (Smith, 2001). Many of the learning communities focused on the first year of college, which is the most critical transition point, especially for students from underrepresented populations. Many target courses were associated with noncompletion and the revolving door: key gateway courses, remedial education, and "graveyard classes," in which large numbers of students received D's or F's, or withdrew (Adelman, 1999).

Today, however, the reach and the level of institutionalization of learning community programs varies. On many campuses, the effort has reached an appropriate scale. On others, administrative turnover and lack of broad faculty involvement has undercut momentum. Also, other agendas have pushed the learning community effort off center stage. Many institutions are not investing enough in faculty development, weathering persistent administrative turnover has been difficult, and the volunteerism that first fueled the effort has ebbed. Many institutions are experiencing large-scale faculty retirements and losing some of the strongest advocates of learning communities. As a result, especially in the current economic environment, many learning community efforts remain fragile.

## Learning Communities and Other Higher Education Reforms

Washington's diversity and assessment initiatives have complemented the learning community effort. Engagement with these state efforts has deepened the learning community movement and kept it fresh and dynamic. Some of the same people have been involved in all three efforts, which has improved implementation and limited the fragmentation of campus-level innovation.

*Assessment*

The learning community effort embraced assessment and evaluation before it became a statewide priority. As a result, when Washington launched a state assessment initiative in 1989, an energetic group on college campuses was already committed to the need to use data to identify what works and improve practice. There was a significant overlap between the college leaders and faculty innovators interested in assessment and learning communities, and similar approaches were used to mobilize people.

After toying with standardized tests, the state embraced local experimentation. Colleges established offices of institutional research and assessment, and faculty conducted assessment projects in many different areas. At the same time, the State Board for Community and Technical Colleges pursued a combined top-down/bottom-up strategy to promote better use of assessment to improve teaching and learning. In addition to seeding campus-level experiments, the board reserved money to bring campuses together to learn from one another. It also linked assessment to broader issues about improving undergraduate education.

*Diversity*

Washington State's higher education diversity initiative has also helped deepen the commitment to and practice of learning communities. In 1991, the state legislature enacted the Minority Participation Policy, which set higher education goals for minority employment, student recruitment, retention, and graduation, as well as expectations about curriculum and institutional climate. Despite the lack of earmarked legislative funding, the community colleges decided to use some of their state-provided quality enhancement funds to focus on diversity. Working with the Washington Center, the two-year college system designed a Minority Student Success Project with a modest budget and reallocated staff time. Twenty-three of the

27 community colleges participated.

In 1992, the Ford Foundation funded the Washington Center for the next step: a project focusing on curriculum and faculty development. The Washington Center joined forces with the University of Washington's American Ethnic Studies Department to create a cultural pluralism project that brought diversity into the curriculum in many institutions across the state and heightened awareness about how to foster student success. Learning communities were a significant vehicle for this new emphasis, especially in community colleges where team teaching was common. The diversity effort had broad spillover effects in faculty recruitment and hiring, faculty development, and new relationships between units, such as student affairs and academic affairs. This left the state's higher education system better prepared when Washington voters approved Initiative 200 in 1998, eliminating affirmative action.

A second diversity initiative followed, focused on building the capacity of institutions to make planning more data-driven. With support from the Washington Center and the State Board, institutional teams identified critical questions about students of color: where they were located in the curriculum, why they tended to leave school, their success rates, and which courses and programs were particularly troublesome. Armed with this information, more strategic interventions became possible.[2]

## Lessons from Washington

Learning communities became widespread in Washington because they responded to a need to better serve students. Learning communities have evolved as a cost-effective vehicle for enhancing quality, promoting collaboration between two- and four-year colleges, and increasing student access, persistence, and achievement.

There are many lessons from this story.

*Structures matter; they can facilitate or impede innovation.* Evergreen's Washington Center and the State Board for Community and Technical Colleges were platforms for cross-institutional collaboration and innovation. Their operating styles and structures suggest ways for policy leaders to work with campuses to promote innovation. They also suggest the need for both long-term resolve and focus at both levels, along with nimbleness and flexibility to deal with unanticipated consequences and opportunities. Long-term goals, embedded in structural changes, keep the work focused, while also allowing it to scale up and down depending upon resources.

*There can be significant synergy between state mandates and campus efforts.* Washington's diversity policy raised awareness but provided few state dollars for implementation. The diversity effort would have been less far reaching if it had not focused on the grassroots. Similarly, state interest in improving undergraduate education and student persistence encouraged campus investments in learning communities. There's a necessary reciprocity here. State mandates only take root when this happens. As the State Board's William Moore put it, "I relied on the campus energy to help catalyze state efforts" (Smith, 2001).

*There can be an important role for a third-party statewide service organization funded by, but independent of, the state.* Acting as a convenor, cheerleader, support, and dissemination system, the Washington Center provided an inter-institutional arena for conversations about improving undergraduate education. To be healthy, growing places, colleges need to think globally and act locally. They need windows on the outside world that broaden their perspectives while finding fertile ground at home to plant new seeds. Focused networks can dramatically speed up dissemination, increase the opportunities for learning across institutions, and build the resilience to weather inevitable ups and downs.

This third-party model is powerful; state officials are usually tempted to assign a much more narrowly defined role to a state office. The flexibility of what is essentially a contract operation may be better. On the other hand, state funding for a center is typically insecure and temporary, particularly in a difficult fiscal environment.

*Think about policies that approach undergraduate education reform in a more targeted and holistic manner.* Faculty and leaders involved in the learning community, assessment, and diversity initiatives worked together to better serve students of color. Learning communities provided a high-leverage structural and pedagogical approach, while the diversity initiative defined the audience. The assessment effort kept the initiatives data-driven, guiding both the initial planning and the end-of-project evaluations.

*Learning communities are one of the most viable solutions to the apparent paradox of raising quality while constraining costs.* The fiscal realities that currently constrain higher education are probably here to stay; thus, finding economical ways to restructure the first year of college is especially important. Learning communities have proven to be an affordable, effective, and flexible approach. States should therefore make learning communities an essential component of their policies to double the numbers, address the revolving door in undergraduate education, and lower the societal costs of losing so many young people in the first year of college.

---

1. A version of this article appeared as "Learning Communities: A Convergence Zone for Statewide Education Reform," in *Reinventing Ourselves*, ed. B. L. Smith and J. McCann (Bolton, MA: Anker Press, 2001).

2. This approach is similar to the diversity scorecard project at the University of Southern California. See *www.usc.edu/dept/education/CUE.*

# SECTION THREE

## Building Support and Public Will for Reform

---

## *Introduction*

The contributors to Section One advanced a number of provocative and bold policy proposals that they believe can help increase the proportion of low-income Americans who complete high school and earn postsecondary credentials. The Section Two authors turned from dramatic prescriptions to fine-grained descriptions of exciting innovations that already exist "on the ground" in schools, colleges, communities, and states. In this section, we look beyond good ideas and emerging practice to confront perhaps the most daunting challenge to "doubling the numbers": the challenge of mobilizing public will for significant improvement in secondary and postsecondary attainment and success.

Innovative ideas, even tested ones, are insufficient in a political and policy environment where resources are scarce, the competition for attention and investment intense, and the public's appetite for complex problems and solutions limited. In these essays, the authors confront that challenge head-on: they suggest ways to spark public concern and commitment to reform as well as policy leadership, so that a campaign to increase secondary and postsecondary success for low-income Americans might gain significant traction.

The four chapters that follow were written by individuals with much experience and perspective on how public policy movements take shape and how urgency can be both communicated and encouraged. Blenda J. Wilson, a former president of a state university in California and now president and CEO of the Nellie Mae Education Foundation, offers advice on the kind of messages and themes that can move a nation to embrace educational change. David J. Ferrero of the Bill & Melinda Gates Foundation addresses the same issue, paying particular attention to the challenges of building broad public will in an era when education is increasingly defined as a consumer good rather than a universal public good. Authors from Jobs for the Future and the National Governors Association suggest specific steps that governors can take to promote the double the numbers goal and, above all, to lead their states toward consensus on new priorities and goals. Finally, Ronald Wolk, the founder of *Education Week*, reflects on decades of disappointing national education reform efforts and gives advice on what a successful public campaign to double the numbers will have to entail.

Blenda Wilson suggests that the double the numbers agenda must be positioned not solely as a matter of private benefit or economic value, but also as a civic and moral obligation in a knowledge-based society. With a public conditioned to skepticism by a "landscape of education reform . . . littered with broken promises, overblown goals, inadequate implementation, and poor accountability," she champions two arguments for education reform that have succeeded in the past: the public good and "fairness," defined as the idea that *all* young people are entitled to the education that leads to a brighter future.

David Ferrero echoes Wilson, warning against overly utilitarian motivations that would make schools "an institutional site for maximizing private benefits to this or that target population." In advocating for the double the numbers agenda, he reminds us of the deep interdependence between an educated and engaged populace and a well-functioning democratic society.

Faced with difficult choices among competing priorities and demands, policymakers tend to rely on economic arguments about efficiency, equity, and growth rather than paeans to democratic values. For governors and state legislators, utilitarian arguments have great appeal, particularly if they hold out the prospect of an expanding economic pie rather than redistribution of a static or shrinking pool of public resources. Richard Kazis, Kristin D. Conklin, and Hilary Pennington focus on how governors and state legislators can be leaders in shaping public will and in fostering policymakers' commitment to policies that drive improved results without huge spending increases. Beginning from a recognition of political and fiscal realities, they point to clear and doable actions that states can take to simultaneously improve student outcomes and increase the efficiency of public secondary and postsecondary sectors. Above all, they point to ways that elected officials can show leadership: charting a long-term course, defining short-term progress, and articulating a vision of the possible around which the public and other officials can rally.

Ronald Wolk concludes by posing two key questions: Is doubling the numbers of young people who attain a postsecondary degree a feasible goal? Can the nation achieve it by 2020? Jobs for the Future commissioned Wolk to attend and observe the 2003 Double the Numbers conference and reflect on it in this essay. He concludes that the conference took an important first step toward assembling the necessary political will by convening "the constituent groups whose collaboration will be essential in meeting the goal: government, business, philanthropy, and all levels of education." Moreover, he notes that the goal of doubling the numbers might be able to gain favor and support from the public and from policymakers: it is "at once simple and straightforward enough for everyone to understand and get behind, yet comprehensive and powerful enough to lever an intractable system of public education onto a path toward significant improvement."

Will our nation find the will to revise our education goals for the new economy? Will we take steps that are needed to make postsecondary success a possibility for all students in this country, not just for a minority? In the end, this will depend on leadership and public will, not just on the rightness of the argument or the soundness of the innovation.

Blenda Wilson quotes approvingly the view of Malcolm Gladwell, author of *The Tipping Point,* that underlying the moment at which a good idea begins to spread and take root is the "bedrock belief that change is possible." It is our intention that this book — and the hard work of innovators around the country whose efforts are captured and highlighted in these pages — will expand the ranks of those who see secondary and postsecondary success for all not only as desirable but necessary, and not only necessary but possible.

*Improving postsecondary attainment is a critically important national goal, given the challenges posed to individuals and our nation by a global information economy. Yet there is no guarantee that public support for this goal will be automatic or sufficiently strong. Blenda J. Wilson asks how public urgency and commitment can be secured. First, a compelling public purpose must be articulated, one that cannot rest solely on economic individualism but also reasserts the essential connection between individual achievement and social benefit. The case for expanding postsecondary success, particularly for low-income Americans, must emphasize two arguments: education as a public good, and fairness as a fundamental national value.*

## 23. Capacity and Public Will: Mustering Support for Postsecondary Reform

### By Blenda J. Wilson

At the turn of the century, 6 percent of Americans graduated from high school. Today 85 percent do so, and three-quarters of graduates enroll in some kind of postsecondary education within two years of receiving their diploma. The nation's stunning success in extending educational opportunity to larger and larger proportions of its citizens is evidence of the importance of postsecondary education in postindustrial America. It also represents a legacy of populism, inclusion, and national purpose that may provide clues as to how we might go about mustering public will on behalf of postsecondary attainment for underserved youth today.

Historically, basic decisions about who should be served by our higher education system have been influenced greatly by government policy. Quite literally, the GI Bill of Rights made a college education the gateway to economic and social mobility for the record numbers of veterans who received government subsidies to attend college. The Cold War and the country's competitive response to Sputnik added another rung to the ladder of educational opportunity through the 1964 National Defense Education Act's extraordinary investments in K-12 education. Later, in response to the civil rights movement and 1960s and 1970s advocacy on behalf of poor and minority populations, state and federal governments made unprecedented commitments to postsecondary outreach, academic support programs, and increased need-based financial aid. In these expressions of federal investment in access and the quality of education, the link between education and the national interest was firmly established.

The nation's remarkable efforts to enable more students to attend college were caught short by *A Nation at Risk*. The provocative and widely acclaimed report warned that the nation's schools had become a "rising tide of mediocrity." Neither increased quality nor educational equity had accompanied increased access. Educators and policymakers have struggled with the twin issues of quality and access to the present day.

The forces driving change in America's education system are enormously complicated. Demographic trends and shifts in the world economy are transforming our society. Technological developments and changes in the job market have challenged not only the pace of education reform but fundamental agreement about the very purpose of education. Ongoing reforms and innovations in elementary and secondary education have influenced political agendas from leaders as ideologically disparate as Bill Clinton and George W. Bush, but none — with the exception of the preference for generic "standards" — has achieved sufficient consensus (or demonstrated efficacy) to frame a compelling course of action.

The eminent social activist John W. Gardner wrote:

> The problem is to achieve some measure of excellence in this society, with all its beloved and exasperating clutter, with all its exciting and debilitating confusion of standards, with all the stubborn problems that won't be solved and the equally stubborn ones that might be. (Gardner, 2003)

Advancing postsecondary attainment is essential to achieving some measure of excellence in our global information economy. It is a fitting goal for the profound transformation we are asking of our postsecondary education system. What are the prerequisites for building broad public support for improvements in postsecondary attainment? Where are the "stubborn problems" that might be solved?

## Self-Interest Rightly Understood

It is almost impossible to find an article or speech about the importance of postsecondary education today that does not base its arguments on the rewards of the labor market. The story line reads something like this:

> In the industrial age it was possible for someone with only a high school education to support his family and earn a middle-class wage. The economy has changed. Today's workplace demands a higher level of skill than ever before.

Then follow the statistics about how much more a college graduate earns than a high school graduate or a dropout.

There is no doubt that the restructuring of the U.S. economy has created greater demands and rewards for "new basic skills," that is, higher-level skills, particularly in literacy and numeracy (Murnane & Levy, 1996). Schools are being held to a different standard than in the past — both to educate a larger percentage of students and to educate them to a higher level of postsecondary preparedness. And higher standards also mean that individuals who do not acquire these skills suffer more severe disadvantage.

However, the economic arguments for educational access and attainment that so dominate contemporary advocacy discussions differ significantly from previous initiatives to expand postsecondary educational opportunities in this country. When the Land Grant movement provided first-time college-going opportunities to the children of farmers and mechanics, for example, the predominant argument was not that these students would be able to make more money or manage bigger farms. On the contrary, the gain to be obtained from a more scientific approach to agriculture and mechanical arts was better food and goods that would be available to everyone. Enrollments in Land Grant institutions were expected to improve the nation's quality of life.

Similarly, while the GI Bill of Rights opened college doors and campuses to veterans in large numbers, its primary political rationale was not to satisfy individual aspiration but to express a nation's gratitude for personal sacrifice. And, even more directly, the goal was to fuel regional and national economic development that would transform the nation from a wartime to a peacetime economy. The GI Bill, therefore, expressed a compelling public purpose.

One last example is the government's response to the scientific challenges of the Cold War, which included chartering the National Science Foundation, passing the National Defense Education Act, and making massive investments in universities as the chosen engines of scientific research. These investments benefited individual students, graduate departments, and faculty members, to be sure, but their political merit was founded in a consensus that the nation's interest was being served.

The expectations of public benefit that accompanied these political decisions about education were not ill founded. The children of farmers and mechanics contributed greatly to the success of the industrial revolution and increased standards of living throughout the country. Returning veterans' access to higher education revitalized the nation's economy after the war and created a new middle class. The movements of the 1960s and 1970s enabled a more diverse work force to contribute new perspectives that energized the entertainment, fashion, and consumer industries, in particular. College graduates of that period contributed to a more inclusive democracy and expanded leadership, particularly in the nonprofit sector, to address issues critical to the poor and disenfranchised.

Some 150 years ago, Alexis de Tocqueville compared America to his native France and concluded that the United States was the one place in the world "where self-interest was properly understood." Americans, he thought, recognized that another's gain might also translate into benefits for oneself and that the pursuit of private goods could produce considerable public benefit.

It is unfortunate that the opposite signals permeate contemporary dialogue about higher education. Consumerism, market forces, large educational debt, and increasing public university tuitions all flourish in an atmosphere that supports individual gain and advantage as the primary purpose of the educational enterprise.[1] As a result, the most contentious educational policy issues are about which group or individuals should benefit most: white students or students of color; middle-class students or the poor; students with high GPAs and scores or students who could benefit most from education; students in liberal arts or those in occupational programs. In elementary and secondary education, too, the national consensus about standards and educating every child belies the tension represented by voucher proposals, charter schools, and failed attempts to equalize school funding.

Despite this shift to an individualistic definition of "who benefits" from education, a national poll of public opinion on higher education, conducted by the *Chronicle of Higher Education*, reported that 91 percent of the respondents "agreed" or "strongly agreed" that colleges are "one of the most valuable American resources" (Selingo, 2003). In a survey by Peter D. Hart and Robert M. Teeter, almost all respondents, 96 percent, believed that a college education is a good investment, and 52 percent reported that our nation's education system is failing to offer young people from all backgrounds a chance to go to college.[2] The pollsters concluded that the public is willing to fund reforms to create a K-12 education system that works better for everyone. That is self-interest rightly understood. To successfully mobilize public opinion in support of doubling access to postsecondary education, educators and public leaders need to engage that part of the American psyche that de Tocqueville discovered long ago. Americans share a history of social transformation through education. In this new century, we need to reassert the essential connection between individual achievement and social benefit.

## Creating a Sense of Urgency

All too often, the case for improving education is framed from the perspective of educational institutions rather than the purposes of the students the institutions are designed to serve. With apologies to the authors of the following quotation, it is not uncommon for institutional goals to convey complexity rather than possibility:

> Picture, if you will, a postsecondary system that serves as a flexible infrastructure for meeting diverse needs in a time of rapid change. This system would be versatile, accessible, attuned to new technologies and economic trends; capable of continuously redesigning itself around the needs of both traditional and nontraditional students; able to try out new things, take initiative and use resources wisely. (Education Commission of the States, 1999)

Where to start? What to pay attention to first? Would such a system really produce better-educated graduates? Starting with a canvas that is too vague and vast undermines efforts to create a sense of urgency or a belief that we can be successful.

When Albert Shanker was leading the American Federation of Teachers in the 1970s, he realized that the idea of vouchers was gaining wider and wider support because poor performance had eroded the nation's confidence in public schools (Kahlenberg, 2003). At the time, traditional union priorities were focused solely on member's rights, salaries, benefits, and protections. In a courageous and insightful act of leadership, Shanker convinced the teachers union to advocate for better schools, saying, "It is as much your duty to preserve public education as it is to negotiate a good contract."

Among the many painful lessons of September 11th must be the realization that everything is global. The discussions about education policy in the United States, however, are all too often limited to internal comparisons among states or between cities. As a result, Americans do not know, for example, that the U.S. high school completion rate among 25- to 34-year-olds has dropped to ninth among 32 industrialized countries, or that U.S. 12th graders perform near the bottom in math and science.[3]

Developing America's brainpower is no less urgent than John F. Kennedy's challenge to the United States to be the first nation to put a man on the moon. The American public is able to understand that the nation cannot continue to enjoy economic, intellectual, and political status in the world if its educational attainment continues to lag behind other nations. The loss of talent, creativity, and perspective if we fail to educate well the next generations of young people is incalculable.

To return to the Albert Shanker analogy, then, we might say that in the global economy of the information age it is our duty to focus our reform efforts on student achievement and performance as the goals of the educational enterprise; it is our duty to hold all students, teachers, and schools accountable to high standards of performance; it is our duty to assure that all students are prepared for college.

These statements are powerful in part because they address education policies and practices over which we have some control. They are goals that we could actually achieve. By committing to programs, policies, and public dialogue around these issues, educators and policymakers could sustain an agenda of reform that has a sense of urgency, serves both individual and national interests, and can muster the support of a skeptical public.

## How to Muster Public Will

In his groundbreaking book *The Tipping Point,* Malcolm Gladwell (2000) describes major social change as "social epidemics" and concludes that "what must underlie successful epidemics, in the end, is a bedrock belief that change is possible."

Because the landscape of education reform is littered with broken promises, overblown goals, inadequate implementation, and poor accountability, garnering and sustaining public support for increasing postsecondary attainment will require a concerted and sophisticated effort to convince a skeptical public that change — appropriate and desired change — is possible. To muster the public will to increase postsecondary access in this environment, policymakers and educators need to adopt the means that have been successful in the past.

Two themes have informed national education policy in the past. They are, first, making the case for education as a public good, and second, making the case for fairness.

## Making the Case for Education as a Public Good

Many social observers have suggested that recent examples of social malaise — including bitter political partisanship, declining financial markets, and scandals in corporate accounting and the media — may make the first half of the 21st century a time of broad social reform and the reinvention of a broad range of public and private institutions.

Ours is a country that self-corrects. If the country is poised to experience another reform era, as it did at the turn of the century and again during the civil rights and Watergate eras, higher education may be ideally positioned to attract public support because the level of public esteem enjoyed by the nation's higher education community remains very high. In this post-Enron period, the need for social stability and noble purpose may translate into greater support for higher education's traditional role.

The public is very weary of win-lose and vested-interest policymaking. Education leaders must be willing to challenge false tradeoffs between education and other investments and to articulate how policy can express what we are for, not only what we are against. The United States has a responsibility to be a leader in addressing the earth's multiple challenges, including global climate change and pollution; depletion of energy sources and the misdistribution of resources; AIDS, water pollution, malnutrition; global terrorism and the protection of civil liberties. A case can be made that a healthy, high-achieving system of postsecondary education is our greatest long-term asset in meeting those challenges. The case can be made — and must be — that the benefits of providing quality education for all are far greater than the costs.

## Making the Case for Fairness

Many Americans remain devoted to the issues of educational equity for underserved populations as a moral obligation and an unfulfilled promise. While their voices may seem muted today by the toll of unrelenting poverty, failed education reforms, the slow pace of incremental gains, and budget pressures, fairness is a fundamental American value. It can be called upon to support the aspirations of new Americans to gain the "new basic skills."

The next generation of youth will be disproportionately poor and composed of students of color. The promise of No Child Left Behind to attain high standards of performance for all children must not obscure the fact that the populations for whom our education system has systematically worked least well will be the majority population in many urban centers. A plethora of federal and state policies, including need-based financial aid, Title 1, and a multitude of federally sponsored support programs, document support for leveling the playing field on behalf of underserved populations. Leadership for our time should invent new policies to support continued progress with that national agenda.

The United States is poised to become the first nation in the world with the capability of educating citizens who represent the full spectrum of ethnicity, language, culture, and color that exists on the globe. Their insights into the dynamics of international commerce and polity could inspire an age of international understanding and collaboration, of global advancement and peace.

Deep in our American hearts is the instinct to enable our most vulnerable youth to secure a brighter future. This value was a central tenet of the recent U.S. Supreme Court decision sustaining affirmative action in university admissions. Writing for the court in *Grutter v. Bollinger*, Justice Sandra Day O'Connor stated:

> In order to cultivate a set of leaders with legitimacy in the eyes of the country, it is necessary that the path of leadership be visibly open to talented and qualified individuals of every race and ethnicity.

Postsecondary education is the only dependable route to that goal. This is a time to call upon Americans to be fair. And to believe that they will be.

---

1. Zemsky (2003) discusses the decline of public purpose in higher education.
2. Peter D. Hart Research Associates and Robert M. Teeter's Coldwater Corporation have conducted qualitative and quantitative research for the Educational Testing Service for the past three years. These statistics are taken from "Quality, Affordability, and Access: Americans Speak on Higher Education," on About ETS at *www.ets.org*.
3. These data are taken from the Gates Education Policy Paper of the Bill & Melinda Gates Foundation, "Closing the Graduation Gap: Toward High Schools That Prepare All Students for College, Work and Citizenship."

*Providing a diverse array of educational settings for students with different needs, interests, and supports has the potential to help more older adolescents select learning environments that motivate and support them to succeed academically. But there are risks to a system of variegated educational offerings. David Ferrero warns of the danger to civic cohesion of a public schooling system that overemphasizes consumer choice and maximizes private benefits at the expense of the civic role of schools to impart a shared sense of the rights and responsibilities of citizens. Will there be a cost in terms of building and sustaining public will?*

## 24. Beyond "Providers" and "Clients": Can Multiple Pathways Advance Civic Aims?

### By David J. Ferrero

Many of the essays in this volume advocate a system of "multiple pathways" to higher education as part of a strategy for doubling the number of college graduates. They argue that different students have different needs and different learning styles, and therefore require different kinds of curricula, instructional modalities, or schools. The multiple pathways system has attracted growing interest among education reformers, along with school autonomy, enhanced professional discretion, and greater choice for students and parents. These innovations stem from a conception of schools that views them as primarily concerned with delivering services to individual students and families who select from among variegated educational offerings in an effort to find schools or programs that best meet their needs, interests, or values.

Such a system would be a good thing, I think, for students and families. It would give students opportunities to attend coherent, supportive schools that offer programs of study aligned with their needs and aspirations. It would also be good for educators, who could practice their craft with like-minded colleagues in ways compatible with the vision of good schooling to which they subscribe. The caution I would like to interject is that schooling is more than a transaction between teacher "providers" and student/parent "clients." Schooling remains a public good charged with pursuing civic purposes. By civic purposes I mean the responsibility of schools to cultivate in students certain knowledge, skills, habits, and dispositions deemed essential to sustaining a liberal-democratic political culture. This formative mandate for public schools implies certain obligations on the part of citizens, including the clients themselves.

Most reform-minded educators recognize the civic mission and sincerely believe in it. But we seem to have acquired certain habits of mind and speech that characterize schools as constituting a marketplace of social services. Families are clients and schools are service providers competing for market share by catering to diverse tastes and preferences while delivering high test scores or admission to college. We don't mean to be so crass. Rather, we are trying to achieve fairness among students who come to school with widely varying abilities, personalities, and social backgrounds. This social services conception of schooling is admirable. It aims to promote distributive justice, which is a fundamental public good. It nonetheless does so by lapsing into a "clientelist" perspective in which schools provide and students consume. And consumers have rights, not obligations. The focus on what schools owe certain students or families — or, for that matter, businesses and other special interests — obscures what those clients might owe in return.

Consider for a moment the current vogue for *underserved* as the term to describe students who come from disadvantaged or dysfunctional backgrounds, suffer from learning disabilities, or are, for whatever reason, unmotivated or disengaged. The term places some onus on schools to reach out to such students rather than push them out. Those who employ it clearly have a missionary motive in mind: the root *to serve* in underserved is clearly intended to signify a moral calling. But in the current American context the term contributes to a flattened public discourse that reduces human interactions with institutions to exchanges between producers and consumers, which cheapens what schools do for, and demand from, students and society. It is difficult to keep the two connotations — missionary and consumerist — distinct. At the same time, the language of "served" and "underserved" has overtones of paternalism, which strips disadvantaged students and families of agency, as well as responsibility. The term also contributes to a widespread notion that schools are remedial institutions tasked with ensuring fairness and opportunity to compensate for failures in other institutional and policy arenas, which are absolved of any responsibility to secure these goods for children or even to provide the basic conditions for student learning.

This attitude is reinforced by another voguish term, *stakeholder*. In contrast to *constituent*, which signifies an entity that makes up part of a greater social or political whole, a stakeholder is another client. It stands apart from schools and from any shared responsibility for the care and socialization of young people. The stakeholder assigns those tasks to schools and participates mainly to ensure that the outputs of schooling meet its specifications.

In other words, a stakeholder's responsibility ends when it secures its self-interest. It is little wonder that most school reform efforts advanced by prominent stakeholder-clients reflect a certain self-centeredness. From standards-based reform to multiculturalism to school choice, proponents consistently seek changes aimed at extracting greater benefits for specific interest groups, be they businesses, ethnic or religious groups, or individual students and families. Champions of these causes usually couch their advocacy in terms of the public interest. Thus, standards are said to boost economic productivity and improve competitiveness in the global marketplace, thereby raising everyone's standard of living. Multiculturalism is said to make schools and society more inclusive and democratic. School choice is couched as the quintessence of liberal-democratic freedom, practically a civil right. These claims have merit. But the main beneficiary is nearly always the group on behalf of whom the reform is advocated. Rarely is there a corresponding recognition of the group's corresponding responsibility to schools or the public culture that schools are supposed to sustain.

It pays to listen for the absences: When is the last time a business group took a stand against corporate tax abatements that reduce local revenues for schools, or an immigrants' rights group conceded a responsibility to master the language of American political deliberation and become familiar with the intellectual traditions that shaped American political institutions? We are much better at articulating our entitlements than our corresponding obligations.

The political philosopher Michael Sandel (1996) and others have argued that this predilection for expanding entitlements while overlooking obligations reflects a more general drift away from public commitment, civic virtue, and the common good in American life. If this critique is correct — and I think it is — then the clientelist view of schools reflects the atrophy of public spiritedness more broadly. This atrophy has provoked commentary on the importance of a robust public culture to the maintenance of liberal-democratic institutions. Liberal values and capacity for republican self-government, the argument goes, actually require active, sustained cultivation from an early age.[1] Children need to acquire the virtues of tolerance and cooperation, develop some degree of autonomy and capacity for public deliberation, and master the essentials of constitutional law and processes. In short, citizens are made, not born. Historically, Americans have viewed public schools as the primary institutional site for cultivating good citizens.

## Balancing Rights and Responsibilities

Does this formative mandate militate against a system of multiple pathways where educators design, and parents and students choose among, programs and schools that correspond to their particular visions or needs? Not necessarily. But it does remind us that the clientelist conception of schooling is insufficient, whether the system provides multiple pathways or just one.

A sizable literature has emerged over the past decade that seeks to make respectable again talk of civic virtue, robust citizen education, and the common good. Yet this body of thought also concludes that a diversified educational landscape may actually be a requirement of a fair and robustly public-minded system of schooling. Many of the philosophers, legal scholars, and political theorists behind this literature explicitly reject clientelist conceptions of schooling, carefully circumscribe the scope of parents' and students' rights, and vigorously defend the interest of the state in cultivating good citizens.[2] Yet when these thinkers turn to public policy, they endorse the differentiation that underlies the idea of multiple pathways without abandoning principles of fairness or the pursuit of common ends.

Eamonn Callan, a Canadian political philosopher and education policy expert, is representative of this. After a lengthy, closely reasoned argument on behalf of common schooling for shared public ends, he concedes, "If the very diversity of provisions makes it more likely that parents, teachers, and children obtain the kind of schooling that will engage their effort and allegiance, it may also make them more receptive to the shared missions when these have become part of the institutions they really care about." In other words, not only can we design multiple pathways without eroding common ends, but such a system, if conceived and implemented well, could actually motivate school constituents to support those ends.

The conclusion for multiple pathways stems from the need to strike a reasonable balance between the liberal-democratic state's interest in producing competent, loyal citizens who will uphold liberal values, and its responsibility to accommodate the pluralism that is inevitable in a free society. In other words, this line of argument takes into consideration something that the somewhat bloodless talk of providers, clients, and stakeholders tends to obscure: different educational models stem more from people's differing values and worldviews than from a dispassionate diagnosis of students' individual learning needs or styles. The inevitability of such *legitimate* value differences in a free society — be they philosophical, ideological, religious, or pedagogical — has been one of the motivations leading many thoughtful people to endorse a greater diversity of publicly supported schools. But it isn't diversity based on consumer preferences, inalienable parents' rights, or even a professional diagnosis of a client's individual needs; it is diversity based on the recognition that schooling is at heart a serious moral undertaking that the state should neither trammel through coercion nor trivialize through consumerization.

In this conception of schooling, pluralism contributes to the good of society, rather than threatening it. It rests on a psychological truism, articulated recently by William Galston (2002): "Genuine civic unity rests on unforced consent. States that permit their citizens to live in ways that express their values are likely to enjoy widespread support, even gratitude. By contrast, state coercion is likely to produce dissent, resistance, and withdrawal."

The theory here is that citizens will give back in loyalty what they gain in liberty. It also assumes that reasonable religious, cultural, and other associative groups will find the resources from within their own traditions to cultivate liberal values and democratic competencies, just as Catholics, Eastern Europeans, and other immigrant groups did in the 19th and 20th centuries.

This widening of liberty by no means precludes the state from exercising its interests in cultivating certain kinds of citizens who meet common standards of learning. On the contrary, the kind of system I am talking about begins with this interest strongly in mind. Fortunately, even the most demanding versions of what a citizen should know, value, and be able to do are limited in scope and reasonable people already subscribe to them. These competencies include values of tolerance, cooperation, and patriotism; knowledge of constitutional essentials; a sense of efficacy, a degree of autonomy, and an ability to deliberate about matters of public import; and literacy, communication, and critical-thinking skills.

These sorts of expectations, if incorporated into school accountability systems supple enough to include them, should protect the state from schools that teach racial or sectarian hatred, anti-Americanism, or uncritical submission to a particular dogma. They should also help ensure that schools seek to provide students with educational experiences that equalize opportunity by preparing them for the demands of college and work. So, if we conceive and execute it right, the effort to double the numbers of college graduates through a system of multiple pathways can substantially increase the number of good citizens as well.

It isn't quite this easy, of course. Defining what we mean by "tolerance," "critical thinking," or "literacy" embroils us in the same controversies that have made common school civic education so tepid and ineffectual. What exactly is a "good" citizen anyway, and how do we make one? The controversies are likely to form along predictable lines. Joel Westheimer and Joseph Kahne (2002) have developed an incomplete but illustrative taxonomy of differing conceptions of the "good" citizen: the *personally responsible* citizen who lives a virtuous, largely private life without necessarily taking an active role in civic or public affairs beyond informed voting; the *participatory* citizen who participates in associations and volunteers in his community; and the *justice oriented* citizen who performs structural critiques of society from the point of view of a critical social theory and organizes political action to bring about fundamental social and political change. Though these conceptions can be integrated to some degree in practice, they nonetheless reflect deep differences in philosophy, ideology, and pedagogy that have significant consequences for how one organizes a school, designs its curriculum, and formalizes relationships between adults and students.

Some of the most exciting public schools of choice in the country embody these differing conceptions. For example, the Northtown Academy in Chicago, the Metropolitan Regional Career and Technical Center ("the Met") in Providence, and the Oakland School for Social Justice and Community Development in Oakland are all avowedly college preparatory high schools, but each has a very different pedagogical philosophy and corresponding citizen ideal. Northtown students study a classical curriculum focused on the historical development of modern Western societies that is threaded with frequent current issues forums where entire grade levels explore and debate controversial topics such as evolution and immigration policy. Met students pursue individualized courses of study and spend 40 percent of each week in internships and community service. The School for Social Justice, meanwhile, offers students courses in "culture and resistance" where they learn about "systems of oppression" and how to organize political action in their communities.

The citizen types these schools aim to cultivate have certain qualities in common (e.g., critical thinking, a taste for public engagement), but are also notably different. Each is "good" according to some defensible conception. These schools demonstrate that as we think about creating multiple pathways to college we can also think about multiple pathways to citizenship.

## Policy Implications

It is entirely possible and consistent for states to require schools to pursue some fully developed conception of the good citizen while setting their own prescriptions more sparingly. States ought to require, for example, that all schools teach tolerance. However, "tolerance" at one type of school might involve organizing an entire instructional program around an anti-racist curriculum, while at another tolerance might be more quietly cultivated and enforced through rules, admonitions, and other aspects of a school's "hidden" curriculum. States could also decide that all schools should aim to cultivate active citizens without attempting to settle disputes over the meaning of "active." Some schools might aim to make students into committed activists armed with critical theory; others might try to make them into compassionate volunteers; and others might simply aim to make them into reflective observers who strive for nuanced understanding of controversial issues. Such an approach to schooling would arguably improve upon what exists in most places now, where schools themselves settle for civic minimalism in order to avoid offending staff, students, and parents.

Assessment could follow the same pattern, with basic tests of literacy and essential constitutional knowledge at the state level supplemented by required assessments that schools would choose or develop themselves. It matters less whether students demonstrate citizen competence by organizing a protest against the closing of a local homeless shelter, satisfactorily performing 40 hours of community service at a local hospice, or comparing and contextualizing Homer's and Hemingway's conceptions of war and heroism in an extended analytic essay, than it does that they demonstrate competence in *some* recognized form of good citizenship.

Nothing in this chapter is intended to cast aspersions on the impulse to serve students or the movement to provide a diverse array of educational settings for students with different needs, interests, or values. In fact, these developments merit strong support. If a system of multiple pathways can accommodate diversity — of learning needs, pedagogical values, conceptions of the good — while upholding liberal principles of basic fairness and republican principles of competent citizenship, then we should affirm it as an integral part of a fair and effective system. This chapter is simply a friendly admonition not to let clientelism overwhelm the civic purpose of schooling and the citizen responsibility it implies.

Schooling is more than an exchange between providers and clients, more than an institutional site for maximizing private benefits to this or that target population. It is also a moral and civic undertaking on behalf of a liberal-democratic political system — a duty to itself collectively as well as to its individual members. If educators and reformers themselves fail to recognize and affirm this broader project — and the balance of entitlements and obligations it entails — then we cannot fault the public for doing so as well. We don't need "stakeholder involvement"; we need responsible constituents. Students do, too.

---

1. See, for example, Macedo (2000) and Gutmann (1999).
2. See, for example, Brighouse (2000), Callan (1997), Galston (2002), Hunter (2000), Macedo (2000), Reich (2002), and Salomone (2000).

*Governors can play a critically important role in mobilizing public and political will to address complex policy challenges. This chapter, based on "Ready for Tomorrow: Helping All Students Achieve Secondary and Postsecondary Success," a Governors Guide prepared by Jobs for the Future and the National Governors Association Center for Best Practices, proposes five specific steps states can take — and are taking — to improve secondary and postsecondary outcomes for young people, particularly those traditionally underserved in higher education. The very first recommendation: state leaders should set a clear, measurable goal for improvements in student attainment and mobilize support across K-12 and postsecondary education sectors and across public- and private-sector stakeholders to reach that goal.*

---

## 25. How States Can Help Promote Secondary and Postsecondary Success in Tough Economic Times

BY RICHARD KAZIS, KRISTIN D. CONKLIN,

AND HILARY PENNINGTON

One of the consequences of the recent crisis in state finance and budgets is the dampening effect on state investments to raise skill and educational attainment. This paradoxical challenge to governors and state leaders increases the importance of efficiency in state education systems.

Never before in this country's history has the quality of human resources — the skills and education of our people — been so important to the economic prospects of states and their residents. Yet, at just this moment, fiscal realities compel states to spend their education dollars more efficiently. Higher education funding has taken a serious hit in most states, and long-standing commitments to K-12 funding increases tied to accountability gains are unraveling.

What is the best way out of this dilemma?

As state after state acknowledges the need for a more highly skilled work force, with every high school graduate ready to succeed in college or a good job, the question becomes: How can states make good on that commitment with limited financial resources? The answer lies in a policy agenda that can simultaneously improve student outcomes and increase the efficiency of public secondary and postsecondary sectors.

At present, the educational pipeline is inefficient, at great cost to individuals and society. States spend, on average, $100,000 for every student's education — but 30 out of 100 young people fail to complete the most basic educational credential, the high school diploma, and only 29 out of 100 earn a bachelor's degree by the time they are 30. For minority, immigrant, and low-income populations, the "leaks" in the pipeline — demonstrated by high school and postsecondary dropout rates, postsecondary remediation, and gaps in college enrollment and completion — are even worse.

Postsecondary success requires steps to improve high schools dramatically — as well as actions that ease the transition to college and incentives for postsecondary institutions based on student learning and graduation. This requires states to change their conventional thinking of K-12 and higher education systems as distinct and to consider the education system as a single pipeline toward postsecondary credentials.

Current state and federal policies are necessary but insufficient steps to improve the odds that more students will earn a postsecondary credential. No Child Left Behind (NCLB) alone won't solve the problem: this act is primarily a K-8 reform package that looks down from high school graduation rather than up to college success. Increased investments in merit- and need-based financial aid make it easier for more low-income students to afford college, but without stronger college preparation, current inefficiencies will continue: one out of three students enrolls in remedial courses, and one-half of all students who start college do not earn a degree within six years, generating weaker return for the public investment in their studies.

So what can governors and other state policymakers do? The National Governors Association and Jobs for the Future have identified five actions that states can take — and that some states have already taken — to dramatically improve postsecondary success rates for young people. Our guide recommends five steps:

- Set a statewide benchmark for postsecondary attainment.
- Better align K-12 and higher education expectations and incentives.
- Create and support an integrated K-16 data system.
- Promote more learning options that provide college-level learning in high school for all students.
- Aggressively pursue strategies to improve the lowest-performing high schools.

Taken together, these strategies to improve high school outcomes and ease the transition to postsecondary learning, coupled with incentives to colleges and universities to increase student persistence and degree completion, point the way toward a more efficient pipeline.

*Set a stretch goal.* The first thing governors can do is to set a statewide numerical target for expanding the number of young people who successfully complete both high school and a first postsecondary credential program. The goal should be ambitious but realistic, focused on completion, not just access, and disaggregated for the population groups least likely to succeed without attention and help: minorities, English language learners, low-income students, first-generation college-goers. A state could, for example, commit to doubling the numbers of low-income young people who achieve a recognized postsecondary credential (e.g., associate's or bachelor's degree, an apprenticeship) by age 26. Iowa governor Tom Vilsack called for just this when he declared that 90 percent of all Iowans should have a postsecondary credential.

*Align K-12 and higher education standards, assessments, and expectations.* While states have made great progress in identifying what young people should know and be able to do at different points in their K-12 education, they have done so with almost no input from the two key consumers of their products: colleges and employers. In many states, standards tested by high school exit exams are below the standards that public colleges use to determine admission and placement. The single most powerful change that states could make would be to better align high school exit requirements with the expectations of colleges and employers.

Oregon has been working on this kind of alignment since 1993 through its Proficiency-based Admission Standards System (PASS). In New York City, the City University of New York (CUNY) system has announced that a Regents math or English exam score of 75 or higher will guarantee entrance to CUNY without the need for remedial coursework. And the California State University system recommends that local high schools administer the system's placement exam to tenth graders, so they and their teachers can understand the university's expectations. Business and education coalitions in Arkansas, Connecticut, Indiana, Maryland, and Oklahoma are now pushing for all high school students to take a college-prep curriculum, as Texas now requires.

Achieving such alignment would be easier if states improved the coordination or integration of the governance of K-12 and higher education, either into a single agency or through a coordinating mechanism with statutory authority and gubernatorial leadership.

*Integrate the K-12 and higher education data systems into a single system.* If a state wants to treat its educational institutions as a single pipeline, it needs to be able to see students' progress along that pipeline as a single trajectory. That can't be done if the K-12 and higher education data systems are disconnected and incompatible. States need to collect and report attainment and achievement outcome across K-12 and higher education for all youth over time. A unique identifier should be assigned to every student in the state when they enter a public institution. Information about dropouts should be kept in the data system; outcomes should be tracked across institutions and across institutional levels. Florida and Illinois are the two states that have gone the furthest in integrating their data systems.

*Promote a diverse range of learning options.* The "one size fits all" comprehensive high school fails too many young people, particularly low-achieving students who enter high school needing to catch up academically if they are to graduate college ready. Some of the most promising reform strategies, particularly for older adolescents, feature smaller schools and blend secondary and postsecondary learning in programs that yield both high school diplomas and postsecondary credentials. Governors have several ways to encourage more and more varied learning options for older adolescents. States can finance the start-up and expansion of new school models through competitive grants, as North Carolina and Texas are doing.

States can also replicate effective models that combine secondary and post-secondary education, as do Ohio and Utah, each of which is committed to opening more than half a dozen early college high schools in the next few years (see "Challenge, Not Remediation," page 213).

*Tackle low-performing high schools aggressively.* If a state really wants to minimize inefficiencies in its K-16 education system, one of the most important steps it can take at the high school level is to help students who are stuck in low-performing high schools. On average, across the 34 states that reported on NCLB performance in the fall of 2003, 80 percent of high schools failed to make "adequate yearly progress" as defined in the law.

Every state has low-performing schools that have the capacity to improve with support and assistance, and there are schools that simply lack the leadership, instructional capacity, and resources to help their students advance. To help support better teaching in low-performing high schools, states can provide incentives for quality teachers to take hard-to-staff positions, as Kentucky and other states have done. Or they can create teaching programs targeted to the skills needed to succeed in urban high school environments, as Boston's district is currently launching.

No less important, states should identify those poorly performing schools that are unlikely to turn themselves around and act aggressively to change their basic "DNA." Maryland officials helped schools and civic leaders in Baltimore reconstitute the dysfunctional Southern High School into a cluster of small high schools co-located on the school's campus. Early data indicate that Southern's four schools have markedly improved students' educational environment, a precursor to longer-term improvements in student achievement. Texas has recently enacted legislation designed to lower dropout rates that requires swift intervention by the state in low-performing districts.

Governors around the country are showing leadership in improving their states' education pipelines. Kansas governor Kathleen Sebelius introduced recent education initiatives with this statement: "To improve education . . . first, we need to look at education as a P-16 system with seamless transitions from pre-K to K-12 to postsecondary." Texas governor Rick Perry recently announced the creation of a $130 million, public-private initiative to increase high school graduation and college attendance rates in school districts statewide.

We may be seeing the early signs of the next era in education reform, an era that continues to push for K-12 improvement, particularly for the lowest-performing students, while linking it clearly and effectively to strategies that will make attainment of postsecondary credentials more common and expected for students from all ethnic, racial, and income groups. The strategies of the current crop of governors — and how successful they are — will reveal a great deal about what the future might hold.

*Like other education reform movements committed to reducing educational inequity and expanding opportunity, "Doubling the Numbers" sets out a challenging goal. Yet it may also be an achievable one, given its incremental character. To succeed, Ronald Wolk writes, will require a strategy that motivates and has clear incentives for leaders across the segments of public education, K-12 and postsecondary, as well as leaders in government, business, and philanthropy. Above all, the campaign will need champions and leaders who use their political capital to turn this rallying cry into concrete actions that move this agenda forward.*

---

# 26. "Be Favorable to Bold Undertakings":[1]
# Next Steps for a Campaign to
# Double the Numbers

## By Ronald A. Wolk

The preceding chapters have raised many of the tough issues that must be addressed if by 2020 we are to double the number of young people who earn postsecondary credentials, particularly among those groups traditionally underserved by higher education.

The paramount question that remains is whether the goal is realistic and how it can be achieved.

The provocative papers in this volume provided the context for an extraordinary meeting convened by Jobs for the Future (JFF) in October 2003 in Washington, DC. At that meeting, and in a related press conference, JFF announced the "Double the Numbers" goal as a challenge to the nation.

The topic attracted more interest than the conference planners anticipated, and the meeting was substantially oversubscribed. Participants represented the constituent groups whose collaboration will be essential in meeting the goal: government, business, philanthropy, and all levels of education.

## A Compelling Case

The contributors to this volume make a compelling case for the new goal of doubling the numbers. It is a critically important goal to achieve, both for the young people involved and for the larger society. Some argue that it is a "moral issue," given the tragic waste of so much human potential. Others see it as a "civil rights" issue, noting that, as always, poor and minority youngsters bear the burden of the system's inequities and failures. Everyone recognizes that it is an economic issue — hundreds of billions of dollars in unrealized national wealth and diminished productivity for the society, low wages and dead-end jobs for the individuals.

An array of statistics powerfully documents the wasteful and "unacceptable leakage all along the educational pipeline" — the deplorable number of youngsters who fall between the cracks in both high school and college, and the human and financial toll that failure exacts on them and on the economy. And there is no doubt that the problem will worsen unless we soon close the gap between the demands of a rapidly changing technological age and the inadequate skills of an undereducated and unprepared work force.

Doubling the numbers of young people who complete high school ready for postsecondary study and go on to earn some kind of credential would be a giant step toward closing that gap.

## Can the Goal Be Achieved?

Is this a realistic goal? Can it be achieved? Those are key questions too often unasked in goal setting. A worthy goal should be a stretch, but if allies are to be recruited to the cause, it has to be reachable with enough hard work and a little luck. Our nation's experience with education goals set previously in this current reform movement give cause for skepticism.

Take Goals 2000, for example. Following the historic Charlottesville summit meeting in the fall of 1989 with the first President Bush, the nation's governors announced six national education goals to be accomplished by the year 2000. Later approved by the U.S. Congress, the goals declared that all children will start school ready to learn. The high school graduation rate will increase to at least 90 percent. All students will leave grades 4, 8, and 12 having demonstrated competency in challenging subject matter. U.S. students will be first in the world in science and math achievement. Every adult

American will be literate. And every school in America will be free of drugs and violence.

The goals were so obviously unrealistic that enthusiasm for them barely outlasted the fanfare that accompanied their announcement. None of them was achieved, the federal government ended its funding for them after four years, and they are now a distant memory.

A decade later, in 2001, Congress approved No Child Left Behind (NCLB) — the reauthorization of the Elementary and Secondary Education Act. The very name of the bill embodies a goal more audacious than any in Goals 2000. Specifically, the new education act declares that the United States will close the achievement gap among the nation's students and guarantee every child a quality education. To help keep that promise, there will be a highly qualified teacher in every classroom by 2006. Poorly performing public schools will either improve or be closed, and students in those schools will have the right to transfer to successful schools. By 2013, every American child will be proficient in reading and mathematics.

Like Goals 2000, No Child Left Behind is likely to fail in meeting its most challenging goals, which schools cannot possibly attain unless the political system solves such profound social issues as poverty and inequality.

Is it realistic to expect every student to be proficient in reading and math within the next nine years, given that millions of our children enter school every year lacking the preparation and motivation they will need to succeed? For many of them, English is a second language, and they struggle — and often fail — to achieve the reading skills they need to learn academic subjects.

Can we produce more than two million highly qualified teachers by 2006 to staff all of the nation's classrooms? Not without a miracle, given that nearly four out of ten secondary teachers lack degrees in their field.

With unprecedented teamwork, imagination, hard work, and massive public support, schools might make genuine progress toward some of the goals of NCLB. But in the end, they will inevitably fall short because solutions are beyond their control.

## The Challenges Are Formidable

Although Double the Numbers seems like a much less daunting goal by comparison, it too will be exceedingly difficult to achieve. As the preceding chapters make clear, formidable challenges confront us at all levels — in the public school system, on our college and university campuses, in our state houses and city halls. The problems are educational, financial, and political, and they must be dealt with simultaneously.

We can't double the numbers of kids who earn a postsecondary credential unless we fix the high school — which Marc Tucker calls "the Waterloo" of education reform and Tom Vander Ark of the Bill & Melinda Gates Foundation cites as the most flawed part of the education system.

We can't increase college access and reduce the horrendous college dropout rate without significantly reforming higher education. But first we face the daunting task of persuading educators and policymakers that colleges and universities need reform. As Peter Ewell puts it, "Higher education acknowledges 'no problem' with America's colleges and universities, except lack of money."

We cannot fix the education system until we address it as a single system. Demographer Harold L. Hodgkinson admonished us two decades ago to treat education as "all one system" — from preschool to the Ph.D. We can no longer afford to ignore that advice. State must take the crucial step of establishing K-16 systems that link schools and colleges.

Government officials at all levels must be called upon to make sound policy and provide the funding necessary to motivate people and organizations to take the steps required to double the numbers.

All of these actions are essential. The goal cannot be met if we fail with any of them.

## The Past Offers Hope

Double the Numbers specifically proposes to increase the number of low-income students who earn a postsecondary credential from 410,000 in 2000 to 920,000 in 2020. (In fact, if the goal is met, the numbers of students from all income levels earning a postsecondary credential is likely to increase somewhat because the kinds of improvements necessary to help low-income students will also help hundreds of thousands of other, higher-income students.)

Past experience offers hope. Except for the past two decades, the United States has doubled the number of college students every 20 years or sooner for more than half a century. From 1940 to 1950, enrollment rose from 1.5 million to 2.7 million. Even more dramatic, enrollment soared between 1959 and 1970, from 3.2 million to 9 million.

Unlike Goals 2000 and NCLB, the success of Double the Numbers may not depend on solving the problems of poverty and inequity. It is within the ability of institutions (aided by sound policy and public support) to meet this goal.

Jay Greene, a senior fellow at the Manhattan Institute for Policy Research, told a session at the Washington conference that black and Hispanic students are underrepresented in college not because of insufficient financial aid or inadequate affirmative action programs, but because the precollegiate education system failed them. "Some may argue that the problem of college readiness can't be solved until poverty, racism, illegitimacy, and a host of other social ills are cured first," he stated. "However, the potential effect — positive or negative — that public schools can have on the college readiness of their students is very large."

## A Sense of Optimism

The challenges and obstacles notwithstanding, participants in the Washington conference were generally optimistic and eager to get on with the job. Perhaps a goal had at last been formulated that was at once simple and straightforward enough for everyone to understand and get behind, yet comprehensive and powerful enough to lever an intractable system of public education onto a path toward significant improvement. Participants described the goal-setting and the meeting variously as "a watershed," "a turning point," and "the right idea at the right time."

It may well be "the right time." The problems we have to solve to double the numbers are not new, but 20 years of concerted efforts to improve America's public schools have created a policy climate in which they are being taken more seriously than ever before. A national conversation about education is underway, and it is raising the level of awareness and expectations among the public and policymakers. Recently, the discussion has been broadening to include the practices and performance of colleges and universities. At least three foundation-supported national studies of higher education are focusing the spotlight on problems within higher education institutions and systems that have been largely invisible to the public and generally ignored by higher education officials and state policymakers.

As the debate about standards and accountability spreads to the loftier terrain of colleges and universities, pressure should build for reform. In addition, the increasing emphasis on gathering and publishing data about the performance of institutions and students is casting in stark relief the inequities of the system and the high price paid by its victims. And as successive efforts to improve the system fail, a growing frustration may prompt more innovation, state policies that are more aggressive, and rising impatience with the sacred cows of the system.

## Signs of Progress

Some progress is being made. Here and there across the country, reformers have established beachheads and planted flags in the struggle not only to expand access to higher education, but also, and perhaps even more important, to increase the number of young people who leave high school college-ready and then go on to complete a postsecondary program and earn a credential. There are some spirit-lifting signs of progress and positive action — a few of them mentioned in this book.

- States are experimenting with incentives to prompt institutions to stress "completion" and motivate students to improve their performance. Michigan, for example, has established a program of merit scholarships for students who do well on an external curriculum-based exam. Early results are positive, showing significant increases in students' meeting the standards and receiving merit awards.
- States are working to beef up a high school education and are creating a consistent set of expectations that span high school classes and entry-level college courses. Oregon's pioneering Proficiency-based Admission Standards System (PASS) and Standards for Success sponsored by the Association of American Universities and The Pew Charitable Trusts are successful examples.
- To meet the demands of standards-based accountability, more states are expanding data collection across the education system. Texas and Florida have set the pace in building integrated "data warehouses" that, as Hans L'Orange notes, "provide 'ready access to public primary, secondary, and

higher education information for purposes of research, planning, policy, and decisionmaking,' from prekindergarten through the bachelor's degree."

• More than 30 states now have laws supporting dual enrollment programs in which thousands of students are combining secondary and postsecondary study.

## Two Competing Strategies

One of the most encouraging aspects of the Washington meeting and this volume of essays is that they bring together two competing reform strategies that have seemed mutually exclusive. One of the key prerequisites for doubling the numbers is the recognition that, while all students should leave high school prepared to succeed in college, the conventional college-prep curriculum in the traditional high school should not be the only route to postsecondary education.

Multiple pathways are essential to accommodate the socioeconomic and cultural diversity of today's students with their different needs, abilities, and interests. It is symbolically important that this book's first chapter is "The Case for Multiple Pathways" by Robert Schwartz, one of the founders and most ardent leaders of the national standards movement.

Advocates of standards-based reform tend to see multiple pathways as undermining rigorous standards. Those who are working to develop multiple pathways argue that these pathways cannot survive if they are forced to meet the often rigid and narrow standards and assessments of states and districts. Both are needed if we are to double the numbers. Somehow, we have to find ways to allow multiple pathways and standards-based reform to coexist.

New pathways include innovative and alternative high schools like the New Vision Schools in New York City, High Tech High in San Diego, and the Met in Providence. The founders of these and several other unconventional schools shared their exciting success stories with conference delegates. Other presenters described blended institutions, like early college high schools, that blur the line between schools and colleges; programs that unite schools, colleges, and employees in providing technology-based credentials; workplace programs run by companies and unions; and service pathways like AmeriCorp and the military.

While high school exit standards may be needed to ensure better student performance, they are not enough. Secondary and postsecondary learning must be integrated. As one JFF document puts it, we must "improve the alignment of standards, assessment, and accountability systems across secondary and postsecondary education" but simultaneously expand "the range of high-quality learning environments for older adolescents through state policies, regulations, and financing mechanisms."

The effort is well underway to create new schools, programs, and pathways that graduate more students prepared and motivated to earn a postsecondary credential. In recent years, reformers have launched a full-court press to overhaul the American high school. The Bill & Melinda Gates Foundation has led a movement to create a variety of new break-the-mold high schools. Efforts are afoot to open space in the existing system to shelter these new, small, innovative schools and let them flourish. Success will require that higher education, government, business, and philanthropy all make significant contributions if we are to dramatically increase the number of college-ready high school graduates.

## Next Steps Are Crucial

A volume like this, along with a successful conference of leaders, is a wonderful start in a long-term effort to establish and achieve a difficult education goal. But the next steps will determine the outcome.

First and foremost, leadership is essential. Jobs for the Future has taken the initiative, but the task ahead will require a division of labor and responsibility that must involve a variety of organizations and constituencies. Perhaps a small coalition of organizations can be assembled, with adequate funding from foundations and corporations, to formulate a plan of action and coordinate the efforts of the many constituent groups that have a role to play in doubling the numbers.

These organizations should represent the key constituencies needed to achieve the goal — state organizations like the National Governors Association and the National Council of State Legislators; postsecondary organizations like the American Council on Education and the American Association of Higher Education; precollegiate organizations like the Council of Great City Schools and the Alliance for Excellent Education;

business groups like Achieve and the Business Roundtable; advocacy groups such as The Education Trust; and philanthropic organizations like the Council on Foundations. Some of these organizations were represented at the Washington meeting.

Here are some of the key tasks that must be carried out:

- Legislative leaders and policymakers in every state must be recruited to the cause. We need policies that encourage greater accountability for postsecondary institutions for student retention and success, and that support emerging models and solutions and advance multiple pathways and dual-enrollment initiatives. Political leaders must refocus the debate from access to success in postsecondary education.
- Postsecondary institutions and systems should work closely with public schools to articulate clearly expectations for student preparation, to align entry requirements with high school exit exams, and to pursue more effective strategies to assure that students stay the course and earn a credential. In addition, colleges and universities need to acknowledge the nontraditional multiple pathways and adapt practices and policies to maximize their contribution.
- The business community should be called on to help establish career ladders, internships, and certification programs targeted to bringing students back into the pipeline to work and postsecondary education.
- The philanthropic community should be urged to provide funding for key initiatives that advance these objectives.

## We Must Stay the Course

It is difficult to be involved in reform movements for very long without becoming a bit skeptical, if not downright cynical. The litany of problems is so familiar that it becomes background noise; the proposed solutions lose their lustrous promise in the inevitable "scholarly debate"; the calls to action tend to become clichés. And the hill we are pushing the stone up seems always to be getting higher.

That makes it all the more important to hang in there and keep trying, because peaceful and successful change is ultimately the lifeblood of a democracy. Doubling the numbers of underserved youth who succeed in a postsecondary program is a goal worth striving toward. It is the most achievable education goal we've set during this reform movement, and the stakes are so high that we cannot afford to fail.

One of the plenary speakers at the conference quoted Franklin D. Roosevelt: "We may not be able to build a better future for our children, but we can build better children for our future." If we double the numbers, we will most surely do both.

---

1. Virgil, 70–19 BC.

# *References*

## CHAPTER 1, MULTIPLE PATHWAYS (SCHWARTZ)

Lewis, A., (Ed.). (2003). *Shaping the future of American youth: Youth policy in the 21st century.* Washington, DC: American Youth Policy Forum.

Ravitch, D. (2000). *Left back: A century of failed school reforms.* New York: Simon & Schuster.

## CHAPTER 2, A CORE CURRICULUM (BARTH/HAYCOCK)

Adelman, C. (1999). *Answers in the tool box: Academic intensity, attendance patterns, and bachelor's degree attainment.* Washington, DC: U.S. Department of Education.

Carnevale, A. P., & Desrochers, D. M. (2002). *The missing middle: Aligning education and the knowledge economy.* Washington, DC: U.S. Department of Education, Office of Vocational and Adult Education.

Frome, P. (2001). *High schools that work: Findings from the 1996 and 1998 assessments.* Washington, DC: U.S. Department of Education, Research Triangle Institute for the Planning and Evaluation Service.

Greene, J. P., & Winters, M. A. (2002). *High school graduation rates in the United States.* New York: Manhattan Institute for Policy Research.

Somerville, J., & Yi, Y. (2002). *Aligning K-12 and postsecondary expectations: State policy in transition.* Washington, DC: National Association of System Heads.

Venezia, A., Kirst, M. W., & Antonio, A. L. (2003). *Betraying the college dream: How disconnected k-12 and postsecondary education systems undermine student aspirations* (Final policy report from Stanford University's Bridge Project). Stanford, CA: Stanford Institute for Higher Education Research.

## CHAPTER 4, THE CASE FOR IMPROVING CONNECTIONS (KIRST/VENEZIA)

Adelman, C. (1999). *Answers in the tool box: Academic intensity, attendance patterns, and bachelor's degree attainment.* Washington, DC: U.S. Department of Education.

Carnegie Foundation for the Advancement of Teaching. (2001). *The Carnegie classification of institutions of higher education.* Menlo Park, CA: Author.

Education Trust. (1999). Ticket to nowhere. The gap between leaving high school and entering college and high performance jobs. *Thinking K-16, 3*(2).

Le, V. N., & Robyn, A. (2001). *Alignment among secondary and post-secondary assessments: A report for Stanford University's Bridge Project.* Santa Monica, CA: RAND.

Mortenson, T. (1998). Freshman-to-sophomore persistence rates by institutional control, academic selectivity and degree level, 1983 to 1998. *Postsecondary Education Opportunity,* 74(August).

National Center for Education Statistics. (1996). *National Education Longitudinal Study, 1988–1994: Descriptive summary report.* Washington, DC: U.S. Department of Education.

U.S. Department of Education. (2001). *The condition of education.* Washington, DC: National Center for Education Statistics.

### Chapter 5, More High School Options (Nathan)

Boyd, W., Hare, D., & Nathan, J. (2002). *What really happened? Minnesota's experience with school choice.* Minneapolis: Humphrey Institute of Public Affairs, Center for School Change.

Center for Education Reform. (2003). *What the evidence reveals about charter schools.* Washington, DC: Author.

Charter School Institute. (2003). *2003 ELA tests.* Albany: State University of New York.

Cohen, M. A. (1996). *The monetary value of saving a high-risk youth.* Nashville: Vanderbilt University, Owen Graduate School of Management.

Education Commission of the States. (2001). *Post-secondary enrollment options: Dual concurrent enrollment.* Denver: ECS Center for Community College Policy.

Greene, J. (2002). *High school graduation rates.* New York: Manhattan Institute.

Greene, J., Forster, G., & Winters, M. A. (2003). *Apples to apples: An evaluation of charter schools serving general populations.* New York: Manhattan Institute.

Kolderie, T. (1990). *The states will have to withdraw the exclusive.* St. Paul, MN: Center for Policy Studies.

Lawrence, B. (forthcoming). *Land for granted: The effects of acreage policies on rural schools and communities.* Washington, DC: Rural School and Community Trust.

Mason-Dixon Polling. (2003). *Minnesota school choice poll.* Available from the University of Minnesota, Humphrey Institute of Public Affairs, Center for School Change.

Nathan, J. (1996). *Charter schools: Creating hope and opportunity in American education.* San Francisco: Jossey-Bass.

Nathan, J., & Febey, K. (2001). *Smaller, safer, saner successful schools.* Washington, DC: National Clearinghouse for Educational Facilities.

Office of Legislative Auditor. (1996). *Postsecondary enrollment options program.* St. Paul, MN: Author.

Rand Corporation. (2003). *Charter school operations and performance: Evidence from California.* Santa Monica, CA: Author.

Raywid, M. A. (1999). *Current literature on small schools.* Charleston, WV: ERIC Clearinghouse on Rural Education and Small Schools.

Rofes, E. (n.d.). *How are school districts responding to charter laws and charter schools?* Berkeley, CA: Graduate School of Education Policy Analysis for California Education.

Steinberg, A., Almeid, C., Allen, L., & Goldberger, S. (2003). *Four building blocks for a system of educational opportunity.* Boston: Jobs for the Future.

Stiefel, L., Latarola, P., Fruchter, N., & Berne, R. (1998). *The effects of student body on school costs and performance in New York City high schools.* New York: New York University, Institute for Education and Social Policy.

Wehrwein, A. (1985, October 23). Critics assailing Minnesota choice plan. *Education Week,* available online at www.edweek.com/ew/ewstory.cfm?slug= keywords=wehrwein

## CHAPTER 6, MERIT SCHOLARSHIPS FOR THE MANY (BISHOP)

Barbett, S., & Korb, R. (1999). *Current fund revenues and expenditures of degree granting institutions: Fiscal year 1996.* Washington, DC: National Center for Education Statistics.

Bishop, J. H. (1999a). Are national exit examinations important for educational efficiency? *Swedish Economic Policy Review, 6,* 349-401.

Bishop, J. H. (1999b). Nerd harassment, incentives, school priorities and learning. In S. Mayer & P. Peterson (Eds.), *Earning and learning* (pp. 231-280). Washington, DC: Brookings Institution Press.

Bishop, J. (2001). A steeper, better road to graduation. *EducationNext, 4,* 56-61.

Cornwell, C., Mustard, D., & Sridhar, D. (2003). *The enrollment effects of merit-based financial aid: Evidence from Georgia's HOPE scholarship.* Athens: University of Georgia.

Dynarski, S. (2000). Hope for whom? Financial aid for the middle class and its impact on college attendance. *National Tax Journal, 53,* 629-661.

Dynarski, S. (2002). *The consequences of merit aid.* Cambridge, MA: Harvard University, Kennedy School of Government.

National Center for Education Statistics. (1993). *Digest of education statistics.* Washington, DC: Author.

National Center for Education Statistics. (2003). *Condition of education.* Washington, DC: Author.

Rohwer, W. D., & Thomas, J. W. (1987). Domain specific knowledge, cognitive strategies, and impediments to educational reform. In M. Pressley (Ed.), *Cognitive strategy research.* New York: Springer-Verlag.

Suskind, R. (1998). *A hope unseen.* New York: Broadway Books.

## CHAPTER 7, AN ACCOUNTABILITY SYSTEM (EWELL)

Burke, J. C., & Associates. (2002). *Funding public colleges and universities for performance: Popularity, problems, and prospects.* Albany, NY: Rockefeller Institute Press.

Cambridge, B. L., Kahn, S., Yancey, K. B., & Tompkins, D. P. (Eds.). (2001). *Electronic portfolios: Emerging practices in student, faculty, and institutional learning.* Washington, DC: American Association of Higher Education.

Dill, D. D. (2000). Designing academic audit: Lessons learned in Europe and Asia. *Quality in Higher Education, 6,* 187-208.

Ewell, P. T. (1998). Achieving high performance: The policy dimension. In W. G. Tierney (Ed.), *The responsive university: Restructuring for high performance.* Baltimore: Johns Hopkins University Press.

Ewell, P. T. (2003). Going for broke: The National Forum on College-Level Learning's Multistate Demonstration Project. *Assessment Update, 15*(3), 8-15.

Johnstone, S. M., Ewell, P. T., & Paulson, K. (2002). *Student learning as academic currency.* Washington, DC: American Council on Education.

Jones, D. P., & Ewell, P. T. (1993). *The effect of state policy on undergraduate education.* Denver: Education Commission of the States.

Jones, D. P., & Paulson, K. (2002). *Developing and maintaining the information structure for state level higher education policymakers.* Boulder, CO: National Center for Higher Education Management Systems.

NCPPHE. (2000). *Measuring up: The 50-state report card for higher education.* San Jose, CA: National Center for Public Policy in Higher Education.

NCPPHE. (2002). *Measuring up: The 50-state report card for higher education.* San Jose, CA: National Center for Public Policy in Higher Education.

Ruppert, S. J. (Ed.). (1994). *Charting higher education accountability: A sourcebook on state-level performance indicators.* Boulder, CO: National Center for Higher Education Management Systems.

Venezia, A., Kirst, M. W., & Antonio, A. L. (2003). *Betraying the college dream: How disconnected K-12 and postsecondary education systems undermine student aspirations.* Palo Alto, CA: Stanford University, Stanford Institute for Higher Education Research.

## CHAPTER 8, FINANCING TIED TO OUTCOMES (LONGANECKER)

Albright, B. N. (1997). Of carrots and sticks and state budgets. *Trusteeship, 5*(2), 18-23.

Burke, J. C., & Minassians, K. P. (2003). *Performance reporting: "Real accountabil-*

*ity" or accountability "lite." Seventh annual survey 2003.* Albany: State University of New York, Nelson A. Rockefeller Institute of Government.

Burke, J. C., & Serban, A. M. (1998). *Current status and future prospects of performance funding and performance budgeting for public higher education.* Albany, NY: Nelson A. Rockefeller Institute of Government, Public Higher Education Program.

Shulock, N., & Moore, C. (2002). An accountability framework for California higher education: Informing public policy and improving outcomes. In *Policy issue report.* Sacramento: California State University, Institute for Higher Education Leadership and Policy.


CHAPTER 12, USING A K-12 ASSESSMENT (KIRST)

Le, V.-N. (2002). *Alignment among secondary and postsecondary assessments in five case study states.* Santa Monica, CA: RAND.

Venezia, A., Kirst, M. W., & Antonio, A. L. (2003).). *Betraying the college dream: How disconnected k-12 and postsecondary education systems undermine student aspirations.* Stanford, CA: Stanford Institute for Higher Education Research.


CHAPTER 14, TWENTY-FIRST CENTURY SCHOLARS (EVENBECK ET AL.)

For more information on the Twenty-First Century Scholars Program, see *http://scholars.indiana.edu/*.

Heller, D. E. (2003). Cost model for revised Michigan Merit Award Scholarship Program. 28 January, Attachment 2 (Plaintiffs' settlement proposal, *White, et al., v. Engler, et al.*). Unpublished document.

Kaltenbaugh, L. S., St. John, E., & Starkey, J. B. (1999). What difference does tuition make? An analysis of ethnic differences in persistence. *Journal of Student Financial Aid, 29*(2), 21-32.

St. John, E. P. (2002). *The access challenge: Rethinking the causes of the new inequality* (Policy Issue Report No. 2002-1). Bloomington: Indiana Education Policy Center.

St. John, E. P. (2003). *Refinancing the college dream: Access, equal opportunity, and justice for taxpayers.* Baltimore: Johns Hopkins University Press.

St. John, E. P., & Chung, C.-G. (forthcoming). Merit and equity: Rethinking award criteria in the Michigan scholarship program. In E. P. St. John & M. D. Parsons (Eds.), *Public funding of higher education: Changing contexts and new rationales.* Baltimore: Johns Hopkins University Press.

St. John, E. P., Musoba, G. D., & Simmons, A. B. (2003). Keeping the promise: The impact of Indiana's 21st Century Scholars Program. *Review of Higher Education, 27*(1).

St. John, E. P., Musoba, G. D., Simmons, A. B., & Chung, C.-G. (2002). *Meeting the access challenge: Indiana's Twenty-First Century Scholars Program* (New Agenda Series, Vol. 4, No. 4). Indianapolis: Lumina Foundation for Education.

St. John, E. P, Mosuba, G. D., Simmons, A. B., Schmit, J., Chung, C. C., & Peng, C.-Y. J. (2002). *Meeting the access challenge: An examination of Indiana's Twenty-First Century Scholars Program.* Presented at the annual meeting of the Association for the Study of Higher Education, Sacramento, CA.

CHAPTER 15, THE NATIONAL SURVEY (BRIDGES/KUH)

Astin, A. W. (1984). Student involvement: A developmental theory for higher education. *Journal of College Student Personnel, 25,* 297-308.

Astin, A. W. (1991). *Assessment for excellence: The philosophy and practice of assessment and evaluation in higher education.* New York: American Council on Education/Macmillan.

Chickering, A. W., & Gamson, A. F. (1987). Seven principles for good practice in undergraduate education." *AAHE Bulletin, 39*(7), 3-7.

Ewell, P. T. (2002). *An analysis of relationships between NSSE and selected student learning outcomes measures for seniors attending public institutions in South Dakota.* Boulder, CO: National Center for Higher Education Management Systems.

Kirst, M. W. (2001). *Overcoming the high school senior slump: New education policies* (Report No. K-16-R-01-01). Washington, DC: Institute for Educational Leadership. (ERIC Document Reproduction Service No. ED 346 082)

Kuh, G. D. (2001). Assessing what really matters to student learning: Inside the National Survey of Student Engagement. *Change, 33*(3), 10-18.

Kuh, G. D., Carini, R. M., & Klein, S. P. (2003). *Student engagement and student learning: Insights from a construct validation study.* Bloomington: Indiana University Center for Postsecondary Research, Policy, and Planning.

Kuh, G. D., Schoh, J. H., Whitt, E. J., & Associates. (1991). *Involving colleges: Successful approaches to fostering student learning and personal development outside the classroom.* San Francisco: Jossey-Bass.

Pascarella, E. T. (2001). Identifying excellence in undergraduate education: Are we even close? *Change, 33*(1), 18-23.

Pascarella, E. T., & Terenzini, P. T. (1991). *How college affects students: Findings and insights from twenty years of Research.* San Francisco: Jossey-Bass.

Sax, L. J., Lindholm, J. A., Astin, A. W., Korn, W. S., & Mahoney, K. M. (2001). *The American freshman: National norms for fall 2002.* Los Angeles: UCLA Graduate School of Education and Information Studies, Higher Education Research Institute.

**CHAPTER 16, BALANCING AUTONOMY AND ACCOUNTABILITY (COUTURIER)**

Almanac 2002–2003 (2002, August 30). *Chronicle of Higher Education.*

Berdahl, R. O. (1998). Balancing self-interest and accountability: St. Mary's College of Maryland. In Terrence J. MacTaggart & Associates (Eds.), *Seeking excellence through independence.* San Francisco: Jossey-Bass.

Berdahl, R. O., & MacTaggart, T. J. (2000). *Charter colleges: Balancing freedom and accountability* (White Paper No. 10). Boston: Pioneer Institute for Public Policy Research.

Colorado School of Mines. (2003a). *Colorado School of Mines diversity plan and update.* Unpublished document.

Colorado School of Mines. (2003b). *Colorado School of Mines diversity plan and update* (January 1, 2002-December 31, 2002). Unpublished document.

Martinez, J. C. (2003). ACLU vows fight ahead, owens backs outlawing college affirmative action. *Denver Post,* July 9, p. B1.

Naughton, J. (2001). St. Mary's grows up. *Washington Post Magazine,* July 22, p. W32.

St. Mary's College of Maryland. (2002). *Significant events in the history of St. Mary's College of Maryland.* Available online at www.smcm.edu/instre-search/OIRweb-0102/TimeLine%202001-2002.htm

St. Mary's College of Maryland. (2003). *Office of Government Relations: Response to issues raised and actions recommended in the Department of Legislative Services Analysis.* Available online at http://www.smcm.edu/govtrelations/template-govtrelations.cfm?doc_id=1220

Schmidt, P. (1998, November 20). Unusual autonomy and unique budget law help St. Mary's College to stand apart. *Chronicle of Higher Education,* p. A27.

**CHAPTER 17, THEME SCHOOLS (MARTINEZ/DONIS-KELLER)**

Adelman, C. (1999). *Answers in the tool box: Academic intensity, attendance patterns, and bachelor's degree attainment.* Washington, DC: U.S. Department of Education.

Ancess, J., Darling-Hammond, L., & Ort, S. W. (2002). Reinventing high school: Outcomes of the Coalition Campus Schools Project. *American Educational Research Journal, 39,* 639-673.

Beales, J. R., & Bertonneau, T. F. (1997). *Do private schools serve difficult-to-educate students?* Midland, MI: Mackinac Center for Public Policy.

Berkner, L., & Chavez, L. (1997). *Access to postsecondary education for the 1992 high school graduates* (NCES Publication No. 98105). Washington, DC: National Center for Education Studies.

Bransford, J. D., Brown, A. L., & Cockling, R. R. (Eds.). (1999). *How people learn: Brain, mind, experience, and school.* Washington, DC: National Academy Press.

Croninger, R., & Lee, V. E. (2001). Social capital and dropping out of high schools: Benefits to at risk students of teachers' support and guidance. *Teachers College Record, 103,* 548-581.

Elliott, M. N., Hanser, L. N., & Gilroy, C. L. (2001). *Evidence of positive student outcomes in JROTC career academies.* Santa Monica, CA: RAND.

Elliott, M. N., Hanser, L. N., & Gilroy, C. L. (2002). Career academies: Additional evidence of positive student outcomes. *Journal of Education for Students Placed at Risk, 7*(1), 71-90.

Gamoran, A. (1987). The stratification of high school learning opportunities. *Sociology of Education, 60,* 135-155.

Gandara, P., Gutierrez, D., & O'Hara, S. (2001). Planning for the future in rural and urban high schools. *Journal of Education for Students Placed at Risk,* 6(1/2), 73-93.

Goddard, R. D., Hoy, W. K., & Hoy, A. W. (2000). Collective teacher efficacy: Its meaning, measure, and impact on student achievement. *American Educational Research Journal, 37,* 479-507.

Hill, P. T., & Celio, M. B. (1998). *Fixing urban schools.* Washington, DC: Brookings Institution Press.

Hill, P. T., Foster, G. E., & Gendler, T. (1990). *High schools with character.* Santa Monica, CA: RAND.

Kemple, J. J., & Snipes, J. D. (2000). *Career academies: Impacts on students' engagement and performance in high school.* New York: Manpower Demonstration Research Corporation.

Lee, V. E., Ready, D. D., & Johnson, D. J. (2001). The difficulty of identifying rare samples to study: The case of high schools divided into schools-within-schools. *Educational Evaluation and Policy Analysis, 23,* 365-379.

Lee, V. E., Smith, J. B., & Croninger, R. G. (1996). *Understanding high school restructuring effects on the equitable distribution of learning in mathematics and science* (rev. ed.). Madison: University of Wisconsin, Wisconsin Center for Education Research.

Lucas, S. R. (1999). *Tracking inequality: Stratification and mobility in American high schools.* New York: Teachers College Press.

McNeil, P. W. (2003). *Rethinking high school: The next frontier for state policymakers.* Aspen, CO: Aspen Program on Education.

New Jersey Department of Education. (2003). *Commissioner Librera, DOE launch 12th grade option pilot program senior-year initiative plays key role in McGreevey administration's education reform plan.* Press release, May, 27.

Newman, F. M., & Wehlage, G. G. (1995). *Successful school restructuring: A report to the public and educators by the Center on Organization and Restructuring of Schools.* Madison: Wisconsin Center for Education Research.

Noeth, R. J., & Wimberly, G. L. (2001). *Creating seamless educational transitions for urban African American and Hispanic students* (ACT Policy Report). Iowa City: ACT.

Pittman, T. S. (1998). Motivation. In D. T. Gilbert, S. T. Fiske, & L. Gardner (Eds.), *The handbook of social psychology* (vol. 1, 4th ed.). New York: McGraw-Hill.

Raywid, M. A. (1994). Selecting the focus on a focus school. *ERIC Clearinghouse on Urban Education Digest, 102.*

Stanton-Salazar, R. D. (1997). A social capital framework for understanding the socialization of racial minority children and youth. *Harvard Educational Review, 67,* 1-40.

Thomas, R. S. (2000). Black students' academic performance and preparation for higher education. In S. T. Gregory (Ed.), *The academic achievement of minority students: perspectives, practices, and prescriptions.* New York: University Press of America.

## CHAPTER 19, DUAL ENROLLMENT (VARGAS)

Bailey, T., Hughes, K., & Karp, M. (2002). *What role can dual enrollment programs play in easing the transition between high school and postsecondary education?* New York: Teachers College/Columbia University, Community College Research Center and Institute on Education and the Economy.

Bailey, T., & Karp, M. (2003). *Promoting college access and success: A review of credit-based transition programs.* Washington, DC: U.S. Department of Education, Office of Adult and Vocational Education.

Kirst, M. (2000). Overcoming the high school senior slump: New education policies. *Crosstalk, 8*(4), 11-12.

Michelau, D. (2001). Postsecondary enrollment options programs. *National Conference of State Legislatures State Legislative Report, 26*(4), 1-29.

Rosenthal, L. (2003). *School choice in Washington: An overview of your options.* Retrieved May 5, from www.greatschools.net

Rylander, C. K. (2000). *Recommendations of the Texas comptroller.* Retrieved January 22, from www.e-texas.org/recommend/ch06/ed11.html

Spurling, S., & Gabriner, R. (2002). *The effect of concurrent enrollment programs upon student success at City College of San Francisco.* San Francisco: City College of San Francisco, Office of Research, Planning and Grants.

Texas Higher Education Coordinating Board. (2002). Texas administrative code, Title 19, Part 1, Chapter 9, Subchapter H, Rule 9.145. Retrieved December 19, from www.thecb.state.tx.us/CBRules

University of Arizona. (1999). *Community college and AP credit: An analysis of the impact on freshman grades.* Retrieved April 11, 2002 from http://aer.arizona.edu/Enrollment/ Papers/dualenr.pdf

Washington State Board for Community and Technical Colleges. (2001a). *Running Start: 2000-01 annual progress report.* Olympia, WA: Author.

Washington State Board for Community and Technical Colleges. (2001b). *Running Start: A progress report from the State Board for Community and Technical Colleges.* Olympia, WA: Author.

Washington State Board for Community and Technical Colleges. (2002). *Running Start: 2001-02 annual progress report.* Olympia, WA. Author.

Washington State Board for Community and Technical Colleges. (2003). *Guidelines for college in the high school.* Retrieved May 6, from www.icrc.wwu.edu/text/formate/ ap/text_hs.html

Windham, P., & Perkins, G. (2001, June 3-6). *Dual enrollment as an acceleration mechanism: Are students prepared for subsequent courses?* Paper presented at the 41st Annual Association for Institutional Research Forum, Long Beach, CA.

## CHAPTER 20, CHALLENGE, NOT REMEDIATION (HOFFMAN)

Adelman, C. (1999). *Answers in the tool box: Academic intensity, attendance patterns and bachelor's degree attainment.* Washington, DC: U.S. Department of Education.

Hoffman, N. (2003). College level credit in high school. *Change, 35*(4), 42-48.

Murphy, L. P. (2004). *The evidence of things not seen: College going for young women from the inner-city.* Unpublished doctoral dissertation, University of Michigan.

Waidtlow, D. M. (2002). *Transition to work and vocational identity among lower income young adults.* Unpublished doctoral dissertation, University of California, Davis.

## CHAPTER 21, PATHWAYS TO CREDENTIALS (ALLEN ET AL.)

Bailey, T., Jacobs, J., Jenkins, D., & Leinbach, T. (2003, April). *Community colleges and the equity agenda: What the record shows.* Paper presented at the AACC national conference, Dallas.

Berkner, L., He, S., & Cataldi, E. F. (2003). *descriptive summary of 1995-96 beginning postsecondary students: Six years later* (NCES Report No. 2003-151). Washington, DC: U.S. Department of Education, National Center for Education Statistics.

Jacobs, J., & Grubb, W. N. (2002). *Implementing the "education consensus": The federal role in supporting vocational-technical education.* Washington, DC: U.S. Department of Education, Office of Vocational and Adult Education.

Toft, G. (2002). *Youth tuitionships: An alternative funding arrangement to improve markets and respect individual learning.* Washington, DC: U.S. Department of Education, Office of Vocational and Adult Education.

U.S. Department of Education. (2003). *The condition of education 2003* (NCES Report No. 3002-067). Washington, DC: U.S. Government Printing Office.

## CHAPTER 22, BEYOND THE REVOLVING DOOR (SMITH)

The premier website on learning communities is http://learningcommons.evergreen.edu.

Adelman, C. (1999). *Answers in the tool box: Academic intensity, attendance patterns, and bachelor's degree attainment.* Jessup, MD: U.S. Department of Education.

Grubb, W. N., Worthen, H., Byrd, B., Webb, E., Badway, N., Cage, C., Goto, S., & Villeneuve, J. C. (1999). *Honored but invisible: An inside look at teaching in community colleges.* New York: Routledge.

Guskin, A., & Marcy, M. (2003). Dealing with the future now: Principles for creating a vital campus in a climate of restricted resources. *Change, 35*(4), 10-21 (July/August).

Massy, W. (2003). *Honoring the trust: Quality and cost containment in higher education.* Bolton, MA: Anker Press.

North Seattle Community College. (2003). Unpublished study.

Sax, L., Keup, J. R., Gilmartin, S. K., Stolzenberg, E. B., & Harper, C. (2002). *Findings from the 2002 Administration of Your First College Year (YFCY): National aggregates.* Los Angeles: University of California, Los Angeles, Higher Education Research Institute.

Smith, B. L. (2001). The challenges of learning communities as a growing national movement. *Peer Review, 4*, 4-8.

Taylor, K., Moore, B., MacGregor, J., & Lindblod, J. (2003). *What we know now about learning community research and assessment.* Olympia, WA: National Learning Community Project at Evergreen State College and American Association for Higher Education.

Tinto, V., Goodsell-Love, A., & Russo, P. (1994). *Building learning communities for new college students: A summary of research findings of the Collaborative Learning Project.* Syracuse, NY: Syracuse University, National Center on Postsecondary Teaching, Learning and Assessment.

Zhao, C.-M., & Kuh, G. (2003). *Adding value: Learning communities and student engagement.* Paper presented at the meeting of the Annual Association for Institutional Research Forum, Tampa.

## CHAPTER 23, CAPACITY AND PUBLIC WILL (WILSON)

Education Commission of the States. (1999). *Transforming postsecondary education for the 21st century: The nuts and bolts of policy leadership.* Washington, DC: Author.

Gardner, J. W. (2003). The full expression of human excellence. In F. Gardner (Ed.), *Living, leading and the American dream.* San Francisco: Jossey-Bass.

Gladwell, M. (2000). *The tipping point.* New York: Little, Brown.

Kahlenberg, R. D. (2003). Philosopher K or King? The ideas and strategy of legendary AFT leader Albert Shanker. *Education Next, 3*(3), 34-39.

Murnane, R. J., & Levy, F. (1996). *Teaching the new basic skills: Principles for educating children to thrive in a changing economy.* New York: Free Press.

Selingo, J. (2003, May 2). What Americans think about higher education. *Chronicle of Higher Education,* p. A10.

Zemsky, R. (2003, May 30). Have we lost the "public" in higher education? *Chronicle of Higher Education,* p. B7.


## CHAPTER 24, BEYOND "PROVIDERS" AND "CLIENTS" (FERRERO)

Brighouse, H. (2000). *School choice and social justice.* New York: Oxford University Press.

Callan, E. (1997). *Creating citizens: Political education and liberal democracy.* Oxford, Eng.: Clarendon Press.

Galston, W. A. (2002). *Liberal pluralism: The implications of value pluralism for political theory and practice.* New York: Cambridge University Press.

Gutmann, A. (1999). *Democratic education* (2nd ed.). Princeton, NJ: Princeton University Press.

Hunter, J. D. (2000). *The death of character: Moral education in an age without good or evil.* New York: Basic Books.

Macedo, S. (2000). *Diversity and distrust: Civic education in a multicultural democracy.* Cambridge, MA: Harvard University Press.

Reich, R. (2002). *Bridging liberalism and multiculturalism in American education.* Chicago: University of Chicago Press.

Salomone, R. (2000). *Visions of schooling: Conscience, community, and common education.* New Haven, CT: Yale University Press.

Sandel, M.-J. (1996). *Democracy's discontent: America in search of a public philosophy.* Cambridge, MA: Belknap Press.

Westheimer, J., & Kahne, J. (2002, August). *Educating the "good" citizen: The politics of school-based civic education programs.* Paper presented at the annual meeting of the American Political Science Association.

# *About the Contributors*

*Lili Allen* is a program director at Jobs for the Future, where she manages several projects related to youth education and transitions. She is author or co-author of several publications related to youth, including *From Large to Small: Strategies for Personalizing the High School; Wall to Wall: Implementing Small Learning Communities in Five Boston High Schools;* and *Involving English Language Learners in Community-Connected Learning.*

*Patte Barth* is the editor of Thinking K-16, The Education Trust's series of reports on important educational policies and practices. She is author of the most recent of these reports, "A Common Core Curriculum for the New Century," and co-author on two others, "Not Good Enough: A Content Analysis of Teacher Licensing Examinations" and "Ticket to Nowhere: The Gap between Leaving High School and Entering College and High-Performing Jobs."

*John H. Bishop* is a professor of human resource studies at Cornell University and executive director of the Educational Excellence Alliance, a consortium of over 325 middle schools and high schools that are studying ways to improve school climate and student engagement. He has published over 80 articles on education reform, the causes of low levels of academic engagement in the United States, the impact of accountability systems on student learning, and other topics in education.

*Brian K. Bridges* coordinates National Survey of Student Engagement activities for the Building Engagement and Attainment of Minority Students Project (BEAMS), a partnership with the American Association of Higher Education, with support from Lumina Foundation for Education. His research focuses on academic leadership and the college presidency, the experiences of African Americans in higher education, and the history of higher education.

*Sheila Byrd* is director of the American Diploma Project. She has worked with over a dozen states on the development and review of their standards, curricula, and assessments, as well as with a number of national and local education policy organizations. From 1996 to 1998, Ms. Byrd was deputy director of California's Academic Standards Commission. Prior to her appointment to the commission staff, Ms. Byrd was the administrator of the Education Leaders Council, a national network of reform-minded state superintendents and state board of education members.

*Kristin D. Conklin* is a senior policy analyst in the Education Division at the National Governors Association's Center for Best Practices. In this role, she provides high school and postsecondary education research, analysis, and consultation to the nation's governors. Ms. Conklin previously worked for the National Center for Public Policy and Higher Education, where she was responsible for the technical development of a 50-state report card on higher education. Ms. Conklin received a master's degree in public policy from Georgetown University.

*David Conley* is an associate professor of educational leadership and policy at the University of Oregon. He is founder and director of the Center for Educational Policy Research and of Standards for Success. From 1994 to 2001, he served in the Office of Vice Chancellor for Academic Affairs of the Oregon University System as executive director of the Proficiency-based Admission Standards System (PASS). His most recent book, *Who Governs Our Schools?*, examines changing roles and responsibilities in educational governance at the national, state, and local levels.

*Lara K. Couturier* is associate project director and director of research for the Futures Project: Policy for Higher Education in a Changing World at Brown University. Ms. Couturier is an associate of the National Center for Public Policy and Higher Education. She previously conducted research for the Harvard Project on Faculty Appointments and worked as a consultant and global marketing manager for Andersen Consulting.

*Christine Donis-Keller* is a research consultant working with the Theme High School Network at the Institute for Educational Leadership. She has worked school reform evaluation projects with the Institute for Education and Social Policy at New York University, including a study of the New York Networks for School Reform and, more recently, an evaluation of Cornerstone, a national school reform model focused on K-3 literacy.

*Scott Evenbeck* is dean of the University College at Indiana University Purdue University Indianapolis (IUPUI). The University College is the academic home for IUPUI's entering students. It is the locus for the Learning Center, Honors, the Career Center, the Advising Center, Precollege Programs, and a wide variety of student support and outreach efforts. Through leadership of University College, IUPUI was named to the Association of American Colleges and Universities Greater Expectations project, which is articulating expectations for the baccalaureate in the 21st century.

*Peter T. Ewell* is vice president of the National Center for Higher Education Management Systems, a nonprofit research and development center on higher education policy in Boulder, Colorado. His work centers on assessment and accountability policies in higher education, a topic on which he has published and spoken extensively. He has worked with over 375 colleges and universities and 23 state systems of higher education.

*David J. Ferrero* is director of evaluation and policy research for education programs at the Bill & Melinda Gates Foundation, where he oversees policy initiatives and program evaluation and co-manages the foundation's national high school program. The foundation is committed to raising high school and college completion rates by supporting the development of small, focused high schools of choice and making scholarships and support programs available to minority students. Mr. Ferrero has worked as a journalist, high school teacher, policy researcher, educational technology consultant, and state policy consultant on teacher quality.

*Sue Goldberger* is responsible for managing and expanding a new body of work for Jobs for the Future: creating social business ventures to expand educational and economic opportunity for low-income youth and adults. At

JFF, she has directed a multicity urban high school reform initiative and several school-to-career enterprises featuring innovative work and learning models. Prior to joining JFF, Dr. Goldberger founded and directed several community-based organizations that advocated for improvements in health care, child care, and economic opportunity for low-wage workers.

*Arthur M. Hauptman* has been an independent public policy consultant since 1981. He is an internationally recognized expert in higher education finance and has written and spoken extensively on issues of student financial aid, college costs, tuition, fees, and resource allocation. He has consulted on higher education finance issues with more than a dozen countries, as well as a number of federal government agencies, state agencies, and higher education institutions and associations in the United States.

*Kati Haycock,* director of The Education Trust, is one of the nation's leading child advocates in the field of education. Established in 1990, The Education Trust does what no other Washington-based education organization seeks to do: speaks up for what's right for young people, especially those who are poor or members of minority groups. It also provides hands-on assistance to urban school districts and universities that want to work together to improve student achievement from kindergarten through college.

*Nancy Hoffman* is vice president, youth transitions, at Jobs for the Future. She leads JFF's activities for the Early College High School Initiative. At Brown University she was a lecturer, director of the President's Office, and secretary of the Brown Corporation. Ms. Hoffman has held posts as vice provost for undergraduate studies at Temple University, academic services dean at the Harvard Graduate School of Education, and program officer at the Fund for the Improvement of Postsecondary Education. She was a founder of and faculty member at the College of Public and Community Service at the University of Massachusetts Boston.

*Richard Kazis,* as senior vice president of Jobs for the Future, leads the organization's policy and research efforts. He has led JFF's multisite initiative on school-to-career models and projects on local organizations that link schools and employers, community colleges and low-income populations, policies to promote low-wage worker advancement, and the emerging role of labor market intermediaries in work-force development. Mr. Kazis has authored and co-authored many works on issues of work and learning for underserved populations, including *Low Wage Workers in the New Economy.*

*Michael W. Kirst* brings years of experience in government education policymaking — at both federal and state levels — to his classrooms and research. He is co-director of Policy Analysis for California Education, a research consortium including Stanford, UC Berkeley, and USC. In this capacity, Dr. Kirst is at the forefront of the PACE agenda to provide analysis and assistance to California policymakers to help build an ongoing picture of California education.

*George D. Kuh* is Chancellor's Professor of Higher Education at Indiana University Bloomington, where he directs the Center for Postsecondary Research, Policy and Planning, home to the National Survey of Student Engagement, the College Student Experiences Questionnaire Research Program, and the NSSE Institute for Effective Educational Practice. His 250 publications and several hundred presentations focus on assessment, college student development, and campus cultures, and he has consulted with about 150 institutions of higher education and educational agencies.

*David A. Longanecker* is executive director of the Western Interstate Commission for Higher Education, a regional compact among 15 western states created to assure access and excellence in higher education through collaboration and resource sharing. Previously, Dr. Longanecker served as assistant secretary for postsecondary education at the U.S. Department of Education. He has also served as the state higher education executive officer in Colorado and Minnesota and as the Congressional Budget Office's principal analyst for higher education.

*Hans P. L'Orange* is director of data and information management and director of the SHEEO/NCES Network. The Network is a collaborative project administered by SHEEO and sponsored and funded by the National Center for Education Statistics at the U.S. Department of Education. Mr. L'Orange serves as a liaison to foster communication, cooperation, and collaboration among the federal government, state higher education agencies, and national associations on issues related to data management and using data and information effectively to develop public postsecondary education policy.

*Monica R. Martinez* is project director for the Institute for Educational Leadership's (IEL) work with the National Clearinghouse for School Reform, the Theme High Schools Network (THiSNET.org), and the Catalog of Research on Secondary School Reform. She is founder of and senior advisor to the National High School Alliance and oversees IEL's work with the Pathways to College Network. Ms. Martinez's experience includes work in a variety of higher education institutions and intermediary organizations that provide programmatic assistance in partnership development, school change, research, and evaluation.

*Seana Murphy* serves as director of the Twenty-First Century Scholars–GEAR UP Program for the state of Indiana. She is responsible for oversight and management of the 16 regional support sites. Previously, she was coordinator for the Central Indiana Twenty-First Century Scholars–GEAR UP Program, coordinating activities for the largest program site in the state.

*Joe Nathan* directs the Center for School Change at the Humphrey Institute, University of Minnesota. Dr. Nathan was an award-winning inner-city public school teacher and administrator. He has written several books and is a regular columnist for the *St. Paul Pioneer Press.* The National Governors Association hired him to coordinate the 1985–1986 report, "Time for Results: The Governors' 1991 Report on Education." His guest columns have been published by, among others, *USA Today,* the *Wall Street Journal, Atlanta Constitution, Detroit News, Sacramento Bee, Philadelphia Inquirer,* and (Minneapolis) *Star Tribune.*

*Hilary Pennington* is co-founder and CEO of Jobs for the Future, where she guides the agency's work on practices and public policies that promote the advancement to and through college for populations most at risk of being left behind in the new economy. A leading advocate for improving transitions for young people into adulthood and for expanding economic opportunity, she has served as a consultant to national foundations, state governments, federal agencies, and corporations as they develop programs on these issues. A member of Clinton's presidential transition team in 1992, she recently co-chaired the Presidential Advisory Committee on Expanding Training Opportunities.

*Donna Rodrigues*, program director at Jobs for the Future, works with the Early College High School Initiative. She has spent 35 years in education as a teacher, department chair of foreign languages, professional development school coordinator, adjunct professor, and, for seven years, planner and principal of University Park Campus School (UPCS). She has presented at conferences across the country as UPCS became a model for standards-based student success, closing the gap for minority students, school leadership, and university-neighborhood-public school collaborations.

*Robert B. Schwartz* is a faculty member at the Harvard Graduate School of Education and directs the master's program in administration, planning, and social policy. From 1997 to 2002, he also served as president of Achieve, Inc., a nonprofit established by governors and corporate leaders to help states strengthen academic performance. He previously served in a variety of education and government roles, including education advisor to Boston mayor Kevin White and Massachusetts governor Michael Dukakis, executive director of The Boston Compact, and education program director at The Pew Charitable Trusts.

*Philip A. Seabrook* is assistant dean of the University College at Indiana University Purdue University Indianapolis. He is responsible for the administration of academic support programs and for the oversight of college-level support programs such as the Student Support Services Program and the Nina Scholars Program. Mr. Seabrook served as the initial director of the Twenty-First Century Scholars Parents' Project, which is a support program for the Twenty-First Century Scholars Program, Indiana's tuition guarantee program.

*Barbara Leigh Smith* is a member of the faculty and former provost and vice president for academic affairs at the Evergreen State College. With Jean MacGregor, she founded the Washington Center for Improving the Quality of Undergraduate Education, a state-supported consortium that disseminates learning community work throughout the nation. From 2000–2004, Ms. Smith and Ms. MacGregor co-directed The Pew Charitable Trusts' National Learning Communities Project.

*Edward P. St. John* is a professor of educational leadership and policy studies at Indiana University. Dr. St. John's research on student financial aid and other postsecondary policy topics has appeared in *Research in Higher Education*, the *Journal of Higher Education*, the *Journal of Student Financial Aid*, and other education research journals. His most recent book is *Refinancing the College Dream: Access, Equal Opportunity, and Justice for Taxpayers*.

*Adria Steinberg* is a program director at Jobs for the Future, where she leads From the Margins to the Mainstream, and is a core partner to the Boston Public Schools in its Schools for a New Society high school reform efforts. Steinberg has 30 years of experience as a teacher, staff and curriculum developer, writer, and academic coordinator. She has authored many publications, including five years as primary writer/editor of the *Harvard Education Letter*. Recent publications include *Real Learning, Real Work; Schooling for the Real World* (with Kathleen Cushman and Rob Riordan); and *City-Works* (with David Stephen).

*Marc S. Tucker* is president of the National Center on Education and the Economy. He authored the 1986 Carnegie report, "A Nation Prepared," created the National Board for Professional Teaching Standards, created the Commission on the Skills of the American Workforce, and helped author its report, "America's Choice: High Skills or Low Wages!" Mr. Tucker was instrumental in creating the National Skills Standards Board and chaired its policy committee. He was co-creator of the New Standards consortium and, with Judy Codding, of the America's Choice School Design.

*Tom Vander Ark* is executive director of the Bill & Melinda Gates Foundation's education initiatives. He is responsible for the development and administration of the foundation's education grant programs and scholarship programs. Previously, Mr. Vander Ark served as a public school superintendent in one of Washington State's districts. He was one of the first superintendents recruited from the private sector to lead a public school district. Vander Ark serves on the boards of the Foundation for Early Learning, Partnership for Learning, James B. Hunt Jr. Institute for Educational Leadership and Policy, and Western Governors University.

*Joel Vargas* is a senior project manager at Jobs for the Future, where he works with the Early College High School Initiative. As a former director of Summerbridge Manchester, Dr. Vargas helped public school youth realize their college aspirations through a program encouraging talented high school and college students from across the country to become educators. He also coordinated a Higher Education Information Center program at a Boston public middle school that promotes college access. In addition, he has been a middle school teacher at the Derryfield School in New Hampshire, a leader within the Summerbridge collaborative of programs nationally, and an editor and research assistant for The Civil Rights Project at Harvard University.

*Andrea Venezia* is a senior policy consultant and project director with the National Center for Public Policy and Higher Education. Her work examines education policy, particularly as related to equity and the transition from K-12 to postsecondary education. Dr. Venezia has worked for a variety of state, federal, and not-for-profit entities, including the Stanford Institute for Higher Education Research, the Texas Higher Education Coordinating Board, and the National Education Goals Panel.

*Blenda J. Wilson* is president and CEO of the Nellie Mae Education Foundation, one of New England's largest foundations and the largest focused exclusively on education. Its mission is to promote the accessibility, quality, and effectiveness of education, from preschool through postsecondary levels, for all ages, especially for underserved populations. The foundation's first president, Dr. Wilson has led it in defining its vision as a major grantmaker, research organization, convener, and policymaker. Dr. Wilson was formerly president of California State University, Northridge, chancellor of the University of Michigan, Dearborn, and executive director of the Colorado Commission on Higher Education. She is past chair of the American Association of Higher Education.

*Ronald A. Wolk* is the founding editor of *Education Week, Teacher Magazine,* and *Quality Counts.* He now serves as chairman of the board of Editorial Projects in Education, the nonprofit organization that publishes those periodicals. He is also chairman of the board of The Big Picture Company, a school reform organization in Providence, Rhode Island, and serves on the board of the Public Education Network. Wolk has served as vice president of Brown University, assistant to the president of Johns Hopkins University, and assistant director of the Carnegie Commission on the Future of Higher Education.